Moses
and the
Journey
to
LEADERSHIP

**OTHER JEWISH LIGHTS BOOKS BY
NORMAN J. COHEN**

*Hineini in Our Lives: Learning How to Respond to Others through
14 Biblical Texts & Personal Stories*

*Self, Struggle & Change: Family Conflict Stories in Genesis and Their
Healing Insights for Our Lives*

Voices from Genesis: Guiding Us through the Stages of Life

The Way Into Torah

Moses
and the
Journey
to
LEADERSHIP

Timeless Lessons of
Effective Management
from the Bible
and Today's Leaders

Dr. Norman J. Cohen

For People of All Faiths, All Backgrounds

JEWISH LIGHTS Publishing

Woodstock, Vermont

Moses and the Journey to Leadership:
Timeless Lessons of Effective Management from the Bible and Today's Leaders

2007 First Printing
© 2007 by Norman J. Cohen

Library of Congress Cataloging-in-Publication Data
Cohen, Norman J.
Moses and the journey to leadership : timeless lessons of effective management from the Bible and today's leaders / Norman J. Cohen.
p. cm.
Includes bibliographical references.
ISBN-13: 978-1-58023-227-2 (hardcover)
ISBN-10: 1-58023-227-2 (hardcover)
1. Moses (Biblical leader) 2. Bible. O.T. Pentateuch—Criticism, interpretation, etc. 3. Leadership—Moral and ethical aspects. 4. Management—Moral and ethical aspects. I. Title.
BS580.M6C643 2006
222'.1092—dc22

2006024842

10 9 8 7 6 5 4 3 2 1
Manufactured in the United States of America

For People of All Faiths, All Backgrounds
Published by Jewish Lights Publishing
A Division of LongHill Partners, Inc.
Sunset Farm Offices, Route 4, P.O. Box 237
Woodstock, VT 05091
Tel: (802) 457-4000   Fax: (802) 457-4004
www.jewishlights.com

To my teacher and mentor at
Hebrew Union College—Jewish Institute of Religion,
Dr. Paul M. Steinberg, *z"l,*
who taught me how one can lead with both vision and purpose,
while manifesting care and concern

Contents

Acknowledgments

Moses was 120 years old when he died; his eyes were undimmed and his vigor unabated. And the Israelites bewailed Moses in the plains of Moab for thirty days. The period of wailing and mourning came to an end. Now Joshua, the son of Nun, was filled with the spirit of wisdom because Moses had laid his hands upon him; and the Israelites heeded him, doing as Adonai commanded Moses.

Never again did there arise in Israel a prophet like Moses whom Adonai singled out, face to face, for the various signs and portents that Adonai sent him to display in the land of Egypt, against Pharaoh and all his courtiers and his whole country, and for all the great might and awesome power that Moses displayed before all Israel.

Deuteronomy 34:7–12

The description of Moses's death at the end of the Torah underscores his uniqueness as a leader. Not only does he enjoy a singular relationship with God, seeing the Divine face to face, but, as a result, he performs miracles and exhibits a power that enables him to save the People of Israel from Egyptian bondage. Witnessing such power and ability, the Israelites recognize that there will never be another leader like Moses. Even when he dies, his vigor, wisdom, and passion are intact.

Therefore, who better than Moses to hold up as a paradigm from whom every future leader can learn? His vision, actions, and skills serve as models for future generations of aspiring leaders, including those of our day. The Israelites fittingly wail and mourn his death.

Yet, in the very biblical passage in which Moses's uniqueness is stressed, we are also reminded that Joshua immediately assumes leadership, commanding the Israelites' respect. Though Moses may have been one of a kind—"There never again will be a prophet like Moses" (Deuteronomy 34:10)—Joshua is also imbued with wisdom, a prerequisite for all successful leaders.

But there is more. Moses actually prepares his disciple to take his place, understanding that continuity in leadership is crucial. All leaders need to cultivate and nurture the next generation of leaders. The most successful leaders are those who share their passion and knowledge with their successors, imbuing them with the skills and insights to assume the mantle of leadership.

As I look back on my own years of service at the Hebrew Union College–Jewish Institute of Religion (HUC–JIR), there were many individuals along the way who had a tremendous impact upon me and my future career. Whatever success I have achieved as a faculty member, dean, and provost is in large measure the result of the wonderful models from whom I learned. As a teenager in the Zionist youth movement, Young Judaea, I had the good fortune to find powerful role models, leaders who not only touched my heart, mind, and soul, but who embodied the essence of what it is to lead others. And as a rabbinical student in the New York School of HUC–JIR and as a PhD candidate in our Graduate School in Cincinnati, I was blessed with many wonderful teachers and administrators who had a profound impact upon me. I owe so many individuals a debt of thanks, but none more than Dr. Paul M. Steinberg, *z"l.*

Paul Steinberg served HUC–JIR for fifty years in a variety of capacities, helping to build and expand its vision and programs in significant ways. But as program director, dean, and vice president on the New York campus, he influenced the lives of generations of rabbinical, cantorial, and education students. As his student and his successor as dean of the New York School, as well as his colleague in the national administration, I consider Paul Steinberg a true mentor. For me, he embodied a deep sense of caring and concern toward all those whom he led and with whom he worked. And through his unflinching support and guidance, I was able to grow in my own roles as an administrator. In succeeding him as dean of the New York School, I inherited a powerfully supportive role model and friend. Of all of Paul Steinberg's contributions to HUC–JIR, none was more important than his gifts of self. Paul embraced me and so many others, as he embraced life itself, up until the moment of his passing, and we shall ever embrace his memory.

I have also learned much from and am grateful to several individuals at Jewish Lights Publishing. Art Kleiner's insightful editorial comments and his many suggestions about the nature of leadership and about the characteristics of leaders have added much to the book's content, for which I am appreciative. Jewish Lights' talented Emily Wichland, through her masterful editing of the manuscript, has markedly improved the book, making it eminently more readable. Like many of the books she's worked on at Jewish Lights, mine has benefited greatly from her wisdom. I am also grateful to copyeditor Diana Drew, whose keen eye for grammar and the technical elements of style helped shepherd this work to final production. Finally, let it be said that none of the books which I have written would ever have seen the light of day without the support, encouragement, and prodding of Stuart M. Matlins, founder and publisher of Jewish Lights Publishing. It was his vision of a Jewish publishing company that would help transform Jewish life and bring the riches of the Jewish tradition to bear on our search for meaning that impelled me through my writing to share the joy of study with a wider audience. I will always be in his debt. It is with a deep sense of blessing, therefore, that I share this work with you, the reader, with the hope that you will recognize the power of the Bible and the rabbinic tradition to respond to enduring questions of meaning that all of us ask, and the relevance of the material about Moses for our understanding of the nature of leadership.

Introduction

Every morning, the newspapers carry a flood of stories about individuals forcibly removed from power because they have either been caught in a web of deceit or they lack the ability to effectively address the difficult challenges faced by all leaders. According to Booz Allen Hamilton's annual study of CEO succession, forced resignations in the world's 2,500 largest companies is up 300 percent since 1995.[1] It is not a stretch to assert that the single most troubling aspect of modern society is a crisis of leadership. In every realm, including politics, economics, and religion, few leaders possess vision and strength, while living lives of integrity based on enduring values.

So where will we find strong leaders—role models who can help us nurture the next generation of leaders for our diverse communities and our world? The events of the twentieth century have shown us that the prevailing assumption that leadership will emerge from what Harvey Cox called the "secular city"[2] is false. Secular culture, which is devoid of ultimate values, has not proven itself to be the panacea that Cox claimed; almost none of its leaders have the skills to solve the many problems confronting us today, even though they may be technologically advanced. So we who are committed to making the world a better place for all of God's creations must seek paradigms of leadership elsewhere.

Our search for values and models by which to live inevitably leads us to the enduring texts of our tradition. These are not merely remnants of an ancient past, but, rather, timeless tomes that can touch us and teach us today. This is especially true of the Bible, which is

1

filled with stories that parallel our own lives.[3] Whether you consider yourself religious and you already know the Bible, or think of yourself as secular and are unaware of most of the Bible's content, there is much to be gained in studying these stories, and that of Moses in particular. As we immerse ourselves in the narratives of the Bible, we come to better understand the stories of our own lives.

In engaging with the biblical text, we come across no more important character and model than Moses, the most celebrated, yet solitary, hero of the Bible. Elie Wiesel aptly characterizes the man and his achievements when he notes that the immensity of his task and the scope of his experience command our admiration, even our awe. Moses changed the course of human history all by himself![4]

As the first leader of the Jewish people, the founder of his people, and as giver of the Torah, Moses exerts a unique force in the shaping of the nation. But he also plays a significant priestly role,[5] is considered the greatest of all prophets,[6] and is the chief magistrate, judging his people at all times. In rabbinic terms, he wears all the major crowns of leadership: *keter* (crown) *Torah, keter kehunah* (priesthood), and *keter malkhut* (kingship or power).[7]

The magnitude of what he achieves seems at first glance so far beyond our grasp that we have great difficulty identifying with it. We see Moses as the redeemer who miraculously delivers his people from slavery; the human being who sees the Divine face to face and survives forty days of intimacy on Mount Sinai; the poet who twice sings the song of his people—at the Red Sea and at the end of his life gazing into the Promised Land; the warrior who leads Israel in battle against the Amalekites and the Moabites; the lawgiver for whom the Torah, the Five Books of Moses, is named (*Torat Moshe*);[8] the mystical figure whose burial site is unknown;[9] the incomparable prophet;[10] and *Moshe Rabbenu*, Moses, our rabbi, the paradigmatic teacher in the rabbinic tradition.

At the same time, Moses is also described in very human terms in the Bible; we come to see his shortcomings as well as his strengths. Therefore, as we deliberately focus on him as the leader of his people, we will pay close attention not only to his great achievements, but also to his very human frailties: his self-doubts, his disappointments, his struggle to balance family with his role as leader, and the many challenges he faces as he leads the Israelites through the desert to the Land of Israel. In the end, we will attempt to understand the longing and bittersweet pride that he feels at not being able to join them as they cross the Jordan River into the Promised Land.

Above all else, Moses's life story reminds us of the one aspect that distinguishes him as a leader of others: His life is not his own. This is something that all leaders must come to accept. Because Moses's life is inextricably bound up with the life of his people and its mission, he has to make choices that are both uncomfortable and self-denying. While this is a reflection of his maturity, it is also a source of personal pain. Moses's life is much more than the story of one human being; it is intertwined with the story of the People of Israel, and what he experiences cannot be easily separated from events of early Jewish history.[11]

Even though Moses's authority emanates from God—he is called and chosen by God to lead his people—his power comes from his relationship with the people, and this defines the essential nature of his leadership, as it does with leaders in modern democracies. The model of Moses's leadership could not be that of a dictator who dominates his people, since the People of Israel themselves are covenanted to God. They are considered Moses's people, especially when they are sinful; as God says when Israel builds the Golden Calf, "Hurry down [Moses], for *your* [emphasis added] people whom you have brought out of Egypt, have acted basely" (Exodus 32:7).[12] Yet, over and over again, they are identified as God's possession, as we read in Deuteronomy, "Yet they are Your very own people, whom You freed with Your great might and Your outstretched arm" (9:29). The mission of Israel is larger than that of any individual leader, even Moses, and this is underscored even—or perhaps especially—when they have not lived up to their part of the covenant. As the intended partner of the Divine in helping to bring the world to completion, they have to be delivered from Egypt and journey to Mount Sinai in order to become the bearers of God's law. Israel's redemption is bound up with God's revelation to the entire world.

Moses is the model of a visionary leader; he articulates the expectations God has of the People of Israel, both as a collective and as individual members of this covenanted community. But he also empowers the people, not only demanding that they themselves take responsibility for living lives according to God's laws (not his), but believing that they possess the ability to do so. He makes clear God's expectations of them, supports them when they fail, and does not hesitate to challenge them to live up to their highest potential as human beings created in God's image.

Moses is an exemplar of the leadership to which we may all aspire, whether we are professional or lay leaders of our religious or communal institutions, or leaders in business, politics, or other arenas. One reason why his model is so accessible to us is that his life is much like ours. We can identify with what he experiences; his difficulties mirror ours, just as his challenges do. Though he successfully guides the People of Israel from the degradation of slavery, through the heat and the aridity of the desert to God's mountain and eventually to the Promised Land, it was not without much personal pain. Despite his great success, he lives through acts of rebellion on the part of his followers and outright rejection of his leadership. There are many moments when he feels isolated from the very people to whom he is devoted, even as he seems to sacrifice the one source of comfort available to most of us—family and friends who accept us unconditionally. In the end, he never sees his dream fulfilled, because he cannot enter the Promised Land, upon which he gazes from Mount Nebo in the Plains of Moab.[13]

Yet, despite all his personal and professional struggles, despite all his own imperfections and limitations, despite many moments of disappointment, he grows immensely over time. Not only does he move Israel from slavery to freedom, from Egypt to the Land of Israel, from serving the earthly king to the service of the Holy One of Being, but he gains in stature in the process. He begins as a lowly shepherd of his father-in-law Jethro's sheep in Midian,[14] but eventually shepherds the People of Israel, first to Mount Sinai, where they experience a revelation that alters human existence, and then to their ancestral homeland, where they will live out their covenant with the Divine.

Moses, through both his frailty and failures as well as his great success, can touch and teach each of us. No matter what our personal circumstances, our upbringing, or our shortcomings, we can learn from his model that we, too, have the potential to move people from places of confinement, like *Mitzrayim* (Egypt), from the narrow places (for which the Hebrew word is *meitzarim,* echoing *Mitzrayim*),[15] in which they are suffering, to the expanse of the desert and to the place of holiness, God's place. By following his example, we can help bring others to the experience of wholeness—*shalom*—peace.

1
Showing the Potential for Leadership
Exodus 2

The circumstances surrounding Moses's birth, as described in the beginning of the book of Exodus, indicate the significant role that he will play in the life of his people. Suffering as slaves under the yoke of Egyptian oppression, the future People of Israel hear a prophecy that they will be liberated through the leadership of one who is born to those very slaves. For fear that they could one day rebel against him, Pharaoh, in an effort both to curtail the burgeoning Hebrew population and to obviate the birth of a potential redeemer,[1] decrees that every male child born to a Hebrew mother should be drowned in the Nile River.[2]

So when Moses is born and his mother sees him to be *ki tov,* usually translated as "that he was beautiful," she hides him for three months, until she can no longer guarantee his safety and then places him in a basket in the Nile (Exodus 2:2–3). But the phrase *ki tov,* that Moses is "good," immediately calls to mind God's description of the Creation in Genesis, prior to the creation of humankind.[3] Moses's mother attempts to save his life, not because of his appearance, but because his birth signals a new beginning, a new genesis. Just as the appearance of Adam and Eve embodied the hope that Creation had the potential for goodness and that it would ultimately be complete, so, too, the advent of Moses will lead to the birth of his people and the transformation of the world.[4]

GROWING UP IN THE PALACE:
MOSES IS EDUCATED FOR A LEADERSHIP ROLE

Even the name given to Moses is indicative of his future role. Having been placed in the Nile by his mother, he is drawn out of the water by the daughter of Pharaoh, who has come to bathe. Later, she calls him *Moshe,* explaining, "I drew him out of the water" (2:10). However, if the name is meant to mean that Moses was "drawn out of the water," it should have been the passive form of the Hebrew verb *Mashui. Moshe* is an active verb that means "drawer," and, therefore, teaches us that he will eventually not only take his people out of slavery, but also draw them through the waters of the Red Sea on their journey toward Mount Sinai and the Promised Land.[5]

Moses is the product of two worlds. He is born to a Hebrew mother, and nursed by her in his early years at the request of the Egyptian princess, who knows that he indeed is a Hebrew. When he has grown (*va-yigdal*) sufficiently, which clearly means that he is weaned, he is brought to the palace, where he matures in the context of Egyptian power and culture (2:7–10). In that environment, he is exposed to a classic Greek education and to models of both authority and leadership. Such experiences will prepare him for what lies ahead.[6] The irony, of course, is that the very knowledge and skills he learns in Pharaoh's house will be used in his confrontation with Pharaoh upon his return to Egypt later on.[7]

If Moses grows physically before being brought to the palace, he matures and gains stature (*va-yigdal*) once he lives there. The repetition of the term *va-yigdal* in the Exodus text underscores Moses's preparation for leadership. The tradition even goes as far as to claim that he holds a position of authority in the royal court.[8] Just as Moses is ready to be reared in Pharaoh's house after he is nursed by his own mother, after this period of maturation, he is ready to confront new experiences and challenges as an adult.[9]

LEAVING THE PALACE:
MOSES IDENTIFIES WITH HIS KINFOLK

Leaving the place of his youth, Moses goes out (*va-yeitzei*) to his kinfolk (2:11). He leaves behind the comfort of the palace to see his brothers and sisters, and in so doing not only changes his life, but will change the life of his people.[10] At times, an individual who aspires to leadership must be willing to give up an easier, less burdensome lifestyle in order to serve the community. And frequently, there is little to gain. Moses, in becoming involved with the Hebrew slaves, has everything to lose.[11]

Think of politicians like Mayor Michael Bloomberg of New York City, who left his highly successful media empire, Bloomberg LLP, and its multitude of radio and television stations and information services, to face the daunting challenges of leading the largest city in the world after 9/11. The mayoralty, as important as it is, is fraught with constant severe criticism and little reward, whether it be financial or otherwise. Even though Mayor Bloomberg, like all politicians, is motivated by self-interest, nevertheless, his willingness to serve should be recognized.

What seems to drive Moses is an intense desire to connect with his brothers and sisters. The text emphasizes that he goes out twice, two days in a row (2:11, 13), indicating his deep need to forge a connection.[12] Though they live in different worlds—he a prince, with rights and privileges of the palace; and they, hungry, persecuted slaves—he feels compelled to join them. This, perhaps, is part of his inherent greatness.[13] Moses is not blinded by the wealth and power of his surroundings. He is able to truly see the enslaved Hebrews as his brothers and sisters, a point brought out by a repetition of the word *echav,* his brothers, in the text. He first ventures from the palace "to see his brothers" and then "saw an Egyptian beating a Hebrew, one of his brothers" (2:11). The second reference to "his brothers" is clearly redundant, since the Hebrew is, of course, one of his kinsmen. They are not "other" to him; he identifies with them.

Moses indeed sees (*va-ya'ar*) them in the fullest sense of the word, and this is the recurring theme in the passage: "He *saw* their burdens ... he *saw* an Egyptian [taskmaster] beating a Hebrew.... He turned this way and that and he *saw* that no one was about" (2:11–12). His first act outside the palace, then, is to see, to understand, and to internalize the suffering of his kinsmen.[14] Truly "seeing

Kazuo Inamori, founder of the Japanese electronics company Kyocera, always stressed his commitment to his employees. He stated that his role as a leader began with "providing for the material good and spiritual welfare of the people."[17]

them" is indeed the focus of this passage about Moses. And he is not able to bear the sight.[15] According to the tradition, he breaks down in tears, saying, "Better that I should die than witness such a degradation of [my] people."[16]

And seeing the heavy burdens that they had to bear, he does not hesitate to help them by shouldering the load with them.[18] He assists the young and old, the men and women, the weak and strong, focusing on the needs of each person.[19] This is an essential challenge for every leader: to be able to know and respond to each of his followers. It is so easy for them to become a sea of faceless, nameless individuals, whose unique circumstances, needs, skills, and contributions fall by the wayside. And if this happens, the group will fail to derive the most from each one.

MOSES INTERVENES: A DEFINING MOMENT IN HIS LIFE

Moses so empathizes with his Hebrew brothers and sisters that it is extremely painful for him to witness an Egyptian taskmaster beating (*makeh*) a Hebrew slave. Turning this way and that, and seeing (*va-ya'ar*) no one there, Moses strikes down the Egyptian (2:12). There is no *ish,* no person in the fullest sense, no mensch present who is willing to intervene. In the words of *Pirkei Avot* (Ethics of the Sages), in a place where there is no *ish,* one must attempt to be a person.[20] Even though Moses fears being caught, as evidenced by his turning from side to side to ensure that no one is watching, he nevertheless is willing to risk his own life to save a fellow Israelite.[21]

In saving the life of the Hebrew slave, Moses demonstrates even at this early stage in his maturation a willingness to act out of a commitment to ultimate values that flow from a recognition of God's presence in the world.[22] The fate of this one human being, one of God's creations, is in his hands, and he is compelled to act.[23] The tradition even emphasizes that he intones God's name at that moment.[24] As a result of his standing up for what is right and just, no matter what the cost, according to the Rabbis, his name is ever to be associated with the institution of justice.[25]

Moses's sense of what is just and his willingness to act upon it is not limited to circumstances in which his own people are threatened. He stands on principle even when it only involves his fellow Israelites. So when he goes out the following day and sees two Hebrews fighting, he accuses the wicked one, saying, "Why do you strike [*takeh*—the very word used to describe the actions of the Egyptian taskmaster] your fellow?" (2:13) But how does Moses know which one is the *rasha*, the wicked one, if he simply observes a scene of two individuals quarreling?[27] Moses exhibits here one of the crucial qualities of a leader: the ability to discern the nature of the circumstances he confronts and to know what to do. When a leader intervenes, protecting one and admonishing another, her action is often resented. The Hebrew whom Moses confronts retorts, "Who made you chief and ruler over us? Do you mean to kill me as you killed the Egyptian?" (2:14) Leaders, like

> The CEO of Southwest Airlines, Herb Kelleher, is known for his concern for each one of his employees. He demonstrates his interest and empathic style by occasionally loading the luggage with the baggage handlers, serving food with the flight attendants, and working behind the ticket counter. He emphasizes that successful leaders "have to be with their employees through all their difficulties; you have to be interested in them personally."[26]

Moses, need to develop a thick enough skin to deflect occasional expressions of harsh anger, when they demonstrate qualities of leadership and concern for the well-being of the group!

Some of the resentment expressed may stem from Moses's age. The Hebrew whom he chastises may simply be saying, "You have not even matured yet! Who are you to lord it over us?" This possible rationale could be based on the seemingly superfluous word in the Exodus text: *Mi samechah le-ish sar ve-shofet,* literally, "Who made you the man/person who [should] be chief and ruler?"[29] Young leaders are often challenged because of their perceived youth and lack of experience, and at times this criticism is a difficult hurdle to overcome.

> The CEO of Nestlé, Peter Brabeck-Letmathe, observes, "There are followers and there are leaders. Leaders have the courage [to] stand up against the barrage of public opinion that comes at them, saying, 'I am not going to capitulate.'"[28]

The tradition emphasizes the difficulty Moses has in understanding the Hebrews' response to him. This is a foreshadowing of how the Israelites will act toward him in the future. When the biblical narrative says that "Moses was frightened and thought, 'The matter became known'" (2:14), it isn't just that Pharaoh will learn that he has killed the taskmaster, but that, for the first time, he considers whether the Hebrews are worthy of his putting himself on the line for them; perhaps they are not worthy of being redeemed at all.[30] When a leader comes to the realization that the people he's leading may not deserve his efforts on their behalf, he faces a difficult issue: How can he continue to lead in the face of such an indictment of his followers? Recognizing the frailty of the Hebrews and understanding that they are not as good or devoted as he hoped they were, how does Moses justify his decision to continue leading the people?

In analyzing the Hebrew's angry response to Moses's intervention, let's consider how Moses himself speaks to the slave. Instead of accusing him of striking his fellow Israelite in the most blatant manner—"Why do you strike your fellow?"—perhaps Moses should have chosen words that would have prompted a different response.[31] For example, he might have framed his words with the recognition that their survival under Egyptian slavery depends on their remaining unified. To a significant extent, the way that leaders handle interchanges with both their followers and adversaries determines the nature of the response. All leaders must be sensitive to their choice of words.

MOSES FLEES TO MIDIAN: ANOTHER STAGE IN HIS DEVELOPMENT

Having acted on his principles and put himself on the line defending his brethren, Moses is forced to give up the comfort of life in Pharaoh's palace. He flees into the desert, reaching the land of Midian (2:15). But though he becomes a stranger in a strange land, his leadership abilities immediately come to the fore.

When he arrives at a well, he witnesses a group of shepherds driving off the daughters of Reuel, more commonly known as Jethro, the priest of Midian, who have come to water their father's flock. He rises to their defense—the text literally says he redeemed them (*va-yoshian*), and watered their flock (2:16–17). The odd choice of words in the Exodus narrative highlights not only Moses's courage and his willingness to act on behalf of those in need,[32] but the role he is destined to play on behalf of his own people: He will redeem them from Egypt.[33] In defending the seven maidens, Moses indeed "rose" (*va-yakom*)—he gains in stature and maturation, overcoming difficult odds in the pursuit of justice and preparing himself to lead a nation out of bondage. As Moses leaves behind the shelter of Pharaoh's palace, and becomes the shepherd of Jethro's flock, he further hones the skills he will need to lead his people through the desert to the land of Canaan.[34]

Moses grows and matures. In Egypt, when he tries to impose a measure of justice, he lashes out at both the Egyptian and the Hebrew struggling with his fellow Hebrew, and winds up alienating both the Egyptians and his own people.[35] In Midian, by contrast, he exercises much more restraint, and the result is markedly different. Here he doesn't seem like a violent vigilante, but rather is viewed as a compassionate, caring person.[36] In fleeing Egypt in the face of Egyptian power, he is cut off from all that defines him, but he is not broken.[37] He rises above the pain of his own exile to defend the persecuted—in this case, in the form of the daughters of the Midianite priest. And in so doing, he continues to develop his capacity for leadership. Often, it is the kind of experience that Moses has in Midian that prepares a person to become a leader. Taken out of a familiar world and immersed in an altogether different one, a leader is forced to adapt and learn to respond to all kinds of people. Learning how to be open and responsive, while navigating in an alien environment, propels a leader's maturation and hones key skills.

Consider the example of Mark Colvard, a UPS manager from Toledo, Ohio, who was assigned to work in the McAllen, Texas, branch in a community of poor Hispanics. He participated in any number of communal activities, including working with incarcerated youth, which made him much more sensitive to individual human needs. As a result of this experience in an unfamiliar environment, he became more open and compassionate, a leader willing to take more time with people.[38]

Yet, as we take leave of Moses in Midian, he is a stranger, lacking all sense of a personal identity. Jethro's family considers him an Egyptian—his daughters tell their father that "an Egyptian saved [them] from the shepherds" (2:19)—and Moses does nothing to disabuse them of this notion. He never reveals his Hebrew birth, or the circumstances under which he fled. Moses is a stranger to the Egyptians, but now he is alienated from his own people as well.[39] This alienation is sealed by his marriage to Jethro's daughter, Tzipporah (2:21).

So we as readers may rightfully ask, "Will the real Moses please stand up?"[40] Who is Moses as he settles into a new life in Midian as part of Jethro's family, and does he yearn to reconnect with his people?

2
The Calling:
Overcoming Self-Doubt
Exodus 3–4

Moses settles into his new family in Midian, married to Tzipporah, Jethro's daughter. Yet, we know nothing about Moses's early life away from his people except for the description of him shepherding his father-in-law's flock (Exodus 3:1). The image of the shepherd implies authority and concern, as it does in the description of God in Psalm 23. However, humility and obedience are also inherent traits of the shepherd, who often does not own his own flock, but works for another. Can Moses, ensconced in a Midianite family, far removed from his Israelite origins and kinfolk, overcome his personal circumstances and fulfill his destiny as the leader of his people? The same question applies to many of us who are leaders. We, like Moses, carry much personal, familial baggage as we assume leadership positions, and we too face the challenge of carrying that baggage with us into our new roles. The families into which we marry—their cultural, religious, and social backgrounds—often affect how we are perceived and function as leaders.

SHEPHERDING JETHRO'S FLOCK:
PREPARATION FOR LEADERSHIP

The text's description of Moses caring for Jethro's sheep points out Moses's role in Midian and its connection to his future role as the leader of God's people. This is further emphasized when Moses is called by God to serve while tending his flock.[1]

Throughout the literature of the Ancient Near East and later, the role of the shepherd symbolizes leadership. People are often compared to a flock or a herd, and shepherding is considered a training ground for those destined to lead.[2] There are numerous references in the Bible to leaders who were shepherds in their early lives; for example, King David. The Rabbis stress that Moses gains the necessary experience to redeem Israel and lead the people to the Promised Land precisely because he has been leading Jethro's flock in the wilderness.[3] Moses is deemed the "faithful shepherd," who will deliver the People of Israel.[4]

The manner in which Moses tends to the sheep indicates the type of leader he will become. The Rabbis underscore his concern for each one of the animals in the flock, even to a fault. One day, according to a widely circulated midrash, a baby goat runs away and Moses pursues the animal until he reaches a stream where the kid drinks his fill.

The founder of the Hard Rock Café, Isaac Tigrett, was noted for hiring people on society's fringe—street people and bikers, for example—and was able to make all of them feel as if they were a part of the "family." Tigrett says, "I didn't care about anything but people." He cherishes each of them, looks after them, and responds to each one's circumstances.[6]

Moses, realizing that the kid ran away because he was thirsty, knows that it must be exhausted and carries it back to the flock in his arms. God sees Moses's concern for the animal and says, "Since you have such compassion for an animal, you shall surely pasture My flock, Israel."[5]

In the way he cares for each animal, Moses shows a great deal of the character, maturity, and capability—qualities needed to be the Israelites' leader. Moses challenges each one of us who aspires to leadership to exhibit kindness and compassion for all those whom we are blessed to lead, especially those in difficult straits.

Moses drives Jethro's sheep into the wilderness, caring for each animal and leading all of them to water. So, too, will he lead the people of Israel through the desert for forty years.[7]

SEEING THE BURNING BUSH: PERCEIVING THE SOURCE OF POWER

Just as Moses is concerned about the plight of the little goat, so does he focus on a lowly bush, a *sneh*, when he comes to Horeb. But since Horeb is identified as the "mountain of God," it is no coincidence that the Hebrew word *sneh* has the same consonants as *Sinai*—the mountain where Moses will later encounter the Divine. As God descends on Mount Sinai (Exodus 19:8), so the Divine descends on Horeb (3:8) and manifests Godself in the most insignificant bush in the desert.[8] God is referred to as the "Presence in the bush" in Deuteronomy 33:16, where it also seems like a play on *Sinai*. No place in the world is devoid of God's presence, of God's power. The *sneh*, the thornbush, is Sinai.[9]

Though Horeb and Sinai are thought by scholars to be different mountains, calling Horeb the "mountain of God" clearly prefigures Israel's experience at Sinai.[10] And the similarity in spelling between *sneh* and *Sinai* only reinforces this foreshadowing.[11] The suspense is heightened by God's appearing to Moses in the form of an angel in a blazing fire in the midst of the bush. Later, God will also appear in the form of fire on Mount Sinai—the mountain itself will be consumed by fire and smoke (Exodus 19:18). The Torah is called the "fiery law" when it is revealed to Moses on Sinai (Deuteronomy 33:2). All this is foreshadowed on Horeb, when God is seen literally in the "heart of the fire," *b'labat aish*. Several midrashic traditions note the use here of the term *labat*, derived from *laiv* or *laivov*, meaning "heart," instead of the expected terms *lahav* or *shalhevet*, meaning "flame."[12] Metaphorically, fire and heart together add up to courage. In order to prepare Moses for the lightning and thunder, the fire and smoke of Sinai, so that he will not be afraid, God gives Moses *heart*,[13] and courage.[14] The experience at Horeb enables Moses not only to survive God's overwhelming presence on Mount Sinai, but also to prepare the people for the

challenges they will encounter. Leaders often develop personal characteristics and skills over time; it takes a series of experiences, each
one building on the others, to ensure growth. Leadership is not born
overnight.

Yet, Moses only comes to appreciate the significance of the fire
in the midst of the bush because he turns aside to look at the marvelous sight. First he has to see the bush aflame. He has to raise his
eyes from the mundane desert sands and look to see. Expressions of
"seeing" occur over and over again in the space of just a few verses
(3:2–4): "An angel of the Lord appeared/was seen [va-yera]"; "He
[Moses] saw [va-yar]"; "I will look [ve-ye'eh] at this marvelous sight
[ha-mareh]"; "And the Lord saw [va-yar] that [Moses] turned aside
to look [lirot]." The rep-
etition of the word ra'ah
(see) in an almost stacca-
tolike manner hammers
home the point that
leadership involves truly
"seeing"— the ability to
perceive the importance
of what one experiences,
to understand it, and
then to internalize it. The
marvelous sight that
Moses "sees" is not
merely a lowly bush
burning, but rather the
awesome presence of
God. What distinguishes
leaders from followers is
their ability to discern the impact of even simple events and actions.
But Moses doesn't simply see the burning bush; he has the impulse to
leave the path: "I must turn aside to look" (3:3). The book of Exodus
tells us that God takes note of Moses's choice to turn aside from the
path (3:4). But what actually does Moses do? According to one
midrashic interpretation, Moses takes a few steps off the road in the
direction of the bush.[15] Yet, another tradition stresses that all Moses

In a modern version of a Sufi story, a
passerby sees a drunk on his hands
and knees under a street lamp, looking for his house keys. Offering his
help, the passerby asks, "Where did
you drop them?" The drunk replied
that he dropped them outside his
front door. "Then why are you looking for them here?" "Because," says
the drunk, "there is no light by my
doorway." In citing this story,
Peter Senge stresses that we all find
comfort sticking to what we
know best.[16]

does is to crane his neck to see the bush burning.[17] With a mere twist of the neck, Moses reorients his entire being. As opposed to those who are stiff-necked—opposed to all that is new—he is ready to witness, to truly see God's presence, and, as a result, God reveals the Divine Self to him.[18] Leadership requires us to look beyond what we know and what we are comfortable with.

Not only is Moses inquisitive, but he goes to the trouble of trying to understand what he is experiencing—the nature of the bush and why it is not consumed by the flames. In so doing, he exemplifies basic qualities and actions necessary for leadership. Moses not only perceives God's Presence in the lowliest bush in the desert, but he also comes to understand that God reveals the Divine Self in the *sneh* as opposed to any other more elevated form of nature; all this in anticipation of responding to Israel's suffering in Egypt and the leadership role he is called on to assume. God informs him in this regard, "I have truly seen [*ra'oh ra'iti*—a doubling of the root *ra'ah*] the plight of My people in Egypt.... I have come down to rescue them" (3:7–8). Just as Israel is forced to go down to Egypt (*Mitzrayim*), to descend (*yarad*) into the place of pain, so God will leave the heavens and descend (*yarad*) in order to share Israel's pain (*tzarah*). God reiterates over and over again, "I will be with [Israel] in distress (*b'tzarah*)."[19]

Moses learns that not only will God witness Israel's suffering, but God actually suffers along with the people with whom the Divine is covenanted: "In all their troubles, [God] was troubled" (Isaiah 63:9).[20] The Rabbis illustrate this symbiotic relationship between God and Israel by arguing that this case is similar to twins: If one is in pain, so is the other. God says to Moses, "I am [Israel's] partner in trouble."[21] Moses's leadership stems directly from his relationship with God, as the framer and keeper of the covenant that represents the destiny of his people. Modern leaders call this "holding a vision"—not of what they have chosen, but of what each one is called to do.

God's suffering along with Israel's guarantees that Israel will survive. Just as the bush is the lowliest of the trees God created, so, too, Israel is downtrodden in Egypt. Yet, the bush burns but is not consumed. Similarly, Egypt will not be able to destroy Israel.[22] Israel will endure because its covenant with God must be fulfilled. The People of Israel will return to this holy ground (3:5), to the *sneh*, to *Sinai*, to receive God's commandments, the sign of God's love.[23]

On Horeb, Moses begins to understand the importance of Israel as God's partner in covenant. God speaks to Moses from the burning bush because of the merit of Israel and its future role as a light among nations.[24] The sole source of Moses's authority, then, is his relationship with God and with the people; his leadership is forever to be intertwined with Israel's mission. This reality clearly determines the nature of Moses's leadership and how he will relate to the people.

MOSES'S FEARS AND SELF-DOUBT

When Moses turns aside to see the burning bush, he marvels at the sight and is frightened by it at the same time. And when God calls his name from the bush, he recoils. He cannot comprehend that God is addressing him directly. After all, who is Moses at that very moment but a simple shepherd caring for his father-in-law's flock in the wilderness? So when he hears his name booming forth from the burning bush, he is speechless.[25] He hides his face and is afraid to look (3:6). His

Patrick Lencioni, a management consultant, defines humility in relationship to leadership as "the realization on the part of leaders that they are no better than the people they lead." He urges all leaders to embrace both ego and charisma, and at the same time to remain humble if they are to be successful.[27]

reticence and insecurity are clearly manifest here, showing how very human he is. As a result, God must call out his name again before Moses responds (3:4). According to the tradition, Moses never totally overcomes his reticence when God calls him. Each time God reveals the Divine Self, God has to call out "Moses" twice before he is able to reply.[26] The Rabbis stress that Moses never loses the humility that characterizes him as a leader: "Now Moses was a very humble man, more so than any other person on the earth" (Numbers 12:3). In his humility, Moses exemplifies the challenge that every leader faces. We, who are called to lead others, by our very natures have healthy egos. We enjoy the spotlight and the accolades. How, then, as we bask in the spotlight, can we retain a sense of humility, which is crucial if we are to truly succeed in responding to others?

Moses's self-doubt is even more evident in his response following God's charge to him: "Who am I that I should go to Pharaoh and free the Israelites from slavery?" (3:11). Moses's reticence to assume the leadership role stems from several factors: He's justifiably afraid of confronting the powerful Pharaoh, who has issued a warrant for his death,[28] but he also fears the People of Israel, God's covenanted partner. How can he possibly lead this benighted people out of Egypt?[29] Stressing his unworthiness relative to the magnitude of God's expectations of him, he is utterly humbled.[30] He is convinced that the Israelites will neither follow him nor listen to him (4:1), even though God assures him that they will (3:18). Moses, in short, is projecting his own fears onto the people.

Moses is at a loss; he feels like an imposter. He is a mere shepherd who believes he cannot find the words to convince the people to follow him.[31] He pleads with God: "I have never been a person of words, either in times past or now.... I am slow of speech and slow of words" (4:10).

Larry Bossidy, former CEO of Allied Signal, cautioned all leaders when he noted: "Being the CEO used to mean you knew everything. But these are very humbling jobs. And the more you search, the more you recognize every reason you have to be humble, because there is an awful lot more to [know and to] do all the time."[33]

How ironic! Moses, who is destined to become one of the most renowned lawgivers and poets in human history, feels at the outset that he lacks the ability to articulate God's vision—the vision the people must embrace if they are to trust in his leadership.[32] How can he possibly lead this people? All of us who are leaders worry at certain times that we are imposters, just as Moses does. Moses's insecurities mirror our own. We are most fearful that those we lead will ultimately discover that we are not as talented, capable, committed, or compassionate as we seem to be (or need to be). As self-assured as most leaders appear, each one is plagued by self-doubt and must work diligently to overcome it. When Moses is racked with such fears, his sense of inadequacy—his concern that he will be unmasked as a fraud—resonates with our own feelings that we lack the skills and knowledge for the position we hold.[34]

Moses's hesitancy in responding to God's call to divine service prompts a protracted negotiation between God and Moses, spanning almost two full biblical chapters, Exodus 3–4. According to the rabbinic tradition, for a whole week, God attempts to coax Moses to undertake the mission to deliver the Israelites from Egypt.[35] For every excuse Moses offers, God has an answer, demonstrating to Moses the power and authority on which he can draw.[36]

WHENCE COMES MOSES'S AUTHORITY AND POWER?

God clearly delineates for Moses the mission for which he has been called. Having witnessed the Egyptians' oppression of the People of Israel, God says to him, "Come, therefore, and I will send you to Pharaoh, and you shall free My people, the Israelites, from Egypt" (3:10). Each half of the verse spells out a separate command and a distinct expectation of Moses: The first half is a command for him to undertake the mission to Egypt, while the second is to deliver the people from slavery. Both address what are Moses's greatest fears— confronting Pharaoh, who has sworn to kill him, and his concerns that the Israelites will not accept his leadership.[37]

Initially, Moses reacts to both commands by expressing his inadequacy:

"Who am I that I should go to Pharaoh and free the Israelites from Egypt?" (3:11).

In response to Moses's feelings of inadequacy, God tells Moses that he is not alone: "I will be with you" (3:12). Even though Moses feels he is not up to the task assigned to him, God is there to support him in every way.[38] Leaders must recognize that they are not alone in fulfilling the mission of the group or the people whom they lead. Others are there to help, to support them in ways that compensate for any shortcomings they may have. No single person—no matter how knowledgeable, innovative, or creative—can be totally responsible for the success of the group or company.[39]

The source of Moses's authority is clear when God continues, "It will be a sign [*ot*] that it was I who sent you" (3:12). But what exactly is the sign that God alludes to—the signal that God is with Moses and is the source of his leadership? Most likely, this is the burning bush on Mount Horeb, which Moses has just witnessed, a foreshadowing of the main event: Israel's receiving the commandments at Mount Sinai.[40] Just as the bush is not consumed, Israel will be delivered from Egypt by God, through the hand of Moses, in order to forge a covenant with God at Sinai and embark on its divine mission. The use of the term *ot*, "sign," as a reference here to the bush on Horeb further underscores that justification for Moses's leadership: God's support of him because of the relationship between the Divine and Israel. Israel's service to God is the real reason why Moses is chosen to lead the People of Israel out of Egypt.[41] Israel is God's people, and the Divine reminds Moses that he is a mere vehicle to bring them to Sinai and then to the Promised Land: "You shall free My people, the Israelites, from Egypt (3:10) ... and when you have freed the people from Egypt, you [plural] shall worship God at this mountain (3:12)."

But Moses doubts that he has the ability to convince the people of his and their close relationship with the Divine. He is concerned that if the people ask him for God's name, he will not be able to respond. If he doesn't even know the name of the Divine, how can he demonstrate his authority, which is linked to the presence and support of the Divine?

In response, Moses is immediately made privy to the full name of the Divine: *Ehyeh Asher Ehyeh*, "I will be that which I will be" (3:14). God reveals the Divine Self in its fullness, but only to Moses, since knowing a name represents power in relation to the bearer of the name. By contrast, when God directs Moses to reveal God's name to the Israelites, God tells him to say, "*Ehyeh* sent me to you." God's singular reality and presence is made known to the leader, Moses, while the People of Israel only come to know God's presence in a limited way.[42]

All religious leaders derive their authority and power from the people's perception of their intimate relationship with God. Each one must be able to claim a place on the continuum of leadership, characterized by intimate knowledge of and relationship with the Divine.

Moses is no different. From the moment God first calls him, God identifies the Divine Self as "the God of your father, the God of Abraham, the God of Isaac and the God of Jacob" (3:6). Moses stands in an unbroken chain of leadership from the inception of the Israelites as God's people. Even though the biblical text mentions the names of the three patriarchs, the term used to refer to them is singular, "the God of your father." The singular term *father* is meant as a collective to emphasize that Moses's authority is comparable to that of all of his predecessors.[43] Hammering the point home, Moses is instructed to tell the Israelites that "the Lord, the God of your fathers, the God of Abraham ... Isaac ... and Jacob has sent me to you" (4:15). God's name, the divine essence, is linked to the leaders of the past, and Moses now draws his power from walking in their footsteps.[44]

When Moses gathers and speaks with the leaders of the people, the elders (3:16), he stresses his connection to the patriarchs, a point God mentions over and over again, as God attempts to convince him that the Israelites will indeed recognize his authority and follow him.[45] To win the people's confidence and support, Moses must be linked to the leaders of the previous generations, whom the people venerate.[46] Leaders not only need to win over the group's spokespeople, they also must bring those representatives into the leadership process. Even though leaders are granted authority, they must still gain the support and participation of at least some of those who hold power already. Therefore, even though his authority comes from God, Moses is directed by God to appear together with the elders before Pharaoh (3:18), just as later he will bring Aaron with him as his spokesperson (e.g. Exodus 5:1).[47] He cannot lead alone.

Yet, with all of God's assurances that his authority will be recognized by the people, Moses nevertheless still harbors doubts: "What if they do not believe me and do not listen to me, but say, 'The Lord did not appear to you'?" (4:1) Like most leaders, Moses remains uncertain about his ability to command the people's respect, even though he has been charged with leading them. All leaders need concrete signs of their authority, and God provides Moses with three signs to demonstrate his power (4:2–9).

In response to Moses's concern that he lacks the authority to make the people believe him, God asks him a simple question: *Ma-zeh b'yadeicha*, "What is that in your hand," meaning, What power do you [already] possess? Moses replies, "*mateh*," a rod (4:2), which is a play on words: *ma-zeh/mateh*.[48] Moses seems unaware that he already has in his hand the power to lead his people; it is part of him. The rod is an extension of his arm; it represents his ability to act. It is also a sign that God is with him, a symbol which, according to the rabbinic tradition, has been in the possession of the leader of every generation going back to Adam in the Garden of Eden. Rabbinic mythology emphasizes that the rod was created in the twilight of the sixth day of Creation, prior to the expulsion of Adam and Eve from the Garden. God thereby provided them and every subsequent leader with the vehicle of redemption, the power to return us to the para-disial place of intimacy with the Divine.[49]

Like all leaders, Moses possesses the rod, and all he has to do is believe that he has the power, the ability, to lead. Once he does, he has to wield that power effectively; he has to be willing to act. So God commands him to cast the rod to the ground, thus transforming it into a snake, and then, even though he is frightened, he must pick up the snake to return it to its original form (4:3–4). Though Moses recoils from the sight of the snake, perhaps from his own power, he surely is strengthened by the demonstration of his ability and God's presence with him. When he "put[s] out his hand and seize[s] [*va-yahazek*] [the snake]" (4:4), he himself becomes strong (*hazak*). And Moses needs to be told to always take the *mateh*, the rod, with him in his hand, with which he would be able to perform the signs (*otot*) in the future to deliver his people (4:17). The rod is an *ot*, a sign of the relationship between the people and God, the covenant, which is his source of power, the essence of his leadership.

But even though he possesses the powerfully symbolic rod, Moses still doubts his ability to lead the people, since he lacks the one skill all leaders need: the ability to speak well. He sees himself as being "slow of speech and slow of tongue" (4:10). To this final, but essential perceived inadequacy, God responds succinctly, yet most poignantly: "*Mi sam peh la-adam*, Who gives the human being speech?" (4:11) Like all leaders, Moses must learn that power and ability do not emanate from him, but rather they originate elsewhere. From the very first human being, *Adam,* as with every one of God's creations, it is the Source of Life that provides us with the characteristics and abilities that make us who we are and sustain us.[50] Each of us is born with qualities that have been developed from the beginning of time and passed down from generation to generation. God, then, is with Moses, as the biblical text emphasizes through the words of the Divine: "Now go, and I will be with you as you speak" (4:12). If we believe that the power rests with us, if we are egotistical enough to think that it all emanates from us and depends solely on us, then Moses is justified in feeling unable to adequately express himself, since he suffers from a speech impediment from his youth. Yet, the power that makes for wholeness is ever with each of us and guarantees that we will be able to find the strength to passionately communicate the message, just as Moses will learn. He is not alone; there is a force in the universe that is with him, if only he can open himself to it. Since his leadership serves a larger purpose, he can tap into a source that is larger than himself.

Yet, despite all of God's reassurances, Moses desperately pleads with God: "Please, O Lord, send someone else!" (4:13). With this short outburst, Moses indicates his essential lack of readiness to assume the role of leader of his people. It cannot be clearer. Moses feels that there must be another person better suited to fulfill the divine mission.[51] God, though angered by Moses's response, makes the ultimate concession to his reticent leader: There is another who

> On his famous exploration of the Antarctic between 1914 and 1916 captaining the *Endurance,* Ernest Shackleton had Frank Wild as his second in command. Without Wild, Shackleton could not have succeeded in bringing all his men home safely. Wild was a perfect number two—he was loyal, cheerful, decent, strong, and experienced, but very different from Shackleton. While the "Boss" was the idea man, the visionary and planner, Wild knew how to get things done.[52]

will serve as his spokesperson; one who is a skilled speaker (4:14–16). Aaron, Moses's older brother, is willing to play second fiddle to Moses, accepting his role as Moses's mouthpiece. Leaders cannot succeed on their own. The most effective leaders partner with capable individuals whose skills and knowledge complement their own, individuals who are comfortable playing second fiddle. In forging a leadership team in every organization, business, or group, the most important choice the leader makes is designating his second in command. The number-two person is the most important hire, and must be someone who balances the leader's strengths and temperament, shows loyalty without being a sycophant, and has a talent for working well with a variety of individuals and groups.

Leaders often find it difficult to share power. Subordinates, meanwhile, may grouse that, given their successes, they should be the ones who receive the ultimate recognition. For the greater good, they should be encouraged to act like Aaron, who revels in his relationship with his younger sibling, even though Moses plays a superior role (4:14–16).

3
The Vision of Leadership
Exodus 6:2–13

Moses and Aaron both go to Pharaoh, requesting that he let their people go, so they can worship God in the wilderness (Exodus 5:1), but Pharoah refuses (5:2). Pharaoh then persecutes the Israelite slaves even more (5:6–14). If Moses is reticent to accept God's call to free his people from Egyptian slavery at the Burning Bush, is it any wonder that Moses's confidence in his mission and his desire to proceed are completely deflated following Pharaoh's refusal to let the Israelites leave Egypt?[1] He lashes out at God, chastising the Divine: "Why did You bring harm upon this people? Why did You send me? Ever since I came to Pharaoh ... he has dealt worse with this people, and still You have not delivered Your people?" (5:22–23).

It is clear, even to the people, that Moses's protestations about the treatment of the Israelites do not mitigate the suffering of his people; rather, they suffer even greater hardship. Moses's anger at God reflects his lack of patience as well as his increasing self-doubt. The focus of his complaint is that he, as the leader and God's spokesperson, has not succeeded.[2] What Moses and every new leader must learn is that courage is not the absence of fear of failure, but rather acting despite the fear. We all have doubts about our ability, especially at the outset of our service and when we are rebuffed for the first time. The test of our leadership capacity comes down to this: How do we overcome our fears and work through them?

CONTINUITY AND UNIQUENESS OF LEADERSHIP

In response to Moses's complaint and his questioning again of why God had sent him (*shalach*) to Egypt, the Divine takes Moses to task,[3] telling him that "he will see what I will do to Pharaoh: He shall let them go [*shalach*] because of a greater might" (6:1). The message again is clear: God's power guarantees the redemption of the People of Israel from Egypt. God speaks to Moses as *Elohim* (6:2), which the Rabbis understand as God's attribute of justice, conveying to him that the Divine will deliver the people who have suffered so terribly.

Yet, at the same time, God identifies the Divine Self as *Adonai,* which represents God's compassion.[4] The phrase "I am *Adonai*" is meant to comfort and encourage Moses, and by extension, the entire people: God has the power to deliver them and will not let Moses fail.[5] Why does God remind Moses of the divine name? To reinforce that Moses's power and authority comes from his relationship with God, who can be relied on to fulfill the Divine's promises. The name *Adonai* signifies that God is the keeper of promises.[6]

So God then directs Moses to speak in the Divine's name—the source of Moses's power—beginning with the words, "I am *Adonai*" (6:6), I am the One who will fulfill the covenantal promise to deliver you from slavery. I revealed Myself to you at the Burning Bush, as the God of your ancestors, promising to deliver your people from the oppression of Egypt, and so it shall be.[7]

Indeed, God emphasizes that the covenant sealed with their forebears, with Abraham, Isaac, and Jacob, in which God pledged to bring their descendants to the land of Canaan (6:3–4), will come to pass, no matter what Israel's response is to Moses's initial efforts.[8] God does not send Moses to Egypt needlessly; his role is to fulfill the promises God made to the patriarchs:[9] "I will bring you into the land which I swore to give to Abraham, Isaac and Jacob ... I am Adonai" (6:8). The covenant with the earlier generations is to be fulfilled now. This is the context for Moses's entire mission: His leadership is an extension of God's promise to those who came before him. Like all leaders, Moses must understand that his role and even his vision stem, in part, from his predecessors. Successful leaders, especially in the context of a religious community, are not afraid to place themselves in a continuum of leadership, building on the achievements and goals of those who came before.

Even though leaders stand on the shoulders of those who came before them, they can reach heights that none of their predecessors did, and every modern leader strives to do just that. Moses knows God in ways that the patriarchs did not: The Bible emphasizes this when God says, "I appeared to Abraham, Isaac, and Jacob as *El Shaddai,* but I did not make Myself known to them by My name, *Adonai"* (6:3). That the patriarchs did not know God by the name of *YHWH* seems to be contradicted by any number of biblical passages.[11] However, that does not seem to be the point here. Rather, with the advent of Moses, a fuller and new sense of God's essence is achieved.[12] Unlike the previous leaders of the people, Moses is able to know God in a new and distinct way: He experiences the Divine as the One who will fulfill promises. In the face of his doubts about his own ability and God's power to deliver, Moses is able to summon the strength and insight to enable him and the People of Israel to overcome their despair and pain.[13] Each new generation of leaders must figure out how to succeed in the context of the challenges they face, some of which previous generations of leaders might never have confronted. Like Moses, they have to identify the sources of their strength and authority so they can respond to the unique exigencies of their day. Leadership, therefore, is the fine bal-

Though Federal Express as a corporation is relatively young, the FedEx management team understands that success depends on a continuity-of-leadership vision. Their corporate literature states, "Our aim is to infuse our managers with the ... philosophy that the company has held to and benefited from for over twenty-five years." They want their current leaders to internalize and build upon the vision that has driven the company throughout its short but successful history.[10]

ance between continuity and change: building on the vision and insights of those who came before, but creating new and distinctive ways to extend the vision and bring it to fruition. It is not merely a matter of moving the inherited vision one step forward, but rather responding to new circumstances and problems by reframing that vision itself.

MOSES'S VISION FOR THE PEOPLE OF ISRAEL

The promise made to the patriarchs will be fulfilled through Moses. In response to Moses's charge that the lives of the Israelites are worse now than before his coming to Egypt and that God is not sensitive to their plight (5:22–23), God reiterates what he stressed to Moses at the Burning Bush: "I now [*gam*] have heard the moaning of the Israelites because the Egyptians are holding them in bondage" (6:5). But the word *gam* means "also," perhaps replying to Moses's chastisement of the Divine: "You, Moses, think you are the only one who hears and is affected by the people's cries? I, too, hear them and will save them!"[14] "Say, therefore (*lichen*), to the Israelite people: 'I am *Adonai.*'" (6:6). Using the word *lachen,* according to the Rabbis, as well as the idiom *nasati 'et yadi,* I raise My hand (6:8), both signify a pledge or oath, indicating God's commitment to act.[15]

God's words are meant as a message of renewed hope, a vision of redemption, articulated by Moses through a series of seven verbs that shift the focus from past to future (6:6–8).[16] The vision of liberation is set in a poetic rhythm involving these seven verbal promises, which follow one another like staccato hammer blows driving home the sense that redemption will come in stages.[17]

The vision of Israel's liberation that Moses is asked to convey spotlights the stages of the journey through which the people—all people—must pass, in ascending order. The first is physical freedom: "I will take [*hotzaiti*] you out from under the burdens of Egypt" (6:6). Before anything else, people must be free from all physical persecution and constraint. The second stage is spiritual freedom: "I will deliver [*hitzalti*] you from their labor [*avodah*]" (6:6). If *avodah* merely meant "labor" or "work," then the text would appear to be redundant, since the previous promise referred to their physical burdens (*sivlot*). Therefore, the tradition understands *avodah* as *avodah zarah*, idolatry, servitude to the gods of the Egyptians: they will be removed from idol worship.

Free both physically and spiritually, they are now ready for the third stage, redemption: "I will redeem [*ga'alti*] you with an outstretched arm" (6:6). Erich Fromm speaks of two kinds of freedom: "freedom from" and "freedom to." Once individuals are free of all constraint, they are ready to choose to align themselves with a higher source of wisdom, which can elevate themspiritually.[18] Having then experienced God's redemptive power, the people now can become God's covenantal partner, the fourth stage: "I will take [*lakachti*] you to be My people and I will be [*hayiti*] your God" (6:7). At this point, Israel is ready for the revelation at Mount Sinai. Once they are redeemed from Egypt, *Mitzrayim*, the narrow places, the People of Israel are poised to be adopted by God as the Divine's people. And finally, with the relationship sealed, God adds a fifth promise: "I will

In the early 1990s, Allied Signal was suffering from a lack of purpose, and decreased morale, and the bottom line was showing. Larry Bossidy, its CEO, asked his employees to make some difficult sacrifices. What made them willing to make these sacrifices for the sake of the future? *Fortune* magazine noted that Bossidy painted a compelling picture of the future similar to that which Moses articulated to the Israelites in Egypt. The employees could see the Promised Land and the stages by which to get there.[20]

bring [*haivaiti*] you into the land ... and I will give [*natati*] it to you for an [eternal] possession" (6:8).

This vision of redemption enunciated by Moses has three essential aspects—the redemption of the people, God's adoption of Israel, and then their settlement of the Land of Israel,[19] though there are clearly five promises embedded in the vision: "I will take you out ... I will deliver you ... I will redeem you ... I will take you to be My people ... I will bring you into the land." So why does the tradition hold that the four cups of wine consumed during the Passover seder symbolize four promises of redemption, ending with God taking Israel as a covenanted partner on Sinai?[21] To be sure, one could rationalize that the process of redemption culminates on Mount Sinai with Israel's acceptance of the Torah.[22] In addition, the Rabbis suggest that the four promises and the four cups correspond to the four decrees of persecution that Pharaoh issued against the Israelites.[23] Yet God provided Israel with four cups of comfort and salvation, not only as an antidote to Egyptian persecution, but also in anticipation of the four exiles that Israel will suffer during its history.[24] Egypt (that is, the narrow, constricted places) is experienced in every generation by each one of us, and the People of Israel, along with all of humanity, ever yearn for deliverance.[25]

But let us not forget that there is a fifth promise: God will bring Israel to the land and they shall inherit it. To the later Rabbis this promise has never been totally fulfilled and therefore is represented by the cup of Elijah, a fifth cup, which is not consumed during the seder.[26] Each year on Passover we pray to return to Jerusalem, the Jerusalem of wholeness and perfection. Like Moses, every leader is challenged to formulate and communicate a clear and compelling vision of the group's future—a vision that will engage, energize, and sustain his or her followers. There is nothing more important than this, and how well it's accomplished will determine the leader's ultimate success or failure. People need to see that they are a part of a community whose mission is not merely to create products or to make money, but rather to enhance the quality of life of people and the overall community.[27]

THE PEOPLE'S INABILITY TO RESPOND TO THE VISION

Moses transmits his vision of hope and redemption to his people, expecting that it will energize and rally the Israelites by convincing them that God is about to free them from Egyptian slavery. Yet his promises of redemption fall on deaf ears.[28] "They would not listen to Moses, because their spirits were crushed and because of the heavy burden of [their] labor [*avodah kashah*]" (6:9). Their reaction is totally understandable. Utterly demoralized because of their suffering, they have given up hope completely.[29]

But the Rabbis understand that the people's suffering as slaves is not the only reason they cannot hear and accept Moses's redemptive vision. When the Exodus text describes the Israelites as not listening to Moses because of *avodah kashah,* the heavy burden of the work, the tradition plays on the words *avodah kashah,* interpreting them as referring to *avodah zarah,* "foreign worship," meaning idolatry.[30] After four hundred years of slavery in Egypt, ensconced in the idolatrous practices of Egypt, the people have assimilated the religious culture of the surrounding society, and it is nearly impossible for them to abandon the known—the familiar religious practices—to worship a God unknown to them.[31] The slaves want to remain slaves, even when the burden of the workload is made more onerous, and the only way they will abandon Egypt and its idols is for God eventually to force them to leave.[32] This is the greatest challenge leaders have to confront: how to maintain hope in the face of their followers' inability to respond to their initiatives and vision. Caught up in their everyday lives or overburdened by responsibility, they cannot even conceive of a better way to live. Therefore, leaders rarely have instant success. It takes time, patience, and powers of persuasion for a leader to convince his followers to embrace the vision he articulates for the group. Oftentimes, the lack of success has nothing to do with the leader's skills. All leaders must learn to persevere, to overcome personal disappointment, when their efforts to move their community do not produce the hoped-for result.

When the people refuse to listen to him and to embrace the vision he articulates in God's name, Moses again begins to doubt his own ability. Moses responds to the apathy of his followers by dwelling on his own lack of eloquence, as he did at Mount Horeb. This will lead to the initial failure of his mission to Pharaoh: "The Israelites would not listen to me; how then should Pharaoh heed me, who am of impeded speech?" (6:12). Though at first he conquers his self-doubts, with the help of Aaron, and gains the confidence of his people (4:31), when their suffering increases, the people lose faith in him.[33] If the Israelites themselves will not listen to him, Pharaoh certainly won't! Moses simply is not worthy of speaking before the king of Egypt, to try to convince Pharaoh to let his people go.[34]

But the Exodus text notes that "the Israelites did not listen to me; neither would Pharaoh. And [as a result,] I am a person of impeded speech." In other words, Moses's inability to speak is due to their inability to truly hear and internalize his message, not the other way around.[35] The leader's ability to articulate a vision in a convincing manner depends in part on whether her followers have the capacity to truly hear. Their failure to listen can weaken the resolve of the leader to express herself clearly and distinctly. The leader must draw strength and inspiration from the people.[36] Many modern leaders have come to understand that no one person—no matter how skilled, knowledgeable, or creative—can succeed on her own. Success derives from a combination of the leader's ability to lead, her followers' ability to hear and internalize the leader's message, and their decision ultimately to act on it.

GOD ENSURES THAT MOSES WILL SUCCEED

The people will not listen to Moses when God commands him to "Go and tell Pharaoh ... to let the Israelites leave his land" (6:11), so Moses reasons that if the Israelites will not listen to him, why should Pharaoh (6:12)! But in response to Moses's contention that if the people do not listen to him, how will the king of Egypt, God reminds Moses that he has support. The Divine speaks directly to both Moses and Aaron, telling them what they should say to the Israelites as well as to Pharaoh. After not mentioning Aaron once in the articulation of the divine vision which is to be conveyed to the People of Israel, Aaron emerges as a full partner. Aaron's role is not limited to speaking to the Israelites, as is implied in the earlier interchange with Moses on Horeb (4:13ff); he, too, will address Pharaoh as well as their Israelite brothers and sisters.[37] Moses will not have to stand alone; Aaron will share the burden and the challenge with him.

Even though Moses is plagued with self-doubt, acknowledges that the people are not listening to him, and therefore needs to involve Aaron in the divine mission to a greater extent, Moses continues to be the leader of the people and God's spokesperson. Moses cannot be absolved of this primary role, since only he was privy to God's revelation of the vision for the future.[38] As the leader, Moses remains the recognized transmitter and embodiment of the people's mission, no matter how useful the people with whom he is surrounded.

According to the rabbinic tradition, the Israelites show their true nature in refusing to listen to Moses and to embrace God's promise for their future. They are obstinate, troublesome, and caught up in their idolatrous ways.[39] Yet God expects him to withstand their abuse, learning to tolerate their inability to break free from idol worship, since God the Divine Self considers them God's children even in their sinfulness.[40] Playing on the verse "God commanded [them] the Israelites and Pharaoh to deliver the Israelites from the land of Egypt" (6:13), some rabbinic texts take it to mean that "God commanded Moses and Aaron [them]"—not the Israelites—charging the two leaders to deal with their people in an understanding and gentle manner. God expects them to be patient with the People of Israel, despite the people's shortcomings.[41] They will succeed in their mission to redeem the people from Egypt if their demeanor reflects the qualities that will enable the Israelites to conquer their own impatience and despair over time. Moses and Aaron grapple with a dilemma common to all leaders: They need to be sensitive to the morale of those whom they lead, both when they themselves fall short of expectations and when they feel personally burdened and oppressed.

Even as Moses and Aaron have to learn to keep attuned to the moods of their fellow Israelites and patient with their shortcomings, they are also instructed to speak forcefully, yet respectfully, to the stubborn king of Egypt. They must learn how to approach the Israelites and Pharaoh in ways that will be most effective in each

Nissan Motors had a union drive in the late 1980s, which the union supporters lost. As soon as the vote was taken, the president of Nissan, Jerry Benefield, went on television with a compassionate message of conciliation: "I asked the supporters of the union to continue to be team members and those on the company side not to gloat, so there would be no animosity whatsoever."[42]

case.[43] At times, leaders have to be understanding and patient, and at other times, forceful and persistent. They have to appreciate that different approaches fit different situations and different constituencies.

4
We Possess the Power and the Ability
Exodus 14:10–16

As a result of Moses and Aaron's forceful confrontation with Pharaoh and the power of the ten plagues, the king of Egypt relents and allows the Israelites to leave. However, once the Israelites flee Egypt, Pharaoh and the Egyptians have a change of heart and give chase. And though the Children of Israel leave Egypt defiantly,[1] Pharaoh and his chariots quickly overtake them (Exodus 14:5–9). As the Egyptians draw near, the Israelites raise their eyes and catch sight of them. In raising their eyes, the Israelites gaze heavenward, once again longing to witness God's protective presence, just as they experienced it in Egypt. But all they can see are the powerful Egyptians in pursuit.

WITNESSING ISRAEL'S LOSS OF FAITH

Seeing the Egyptians bearing down on them, the Israelites become greatly frightened, *va-yir'u* (14:10). Here their vision leads to fear, indicated by a subtle wordplay on the Hebrew roots *ra'ah* (see) and *yarah* (fear).[2] They cannot see their way out of the predicament at the sea and therefore lose their faith. Even though they are saved from Egyptian slavery through the actions of God and Moses, all they can now envision is dying in the desert at the hands of the very Egyptians from whose clutches their God released them. As a result, they challenge Moses, asserting, "Was it for want of graves in Egypt that you brought us into the wilderness to die? What is this that you have done to us, taking us out of Egypt? ... It is better to serve the Egyptians than to die in the desert" (14:11–12). They prefer to be persecuted and die of their suffering in Egypt, than die in the barrenness and aridity of the desert.[3]

Forgetting all that God has done to redeem them from Egypt, including the awesome power exhibited by God through the ten plagues, the Israelites cry out (*va-yitza'ku*) to God (14:10), just as they had during their persecution by the Egyptians prior to the redemption.[4] They revert to a pattern of recrimination that preceded their experience of God's redemptive power, and to expressions of doubt that reflect their earlier response to God's promises: "Is this not the very thing we told you in Egypt, saying, 'Let us be and we will serve the Egyptians, for it is better to serve the Egyptians than to die in the wilderness'?" (14:12). Although the Israelites never actually say these words to Moses while they are Egypt, they surely reflect the doubt that they must have felt when they are first assured that God will free them from Egyptian slavery. They now believe that it is better to suffer the pain of slavery than die at the hands of the Egyptians, especially in the desert where they cannot even be buried with dignity.[5]

The double irony here is that the expression *va-yitza'ku* (they cried out) generally means in the Bible that the Israelites prayed to God.[6] But just when we think that they are again praying for God's intervention, their words are actually directed against Moses in a most sarcastic manner,[7] as they continue addressing Moses directly (14:11). Nachmanides goes as far as to posit that even though they prayed to God, still believing in the Divine, they begin to doubt Moses and his authority and intentions.[8] Philo's extension of Israel's sudden accusations against Moses points up how the people's fear is turned into anger directed against their leader: "Is not ... slavery a lighter ill than death? You enticed [us] with the hope of liberty, and then have saddled it with the greater danger that threatens [our] lives. Did you not know that we were unarmed, and [did you not recognize] the bitterness and savage temper of the Egyptians? Do you not see how great are our troubles; how impossible to escape? What must we do? Can we fight unarmed against the armed? Can we fly, surrounded as in a net by merciless enemies, pathless deserts, seas impassable to ships, or, if indeed they are passable, what supply of boats have we to enable us to cross?"[9] The people, facing crisis in the desert, immediately question Moses's authority and leadership, and voice the desire to return to Egypt.[10] This is a challenge addressed most personally to Moses, as seen by the clear emphasis in the text: "You brought us to die in the wilderness ... What is this that you have done [*mah zot asita*] to us? ... Is this not the very thing that we told you in Egypt?" It is all Moses's fault; the result of his megalomania![11]

Ironically, the Israelites, in their condemnation of Moses, echo the Egyptians when they express regret at letting the slaves leave: "What is this that we have done (*mah zot asinu*)?" Both the Israelites and the Egyptians agree that the People of Israel are better off in Egypt. In fact, in attacking Moses's unwise, miscalculated, and dangerous initiative, the Israelites utter the name of Egypt five times, falling back on what they know, rather than trusting Moses. They can hardly mention *Egypt* often enough.[12] Great leaders rarely accomplish their mission without encountering internal opposition, which sometimes takes the form of personal attacks. Adversity can easily derail a leader who lacks fortitude, but it only energizes leaders with a strong purpose.[13]

Opposition and complaints assail Moses nonstop. Every time things go awry for the Israelites in the desert, they blame Moses. It is Moses, not God, who led them out of Egypt.[14] Even after the miracle of the splitting of the Red Sea and the jubilant song of praise that follows, the people's anger is again directed at Moses. They use the interrogative, *Mah*, "What shall we drink?" (15:24). The Israelites are caught up in themselves and their own needs. It is always about them, and the people's contrarian nature seems to justify Moses's earlier skepticism about them.[15]

But the rabbinic tradition does not view the People of Israel as a monolith. It is hardly possible, according to the Rabbis, for Israel to plead for God's deliverance and at the same time complain so bitterly against Moses. So perhaps these sentiments reflect different segments of the people; those who believe in God's redemptive powers pray to the Divine: "*Va-yiz'aku Bnai Yisrael* [literally, they cried out] ... *el Adonai*," while others cry out and complain against Moses.[16] In fact, there may have been multiple voices present among the people, and the Rabbis pass down a tradition through the centuries that Israel was divided into four different camps as it stood before the Red Sea: "One camp said, 'Let us throw ourselves into the sea.' One said, 'Let us return to Egypt.' One said, 'Let us fight them.' And one said, 'Let us cry out against them.'"[17] Moses's words to the People of Israel at the Red Sea are the basis on which the Rabbis build the notion that there were four different attitudes among the Israelites, and his words are understood as embodying his responses to them. Moses is pictured as responding to each camp in unique ways, addressing each of their doubts, fears, and complaints. The camp that says, "Let us throw ourselves into the sea," is told, "Stand still and witness the deliverance of the Lord" (14:13). To the one that calls out,

Dave Komansky, CEO at Merrill Lynch, stated that it is essential for people to know that you care about them. That does not mean you have to pander to them, or that you don't call attention to things that go wrong, or that you are afraid to say no. But they have to know that you care about them as individuals and respond to each in appropriate ways.[19]

"Let us return to Egypt," Moses says, "For the Egyptians you see today, you will never see again" (14:13). The one that cries, "Let us fight them" is told, "The Lord will fight for you" (14:14). And to the one that asserts, "Let us cry out against them," Moses replies, "You hold your peace" (14:14).[18] One of the most difficult challenges that every leader faces is to recognize the uniqueness of each individual. Too often, we tend to treat constituents as a unit—nameless faces without unique needs and individual stories. In Moses's responses to the various concerns expressed by the people, he models how to allay people's fears and guide them toward consensus. Would that we all could be so wise and insightful.

MOSES IS OVERCOME BY DOUBT

Moses responds to his people, addressing all their concerns, and ends by directing them to hold their peace. When they cry out to God, *va-yitza'ku el Adonai* (14:10), Moses urges them to be silent, *taharishun* (14:14). But then, the next thing we read in the biblical text is God saying to Moses, "Why are you crying out [*titz'ak*] to me?" (14:15). The irony is that the very action symbolizing the people's doubts and fears, *tza'ak*, cry out, is now used by God to describe Moses's state of mind and actions. Moses himself cries out to the Divine.[20] Although God has guaranteed Moses that the Divine will triumph over Pharaoh (14:4), Moses experiences doubt himself. Facing the sea with the enemy in pursuit, Moses seems not to know what to do and he himself cries out to God.[21] Moses prays to God: "Master of the Universe, I am like a shepherd who took his sheep from the level plains, and led them on high mountains, from where I can no longer bring them down ... I simply do not know what to do. We are trapped between Pharaoh's armies and the sea with no place to turn."[22] There are times when even the greatest leaders are lost and begin to doubt their own ability. No matter how much power Moses is able to wield in Egypt, confronted by the people when they behold Pharaoh's army in pursuit, he begins to cry out to God. And God responds to him: "Why are you distressed?" You have the ability to act.[23] Each and every one of us must realize that we possess the power to act, even when we face difficult challenges.

However, since Moses has just urged the people to stand strong and not fear the Egyptians, promising that God will lead the battle against them, thus ensuring victory (14:13–14), it is possible that his cry is not directed against God, in whom he continues to trust, but rather against the people. He may have been devastated by their challenge to his authority and their lack of faith.[24] He doesn't believe that they have the faith to enter the sea. In reaction to Moses's cry, God then says, "Why are you crying out to Me? Why are you so distrustful of your people? Just speak to them and they will move forward [into the water]. They will not disobey you!"[25] But just in case there did exist some doubt on the part of the Israelites concerning Moses's power and authority, God then directs him to raise his rod and extend his arm over the waters of the Red Sea, thus recalling the miracles he performed in Egypt, which all began with his use of the *mateh,* the rod, as he stood before Pharaoh.[26]

MOSES, AS LEADER, RESPONDS
TO THEIR FEARS AND DOUBT

Despite his anger against the people because of their lack of belief in God's power and trust in his leadership, Moses is not dispirited, neither by the danger inherent in the moment nor by the censure of his people.[27] He is still able to understand their doubts, given the predicament they are facing, and he responds to them.[28] The tradition emphasizes his ability to pacify the myriad of Israelites, responding directly to each of their fears: "Don't fear [*al tir'au*]. Stand firm and see [*re'u*] God's deliverance" (14:13).[29] Moses acknowledges their fears, but encourages them to "see" their situation differently. The sound play on *tir'au* and *re'u* underscores his response to his people: They have nothing to fear,

Facing tremendous loss of sales and the possible closure of the plant in Mexico, Peter Brabeck-Letmathe, CEO of Nestlé, needed a new, courageous manager for the company's Mexican operation. He hired an individual who had his doubts about whether the operation could succeed, but possessed a courage that was greater than his fear. The manager conveyed in a measured but firm way to each employee his resolve and confidence, and assured Brabeck-Letmathe: "If you have confidence in me, I will get it done."[31]

for they will indeed no longer see the Egyptians again in the same way, as God will defeat them. The threefold occurrence here of the verb *to see* [*ra'ah*] is not coincidental. Fear is the product of a way of seeing, of perspective; a change in the way they see will change their feelings and thinking.[30] Like every great leader, Moses had to subordinate his own feelings of disappointment, hurt, or even rejection by his followers in order to fulfill his role as leader. It is difficult to suppress one's own ego and even personal comfort in the name of the larger mission—in this case, the deliverance of the People of Israel from bondage. Perhaps Moses's ability to tolerate the people's fears, doubts, and even their challenges to his authority comes from the recognition of his own human misgivings and his self-doubt.

Fearing an all-out and seemingly futile battle against Pharaoh's soldiers, Moses offers the simple visionary declaration: "God will do battle for you; you simply hold your peace" (14:14). The Israelites no longer have to murmur and groan about their situation,[32] since God will protect them as the Divine did in Egypt. God will act and all they have to do is stand by and witness God's redemptive power. It is the powerful simplicity of Moses's words and actions that bolster his people as they face the enemy and the sea.

Herb Kelleher, Southwest Airlines' CEO, said, in this spirit, "You have to be willing to take risks for your people. If you won't fight for them, then you can count on the fact that your people will [not support you]."[37]

After responding to his people's fears and complaints, assuring them that God will save them, Moses turns to God, as we can see from God's reaction: "Why do you cry out to me?" (14:15). Moses cries out on behalf of his people, embodying their fears and needs.[33] When they cry out, he also cries out.[34] The tradition consistently understands Moses's cry as his praying on behalf of the people.[35] When Moses tells them that God will save them, the people do not have the strength of belief to await God's intervention and redemption. As a result, Moses prays to God to show them the Divine's power. According to a rabbinic legend, God shows them the accompanying ministering angels who will defend Israel against the Egyptians.[36] Leaders have to lay themselves on the line for their people, especially when the people face tremendous challenges to their success or even their survival. Leaders have to be able to articulate the hope that the people's mission will be fulfilled and communicate to the people their essential belief in them.

MOSES MUST ACT IF THE PEOPLE ARE TO BE SAVED

Moses believes with his entire being that God will intervene on behalf of the Jewish people, destroy the Egyptians, and enable his people to cross the Red Sea. He is convinced that he and the Israelites merely have to stand by and quietly observe the manifestation of divine power, just as they did during the ten plagues in Egypt. Yet after telling his people that God will do battle for them, nothing happens. There appears to be a gap in the biblical account, since the very next thing we as readers learn, following Moses commanding the people "to hold their peace," is that God asks Moses, "Why are you crying out to me?" (14:15). One moment Moses is telling his followers that they are about to witness God's redemptive power, and the next he appears to be crying out to God when the Divine has not yet acted. In this gap in our story, Moses himself perhaps begins to become anxious as he awaits divine intervention and none of the tribes of Israel is daring enough to enter the waters of the sea.

Facing the perils of the Antarctic, Ernest Shackleton frequently contrived ways for each of his crew members to play some kind of meaningful role. He recognized that they all had to feel that they were doing something important, even if they weren't. For example, when their ship was trapped in ice, he had the men attempt to pick, saw, and ram their way out, even though he knew that they would most likely have to wait for the thaw.[39]

The Rabbis in the Midrash say that one person, Nachshon ben Aminadav, the head of the tribe of Judah, is brave enough to jump into the Red Sea. When Moses sees, however, that Nachshon is drowning, he begins to cry out prayerfully to God to save Nachshon and, by extension, all the people. It is then that God finally responds to Moses, saying: "Moses, my friend—Nachshon? ... the people as a whole?—is drowning in the water, the sea is closing in upon him, the enemy is in close pursuit, and you stand there praying! Do something!" Moses responds to God: "Ruler of the universe, what can I possibly do?"[38] Moses, who is every leader and every person, doubts that he has the power and ability to ensure his people's deliverance. But what he doesn't understand is even more critical: The Israelites will not be saved if they merely stand idly by and wait for God to act. There is no such thing as passive redemption!

It is said that Winston Churchill's supreme talent was in motivating people to act. He understood that nearly all human organizations are subject to inertia, which results in an "it-can't-be-done" attitude, and he found this totally unacceptable. He knew how to communicate to people in order to goad them into giving up their reasons for not acting. Churchill once urged a diplomat: "Continue to pester, nag, and bite. Demand audiences. Don't take no for an answer."[41]

As a result, the first thing that God commands Moses to do is to "speak to the Children of Israel." If he does so, God guarantees him that "They will move forward [into the water]" (14:15). Every leader must clearly communicate his expectations to the group; only then will they respond positively and act. Articulating a vision—in Moses's case, what God expects of the people and what will happen if they act—is foremost if change is to occur.

At this moment, crying out to God in prayer—even speaking to the Israelites—is not enough. When God silences Moses by saying to him: "Why are you crying out to me?" (14:15), it is clear that words are insufficient to ensure Israel's redemption. This is no time to pray or to speak with the Israelites, since Israel is in grave danger.[40] God, in effect, is saying to Moses: "Stop talking and act!" And the emphatic, *ve-atta*, "And as for you, Moses," which stands as a counterpoint to Moses's statement to the people, *ve-attem*, "And as for you [pl.], hold your peace" (14:14), underscores Moses's most important role: to act himself. It is not enough for him to speak to the Israelites; he must be a model of action. Therefore, God continues commanding him: "Raise your rod and extend your hand over the sea" (14:16). It is as if God were telling him, "You should have acted on your own initiative, by instructing Israel to proceed into the water, instead of crying out to Me. You should have used your staff to bring about the means for such a crossing of the Red Sea."[42] Leaders must exemplify action in the face of adversity if they want their followers to learn that they, too, must act to improve their world. Mustering the courage to act, the leader inspires her followers to take similar corrective action.

Every leader, including Moses, must learn that he possesses the power to act. Moses has to raise his rod—the symbol not only of God's presence, but also of Moses's own ability—and place it over the waters of the sea, and they will indeed part (14:16). And lest the people, or even Moses himself, believe

Jon Carlzon, CEO of SAS Airlines, when standing up to Air France, which threatened to stop SAS from flying to France, noted: "We had the courage to act ... and once we dared to take the leap, we gained much more than we ever could have imagined." His ability to act in the face of severe challenges was a tremendous morale booster for SAS and united his staff behind him.[43]

that he can only perform miracles using the staff of God, God gives him the double command: "Raise your rod," and then adds, "and extend your hand over the sea." Only then will the sea split. In a sense, Moses has to divest himself of the rod and then extend his empty hand over the waters.[44] Moses's hand channels, or even becomes, God's own hand, which is described as being extended [over the waters] in the Song of the Sea (15:12).[45] Or perhaps it is God's hand that guides Moses's hand and causes the waters to part.[46] In any event, when Moses stretches out his hand, God parts the waters (14:21). If only all religious leaders—even all human beings—would learn that when we act in the world, we act in God's stead and, in those moments, we fulfill our divine potential. And we, like Moses, must also learn that if we do *not* act, nothing will happen. The Rabbis emphasize that if Moses had not raised his rod and extended his hand over the waters, the sea would not have been divided.[47]

Yet another tradition put forth by the Rabbis emphasizes that the sea splits only when the Israelites themselves move into the waters.[48] According to one version, the miracle occurs when the waters reach their nostrils, that is, when they are ready to sacrifice their lives.[49] When they overcome their doubt and faithfully take the first step into the Red Sea, Moses is finally able to perform the miracle of dividing the waters.[50]

The people need to feel that they are participants in this pivotal moment, that they have a role in ensuring their own survival. The tradition therefore stresses that even when Moses commands the people to "be silent and witness God's redemptive power" (14:14), the people should have acted by raising their voices in praise and exaltation of the Divine.[51] A leader must make her followers feel that they are contributing in a meaningful way, especially when they are facing serious challenges. A leader has to truly understand—and then convey to her followers—that their actions will make a difference. At times it may be difficult to find something worthwhile for everyone to do, but giving everyone a role is one crucial psychological aspect of leadership.

The People of Israel continue to grumble, even after the parting of the Red Sea and their miraculous deliverance from the hands of the Egyptians. As noted earlier, after they leave the sea and set out on their journey through the desert, they complain again to Moses that they have nothing to drink! (15:24) Dwelling more on their own immediate situation and needs, they fail to recognize God's protective presence and Moses's leadership ability.

So if the Israelites have not changed, why does God deliver them in the first place? The answer may be twofold. First, God always acts for the meritorious few—those in every generation, like Nachshon ben Aminadav, who commit to action because of their unwavering belief.[52] Second, God always keeps faith with those of earlier generations, to whom God promised the deliverance of their progeny—individuals who embody

Winston Churchill infused his leadership with historical perspective. "The longer you can look back," he wrote, "the farther you can look forward." He also noted, "I have tried to [bring] history up a little nearer to our own times ... that it should be a helpful guide in present difficulties."[53]

a belief that leads to action—such as Abraham's circumcision of or his binding of his son, Isaac.[54] These ancestors served as models by which those of a later generation, leaders and followers alike, can learn what is expected of us all, thus ensuring Israel's future.

5
The Leader's
Unique Song
Exodus 15:1–21

Passing through the Red Sea, the Israelites witness God's power. While they walk on dry land, with the waters forming walls on their right and left, the Egyptians are inundated by those very waters and obliterated. The children of Israel see (*va-yar*) the strong hand (*yad*) of God, which delivers them from the hand (*yad*) of the Egyptians, from the Egyptians' power (Exodus 14:28–31).[1]

Though it is God who seems to act, nevertheless it actually is Moses's hand that divides the waters: "Then Moses held out his hand over the sea and the Lord drove back the sea with a strong wind … and turned the sea into dry ground. The waters were split" (14:21). And it is Moses's hand that destroys the Egyptians: "The Lord told Moses: 'Hold out your hand over the sea, that the waters may come back over the Egyptians" (14:26). Moses is described in God-like terms: Just as God divides the waters on the second day of creation, thereby creating the earth, now Moses creates a new patch of dry land in the midst of the waters of the Red Sea, partnering with God in this moment of redemption. The creation cannot come to fruition—God's plan for humanity fulfilled—without the actions of leaders like Moses.[2]

So the Israelites, many of whom have doubted Moses's ability and motivation, and have been highly critical of him, now see him as

God's partner in this redemptive moment: "They believed in the Lord and in Moses, [God's] servant" (14:31).[3] He is perceived as the faithful instrument of God's will, and therefore it is fitting to refer to him by the title *Eved Adonai,* God's servant.[4]

To have faith in one implies the faith in the other, and, by extension, to doubt or speak against Moses is tantamount to speaking against the Divine.[5]

THE NATURE OF THE SONG AT THE SEA

The Israelites witness and understand the ramifications of the miracle God has wrought for them as they face the waters of the sea and are pursued by Pharaoh and his Egyptian soldiers, and, as a result, their faith in God and in Moses, their leader, is renewed. As a reward for their faith, the rabbinic tradition emphasizes that the spirit of God's Presence rests upon them, enabling them to sing a song of praise and redemption. As they read the biblical text, the Rabbis frequently point up that contiguous passages have a causal relationship. The verse "They believed in Adonai and in Moses, [God's] servant" (14:31) is immediately followed by "Then sang Moses and the Children of Israel" (15:1), as if the people's ability to sing was the product of their belief.[6]

Their words of song and praise, as the Rabbis note, are the result of God's Holy Spirit resting on the Israelites and Moses. This meaning is underscored by a poignant wordplay: Then Moses and Israel are able to sing (*yashir*) the song (*shirah*) because God's Spirit rests (*sharta*) upon them.[7] God's Shechinah is the source of the song of praise, creating a powerful irony: God is both the source and the object of the song! Their faith in both God and Moses leads to their ability to sing, as noted by the use of the simple word *az,* which can be understood as either "then" or "therefore." Here we can translate: "Israel believed ... therefore (*az*) Moses and the Children of Israel sang" (14:31–15:1).[8]

Perhaps it is the faith that the people have in Moses as their leader that enables him to sing this majestic song of praise to God. How is it that Moses, who describes himself by saying, "I am not a person of words ... I am slow of speech and slow of tongue" (4:10), suddenly turns into Israel's singer of God's song?[9] And not only does he give voice to *Shirat ha-Yam,* the Song at the Sea, but some sources claim that he composes the entire song by himself. He finds the words to express what all the people are experiencing and feeling.[10] Even great leaders often need the support and faith of their followers to find the strength to overcome obstacles, such as, in Moses's case, a speech impediment. Without the sense that the people care about them, leaders are often overwhelmed by the myriad personal challenges they face.

Many modern-day leaders suffer from speech impediments and work hard to overcome them. Winston Churchill had a lisp, which he struggled to correct. And Churchill perhaps will best be remembered for his inspiring speeches during the battle of Britain. Part of what enabled him to become such a great communicator was how the British people responded to his leadership initiatives.[11]

But precisely how is the song uttered? Do Moses and Israel sing while they are still in the midst of the waters or do they praise God once they emerge from the Red Sea and have witnessed the Egyptians drowning? It is possible that the people of Israel sing praises to God as they are crossing the sea. If so, they utter the words of the song while still unsure how it will all turn out. Their fear and anxiety, their sense that their fate is hanging in the balance, all suffuse the notes of the Song, as do their hope and faith.[12] When Pharaoh's chariots and soldiers enter the sea (15:19) ... then Moses and Israel sang (15:1).[13] As they walk on the dry land, discovering that deliverance from the hands of Egyptians is indeed possible, Moses and Israel begin to utter praises of God.

Most commentators assume that Israel and Moses sing this song of redemption after their salvation is guaranteed. It involves a retrospective understanding and internalization of all that they have experienced and what it will mean for them in the future. It encompasses a sense of the past and present, which points them toward the future, captured by the initial verb in the future tense: "Then Moses sang/will sing [*yashir*]" (15:1).[14]

But not only does the future tense verb *yashir* indicate that this song will be sung again in the future, as if it were a paradigmatic song to be repeated by future generations, but this interpretation gains greater force by the use of the word *az,* here translated as "then." Though *az* can be taken to refer to both the past and the future, the tradition enumerates many of those verses in which *az* clearly points us to future events.[15] In fact, the Rabbis say that young infants, and even embryos in their mothers' wombs, open their mouths and sing at the sea.[16] Also indicating that the song will be repeated by future generations is the addition of the redundant phrase *va-yomru laimor,* "and they said, saying," before the song's opening words (15:1). In the midrash, the Rabbis emphasize in this regard that "We shall tell our children and our children will tell their children that they should recite a song such as this when God performs miracles for them."[17]

The word for song, *shir,* is close to the root *shur,* which means "to glimpse into the future." As Moses leads Israel in this song marking their deliverance from the hands of their Egyptian taskmasters, he enables them to see the possibility of ultimate redemption. As Miriam demands of them, "Sing to the Lord," *Shiru l'Adonai,* we are tempted to complete the imperative with the messianic phrase from Isaiah 42:10, *shir hadash,* "a new song." According to the rabbinic tradition, ten songs span all of human history, moving from the redemption from Egypt to the coming of the messianic age, of which *Shirat ha-Yam* is one. This series culminates with the song of redemption in Isaiah 42, which is also enunciated in Psalm 149:1.[18]

WHO SINGS THE SONG?

As we have already noticed, it is not clear whether the words used at the outset of the song refer to the past or to the future. However, there is an even greater lack of clarity when it comes to who actually is singing. The verbs are both singular (*yashir*—he sang; *ashirah*—I will sing) and plural (*va-yomru*—they said). Therefore, we as readers are left in the dark as to exactly how the Song at the Sea is performed. When it says, *"Az yashir* [singular] *Moshe u-Venai Yisrael,"* and then *"ashirah l'Adonai,"* does it mean that only Moses sings and the

People of Israel merely listen passively, or do the singular verbs somehow indicate that both are involved in some way? Adding to the confusion as to who performs the song is the phrase *va-yomru laimor,* "and they said, saying" (15:1). This confusion, however, gives rise to several alternative leadership models, each of which can be instructive for us.

The powerful singular verbs lead some commentators and midrashic sources to stress that Moses and Israel sing in unison. Inspired by God's miraculous deliverance and the presence of the Shechinah, they raise their voices as if one person were singing.[19]

Ohe of the most unusual aspects of Ernest Shackleton's Antarctic expeditions was the absence of any leadership hierarchies. He emphasized that everyone was equal and all would share equally in the division of labor throughout the voyages. Everyone did not have equal status, but all were equally valued and involved. On Shackleton's boats, all hands took turns scrubbing the floors and caring for the dogs.[21]

Moses and Israel are seen as being equal, *shekulim.*[20] This model breaks down traditional hierarchy in leadership and creates greater unity among the group.

According to one tradition, the People of Israel, deferring to their leader, request that Moses begin the song, but he declines, saying, "No, you shall begin for it is a greater mark of honor for God to be praised by the multitude than by one single human being." At once, the people sing to God. And only after they finish does Moses also praise God's name for the signs and miracles that he had been shown.[22]

However, the dominant rabbinic tradition holds that Moses is the one who actually begins to sing the words of *Shirat ha-Yam,* and the People of Israel in some way follow his lead. The song is recited antiphonally, though the tradition is not clear as to how that works. The most prevalent view among the Rabbis is that Israel merely echos Moses's words. The leader creates the song alone and the people simply repeat what he sings. Though the teachers to whom this tradition is attributed vary, it appears very early and is repeated over the centuries.[23] Occasionally, there is a debate as to what the people repeated—is it all of Moses's exact words or simply the initial key-word signifiers?[24] The notion that it is Moses who sings and Israel who merely echoes his words and melody is a masculine model of the strong frontal leader who transmits a vision that the people are to follow. Moses is the "I" standing before the people, leading them in song.[25] In this model, only the leader possesses the wisdom and insight to articulate what they must believe and how they must act.

However, some traditions suggest that Israel does not simply mimic Moses's recitation of the song. A number of sources emphasize that, following Moses's singing of a particular phrase of *Shirat ha-Yam,* Israel repeats what Moses has sung and then completes the line, illustrating another form of leadership. They follow his lead, pick up his melody and words, and then add their own. Moses, for example, sings, "I will sing unto the Lord, for He is highly exalted," and the people repeat after him and then finish the line, "I will sing unto the Lord, for He is highly exalted. The horse and rider He has thrown into the

Paul Russell of PepsiCo points out the importance of the individual you place in front of the people as their leader. People need "icons," world-class people whom everyone looks to as the leader or expert and is willing to follow.[26]

Larry Bossidy, former CEO of Allied Signal, realized that developing new leaders is the key to profitability as well as the sustainability of a company. Can those you lead initiate change on their own? Protégés, such as Mary Petrovich, were encouraged by Bossidy to devise their own methods for achieving the company's goals once they had been trained. He understood that there was a difference between mentoring future leaders and telling them exactly what to do.[27]

sea" (15:1).[28] This is a powerful example of leadership development and underscores the nature of the leader's mentoring role.

MIRIAM'S SONG AND MODEL

The notion that the Israelites sing antiphonally at the sea is first suggested by Philo of Alexandria, who imagines that they form two choruses, Moses leading the men and his sister, Miriam, leading the women.[29] Though Miriam's song is relegated to two verses and one line of actual song (15:20–21), its content is exactly the same as the first line of Moses's song: "Sing to the Lord, for He is highly to be praised. The Horse and rider He has thrown into the sea" (15:21). It seems that Miriam essentially plays the same role—leading the women, who follow her, as Moses does for the men.[30]

Yet, Miriam plays a unique role, even compared to her brother, Moses, since the biblical text emphasizes that all the women go out after her with their timbrels, and they praise God through ecstatic dance and song. Miriam is here identified by name for the very first time in the Bible and she is referred to as *ha-Neviah*, the Prophetess, and as the "sister of Aaron." The tradition interprets these titles as signifying that Miriam prophesies the birth of Moses (she is five years old when Moses is born) for she is "only the sister of Aaron when she utters the prophecy."[31] Yet, it is significant that at the moment of Moses's greatest triumph Miriam is also identified as a prophet, like her brother, and is thought of as Aaron's sister. We would expect her to be called "Moses's sister"![32] This stresses the special role Miriam plays.

Miriam's song is clearly different from Moses's song. Moses's singing is described by the verb *yashir*: He sang his song to the people, while Miriam, by contrast, is said to literally "respond" to [the women] (15:21).[33] The word used is *ta'an*, which comes from the root *anah* (answer). Moses sings in front of the congregation, but Miriam reacts to those around her, responding to them and their songs. Hers is a feminine model, one of sensitivity and response, through which she encourages her sisters to sing their own song. Her empowerment of the women to sing their song is clear from the words she utters. In contrast to Moses leading the people by himself, *Ashirah l'Adonai,* I will sing to God, Miriam urges her sisters to sing them-selves, *Shiru l'Adonai,* "Sing to God!" Miriam's model as a leader is clear: to enable those around her to find their own voices through which to praise God. They need not merely emulate or echo the leader's song.[34] Great leaders understand that each person must be encouraged to raise his or her voice.

The tradition goes even further in positing the uniqueness of the song of Miriam and the women. Though it is only one line, in con-trast to the nineteen lines of the song of Moses, the Rabbis stress that Miriam and her sisters actually sing an entire song by themselves, which is different from Moses's song.[35]

The women's song is distinctive because they utilize *tuppim,* drums or timbrels, to accompany their song and dance. According to a frequently cited tradition, the women anticipate that God will per-form miracles for them and that even though they leave Egypt in the middle of the night, in such a rush that they aren't able to prepare food for the journey, they make sure to bring along musical instru-ments.[36] Like all other righteous individuals, they are prepared for the moment of redemption![37] The song of the women is echoed in the drums they carry with them from Egypt; this is understood as expres-sive of their innate faith in the future. As women, understanding the potential of birth as a means of overcoming past suffering and death, they are ever attuned to possible moments of transcendence. They are always ready to break into song.[38] They teach us that all leaders need to have the capacity to celebrate the potential inherent in every new moment as well as the coming to fruition of their vision.

DRAWING FROM THE TWO LEADERSHIP MODELS

Miriam's entire life is associated with water. Not only does she first appear at the Nile to save Moses's life, but her very name (Miriam—*mar yam,* bitter sea or water) is perhaps tied to *Marah,* the place of bitter waters, mentioned, as we will shortly see, immediately after *Shirat ha-Yam* at the end of Exodus 15. It may also be hinted at in Exodus 17, when Israel complains that there is no water to drink when they reach Rephidim, also identified as a place of strife and bit-terness (17:7). Furthermore, in recognition of her song, the tradition envisions a well springing up in the desert that accompanies the Israelites on their trek through the wilderness for most of the next forty years. It is therefore called "Miriam's well."[39]

According to the Rabbis, this well, due to the piety of Miriam, dates back to the beginning of the world, having been formed on the second day of Creation, when God separated the waters, and all the patriarchs and subsequent leaders of the people had access to it.[40] And finally when Miriam dies at Kadesh, the well and its life-giving waters disappear (Numbers 20:2).

As the Israelites proceed on their journey through the desert, they carry with them both the song of Moses, the powerful singular song of the male, as well as the responsive chords of Miriam, who empowers others to sing their songs. The challenge for each of us who are blessed to play any kind of leadership role is to recognize that there are two different leadership models—one masculine, the other feminine—both of which we must tap. But to do so, we have to get in touch with that other side of ourselves and strive to make it a more active part of who we are as leaders. Those of us who are men must search for the softer, more open and responsive part of our being, so as to help us respond better to others. This will enable us to show others that they, too, can raise their voices in song. Those of us who are women can begin to draw on the more assertive sides of ourselves that will enable us to take a stand when necessary, share our vision, and help us to speak our minds and hearts when necessary.[41]

6

We Can Survive the Desert and Sweeten the Waters

Exodus 15:22–27

It is at the Red Sea that Israel experiences the redemptive presence of God and, as a result, utters a song of praise together with Miriam and Moses. The water of the sea, which at first looms before them as an obstacle that will seal their doom as the Egyptians pursue from behind, is transformed into life-giving waters that ensure their survival at the outset of their desert journey. Yet, the desert does lie before them, with its unbearable heat and aridity, threatening to prevent them from ever reaching the land of their forebears. What will it take for them to leave the Red Sea, which is surrounded by freshwater springs, and take the first step into the desert, without any surety that they will survive? Can they even reach an oasis before their water skins dry up?

THE PEOPLE FOLLOW MOSES INTO THE DESERT

The difficulty of leaving the sea and its life-giving waters is captured in the first words following Miriam's song: "Then Moses caused the Israelites to set out from the Red Sea" (Exodus 15:22). This is the only place in the Bible's description of Israel's trek through the desert in which they are said to journey at the command of Moses, not God. It emphasizes that Moses prompts them to move into the desert.[1]

Even if it were at the instigation of God that they move away from the sea, it is Moses who gives them the direct command, which the people obey without question.[2] The Israelites could have argued with Moses, saying, "How can we possibly set out into the barren desert, without having adequate provisions for the journey?" Yet, our text demonstrates the People of Israel's greatness, in that they do not utter even one word of complaint at this point, showing their essential faith in their leader, Moses. They follow his lead, moving away from the sea, entering the wilderness of Shur, and the people's trust in Moses and God is later enshrined by the words of the prophet Jeremiah, who pictures God proclaiming: "I accounted to your favor the devotion of your youth … how you followed Me in the wilderness, in a land not sown" (Jeremiah 2:2).[3] This is the essential test of all leaders: Can they command enough respect for their people to follow them, even under difficult circumstances?

One of the major reasons why Sir Ernest Shackleton was so successful as a leader was that he inspired faith and trust among his crew members. They overcame life-and-death challenges because of his optimism and leadership. Shackleton wrote: "If you are a leader and want others to follow, you've got to keep going [under all conditions]." And he was the source of his crew's strength.[4]

The use of the causative, "Moses caused [va-yassa] the Israelites to set out," leads several midrashic texts and classical biblical commentators to argue that Moses actually has to force the people against their will to move away from the Red Sea. Some accounts even stress that they linger at the Red Sea, not just because they don't want to venture into the desert, but because they are caught up in gathering all the jewels and riches of the drowned Egyptians, which have washed up on shore. They are taken by the sight of the dead Egyptians, and some even think about returning to Egypt and its sustenance.[5] As a result, it is even said that Moses has to hit them with his rod in order to force them to walk away from the Red Sea and enter the wilderness of Shur.[6] Oftentimes, the role of the leader is to push the people away from places in which they have a tendency to remain, places of comfort, in order for them to expand their horizons and experiences, and grow. Although taking the firsts steps away from familiar situations may be difficult, even frightening, it is the only way any of us can move forward and not stagnate.

The Israelites are reticent to leave the sea and its life-giving waters and journey into the desert of Shur, a place full of serpents and scorpions, a land of drought and the shadow of death,[8] even though they have been told that the desert will be where they will join in covenant with God, receive the Divine's commandments, and find their way to the Promised Land. The name *Shur,* itself, means "to glimpse into the future," thereby intimating that ultimately they will experience the messianic age. Even removed from the waters of the Red Sea, they can continue to sing (*shir*) God's song in the midst of the heat of the desert.

Winston Churchill believed that human organizations and groups are prone to inertia. They must be driven forward relentlessly by trustworthy leaders whose sheer willfulness propels the people's progress. It was precisely Churchill's resolve and forcefulness that ensured Britain's survival when it stood alone in 1940.[7]

FINDING WATER IN THE DESERT

The trek through the aridity of the desert is challenging, and after traveling for three days, the People of Israel find no water (15:22). This is ironic, since only three days before they were immersed in the waters of the Red Sea.[9] They had all the water they needed to cleanse themselves from the Egyptian experience and carry them to the opposite shore, the beginning of their journey to the land of their patriarchs and matriarchs. Yet, after three short days in the heat of the desert, there is no water to be found. One tradition understands this to mean that the water which they have with them in their water skins has evaporated. They fill their skins with fresh water from the springs near the Red Sea and think that they have ample water for their journey in the desert. Yet in three days, their vessels are empty.[10] Metaphorically, they cannot sustain their experience at the sea in the heat of the desert sun. In a sense, they themselves are empty.

We should note that the biblical text does not say that "There was no water"; rather that "They found no water." The implication of this choice of words seems to be that water is present, even in the desert, if only a traveler has the strength and desire to look for it. Rabbi El'azer is quoted in the rabbinic tradition as interpreting this Exodus passage by saying that "Water was present under their very feet, since the earth floats on water," as Psalm 136:6 states: "To [God] who spreads forth the earth above the waters."[11] This, then, is more of a comment on the spiritual and emotional state of the Israelites—they seem to quickly lose hope as they suffer on their journey through the wilderness of Shur. They become disappointed, even despondent and broken in spirit, because of their inability to find a source of deliverance, as they had while passing through the Red Sea.[12] Simply put, all this indicates the aridity

Anita Roddick, the founder of The Body Shop, not only encourages her employees to achieve in their daily tasks, but to understand that they have the ability to overcome all challenges. She has intentionally sent her staff on missions to war-torn places like Kosovo to convince them that they can help change the world. "It has everything to do with the human spirit," said Roddick, "and the energy generated is unstoppable."[14]

of the people spiritually.[13] Perhaps, then, it is the role of Moses and Miriam, their leaders, to show them that even in the parched desert they can find life-giving water. If only they open their eyes, they will see Miriam's well, and find the source of their own salvation. All leaders must be able to encourage their followers, especially when they face adversity, to see their own potential for overcoming situations that seem to be insurmountable.

The Israelites can't find any water, but suddenly they come upon an oasis, though it is called Marah,[15] because its water is bitter (*marim*) (15:23). The name is mentioned three times, corresponding perhaps to their journey of three days, and underscoring their inability to find water to sustain them. The repetition of the name *Marah* highlights the people's increasing desperation.

How utterly ironic—to finally chance upon a seeming source of survival, only to find the water undrinkable! What they think will enable them to survive the desert turns out to be illusory. It is so easy to be misled when life is at stake. And the disillusionment and increased sense that they might die in the desert rather than live in the fleshpots of Egypt, no matter how lowly their status and how great their suffering, make them even more bitter.

Keep in mind that since *water* (*mayyim*) is a plural noun in Hebrew, the plural adjective *marim* (bitter) agrees with either "water" or "the people"—meaning then that "they could not drink the water of Marah because it [the water] was bitter" or "because they [the Israelites] were themselves bitter" (15:23). *Marim* is also very close in sound and identical in its consonants to the word *morim*, meaning "rebels," which is frequently used to describe the rebelliousness of the People of Israel in the desert. For example, following Miriam's death, when the water gives out and the people complain that there is nothing to drink, Moses says: "Hear, O you rebels [*morim*]" (Numbers 20:10).[16] Also, in most cases when a place name is explained—that is, when an etiology is provided—it is the historical event or the actions associated with the place that give rise to the name, and not its natural condition.[17]

THE PEOPLE'S COMPLAINT AND MOSES'S RESPONSE

Certainly, having no water to drink is a serious matter and, therefore, we should not be too harsh on the Israelites for their reaction at Marah.[18] For when they complain to Moses, saying, "What shall we drink?" one interpretive strain in the tradition, attributed to Rabbi Joshua, plays down the pejorative nature of the comment by stressing that Israel's mistake is simply one of protocol. Instead of complaining directly to Moses, they should seek counsel elsewhere. By contrast, Rabbi El'azar, who highlights their faithlessness and rebellious nature throughout, describes the Israelites as habitual complainers.[19]

No matter how deep-seated the Israelites' rebelliousness is, all their negative feelings are directed against Moses and not against God. Since it is Moses who leads them out of Egypt and directs them away from the Red Sea and into the desert, it is he who bears the responsibility in their eyes, and it is upon Moses (*al Moshe*) that they heap their complaints.[20] Since they depend on him as their leader, it is he who bears the brunt of their faithlessness.[21] Leaders must have thick skins, since they frequently are the target of their followers' criticism, whether or not it is justified. It goes with the turf: Those who take on the mantle of leadership set the path that the people pursue: therefore, when faced with any challenges or difficulties along the way, they are the object of all ill feelings.

Occasionally, leaders even internalize the doubts expressed by others and are caught up in the criticism themselves. In one rabbinic tradition, Moses is pictured as saying to God at Marah in the face of the people's complaints, "Why were these waters created if they are bitter? What earthly use is there for them? Would it not have been better if they had not been created? Why did You have me lead the people here?"[22] He, too, seems to reveal his own doubts, both about God and his own actions. Since the Israelites depend not only on God, but on him as well, he feels that he could have led them to a better place! Redemption will come through both divine and human action. Yet sometimes the leader's self-criticism helps clarify issues for everyone.

Winston Churchill said about himself: "Every night I try myself by court martial to see if I have done anything effective during the day. I don't mean just pawing the ground ... but something really effective.... Criticism, especially self-criticism, is like pain in the human body. It is not pleasant, but where would the body be without it?"[23]

It is crucial for every leader to hear the voices of the people, even if they are raised in complaint about that very leader's actions. When they complain to Moses that there is no water to drink, surely the Israelites expect Moses to listen and then relay their complaint to

God.[24] And indeed Moses responds by immediately crying out to the Divine (15:25). The Rabbis stress that Moses's willingness to turn to God after he hears the people's cries shows that true leaders are ready to hear complaints and accept criticism in order to make things better.[25] Moses does not get angry with them; rather, he prays to God on their behalf.

Does Moses cry out to God in order to convey his people's needs? Is he truly acting as the responsive leader who cares about his followers, or is something else going on? Moses's crying out can as easily be understood either as his own inability to deal with the Israelites' complaints—he simply may be expressing his exasperation with his people or his very human feeling of being lost, even though it is early in the journey through the desert. He may even have his own doubts about God's presence. Moses, in expressing his own pain and frailty, challenges all leaders: Are we capable of articulating our own feelings of inadequacy as we confront impatient and even critical followers? How often do so-called strong leaders express their own self-doubts, and to whom do they vent such deep and personal feelings? Who listens to the leader, as she cries out in pain? Where will her support come from?

Andrew Grove of Intel understood the value of listening to those who were critical of him. He said, "It is important ... to listen to people who bring you bad news ... who complain, and to know that these people are often in the lower ranks of the organization. Unless you welcome their contrarian views ... you will never learn from these useful Cassandras."[26]

LEARNING THAT WE HAVE
THE POWER TO SWEETEN THE WATERS

Confronted by his people, Moses cries out to God for help. He needs to learn how to transform the bitterness of Marah—the bitterness and rebelliousness of his followers—into consensus behind his leadership. The first thing Moses has to do is to remain optimistic himself, believing that the waters can be made sweet. The bitterness that they encounter at Marah is just temporary and can be overcome.[27] This is important for every leader—to remain positive and focused no matter what he might be feeling—in order to move the people forward.

In response to Moses's plea, God shows Moses a tree (*etz*) that can be used to sweeten Marah's water (15:25). The Rabbis of the tradition go to great lengths to identify which kind of tree is shown to Moses as a way to change the nature of Marah. Even trees that are bitter are suggested, to show that God's ways are different from ours.[29] Rabbi Gunther Plaut, in his masterful Torah commentary of the Reform movement, suggests that the tree might have been an oak tree, because of its high tannin content; tannin can neutralize the albuminous content of water, making it sink to the bottom.[30] Though there may have been trees at the oasis of Marah, the text should

Ernest Shackleton always set a positive example for his crew, regardless of the circumstances they confronted and his own deep feelings. He was a tower of strength to all, especially when they were in dire straits. And those who served directly under him internalized his example. Frank Wild, his second in command, when left in charge of the crew on Elephant Island during the final expedition of Shackleton's boat, *Endurance,* always set a positive example, regardless of his own feelings. The crew described him as being "unfailingly optimistic and a source of strength even when they were exhausted." [28]

be viewed less literally. After all, the question is this: How can the Israelites journey from Egypt (*Miztrayim*) to the Promised Land, through the aridity of the desert, without any means of survival? How can any of us move from the narrow places of our lives (*meitzarim*) through the desert and come to wholeness?

The Rabbis assist us here in pointing out that the text actually says, "God showed [*va-yoreihu*] Moses a tree," the root of the verb being *y-r-h,* which actually means "to teach."[31] The biblical text does not use the similar but more expected word *va-yareihu,* from the root *r-a-h,* meaning "show." What then does God symbolically teach Israel? What does the *etz,* the tree, represent? Of course, it is understood as the *etz chayyim*—the Tree of Life, the Torah, which God imparts to Moses—that sweetens the bitter waters of their lives. But why does this rabbinic interpretation work? Because the Rabbis pay attention to what follows in the text: "There [God] made for them a statute and ordinance, *hok u-mishpat,*" the law, namely, the Torah (15:25). According to the tradition, God reveals to Moses some of the laws of Torah at Marah before the revelation at Sinai.[32] Torah can enable us to overcome Marah (the bitterness in our lives) and facilitate our journey through the desert to God's place (a sense of wholeness and peace—*shalom*). Yet Moses had to use the "tree," making it his own by casting it into the water for it to be effective. God surely could have performed the "miracle" at Marah, but it is crucial for Moses, the leader, and for the Israelites to use the tree, the Torah, and act themselves. This, too, is the challenge of every leader—to lead by acting, especially when facing physical, emotional, and spiritual adversity. To lead others, a leader must be a model of action.

Facing a threat to his plant and employees in Quebec following severe icestorms, Charles Heimbolt of Bristol-Myers did not sit in his comfortable office in the States, but rushed to Canada to do all that he could personally. In effect, he was saying to his employees, "You are in need. Whatever you want me to do, I'll do." He understood that to manage others, leaders have to perform reliably themselves.[33]

This then seems to be the ultimate test of both the leader and the people: Do they possess both the strength of belief and the willingness to act in the face of severe challenges to their very existence? God's testing of Moses and the Israelites is stressed here in the biblical text: "There [God] made for him/the people [*lo*] a statute and ordinance, and there [God] put him/them to the test [*nisa'hu*]." And God then specifies, "If you will heed the Lord your God diligently, doing what is upright ... giving ear to [God's] commandments and keeping all of [God's] laws" (15:25–26). If Moses and Israel are willing to use the tree, that is, observe the laws of the Torah, then they will survive the bitter waters of Marah and the journey through the desert.

Clearly, the ending of our passage is ambiguous in the Hebrew: "[God] made for him/them [*lo*] ... and put him/them to the test [*nisa'hu*]." Both grammatical objective endings can be read as singular, setting up the possibility that the text is speaking about Moses or the people as a whole. Indeed, the ambiguity may be intentional, thereby stressing the tie between the leader and the people. God tests Israel's faith in both Moses and God, for which the people are praised following the miraculous splitting of the Red Sea (14:31). Now that they find themselves in the desert, seemingly without any water to drink, will they continue to trust in God's presence and Moses's ability to deliver them?[34] Similarly, God may also be testing Moses, to see how he will react when the people begin to complain so soon after the crossing of the sea and the jubilant singing of the song of redemption. To what extent will he be able to deal with the Israelites' grumbling against him and their direct challenge to him as their leader?

It is only if both the people and their leader pass these tests that their future will be assured, and that they will attain greatness. This crucial test is distinguished in the biblical passage by a subtle play on one word: *nisa'hu* (God tested him/them). The root of the verb in the biblical text is *n-s-h* (test), with the middle letter being a *samech*. But, if it were spelled with the Hebrew letter *sin* instead, the word would mean "to raise them up," or, less literally, "to give them greatness."[35] Moses and Israel will only survive the trek through the desert and reach the land of their forebears if they remain firm in their faith and then heed God's commandments, if they recognize the power of the tree, the Torah, and act on it.

Unbeknownst to the Israelites, who complain that they can find no water to drink, not far from Marah, at Elim, there are twelve springs of fresh water and some seventy palm trees, and they are able to camp there (15:27). Though some traditional sources describe Elim as barren and sandy, and note that its wells are insufficient to provide sustenance,[36] the Rabbis tend to see Elim as an oasis that has enough water to sustain the entire people. The twelve springs mentioned in the Bible are interpreted as symbols of the twelve tribes, the entirety of Moses's people, and the seventy palm trees correspond to the seventy elders, the leaders of the people.[37] So when the 600,000 Israelites encamp at the springs at Elim, they have enough to drink and eat to prepare themselves for the rest of the journey.[38] What the people have to learn is that what they lack is not water, but rather faith and strength of conviction. Standing at Marah, they do not know what lies ahead of them, yet they raise their voices against Moses, complaining about their lot.[39] Had they remembered the miraculous divine deliverance at the Red Sea and maintained their strong belief in Moses's ability to lead them and in God, they might have found the water without having to challenge Moses. Elim, which echoes the word *alim*, meaning strong or powerful, is nearby and waiting to sustain them. It is through the leadership of Moses and Miriam that their faith and conviction will be galvanized. This may be the most essential role that every leader plays within the group that she leads.

7

The Burden of Leadership

Exodus 17:1–7

After witnessing events of cosmic proportion—the plagues that free them from Egypt, the splitting of the Red Sea, and the transformation of the water at Marah, the Israelites nevertheless seem totally unimpressed.[1] Even worse, though God provides them with water to quench their thirst at Marah and raises them up (*nisa'hu*) (15:25), at Rephidim, again the people complain to God about the lack of water and test (*t'nassun*) the Divine (17:2).

THE PEOPLE'S DEEPENING BITTERNESS AND DOUBT

Rephidim is the fourth in a series of Israelite grumblings against Moses and God: The first is when they catch sight of the Egyptians pursuing them at the Red Sea (14:10–12); the second occurs when they arrive at Marah (15:22–24); the third happens when they crave to return to Egypt (16:2–3); and now at Rephidim, they demand, "Give us water to drink!" (17:2).[2] Over time, the rhetoric has grown stronger and more threatening; here they even question God's omnipotence (17:7).[3] The people do not merely grumble (*va-yalen*) against Moses (17:3), as they have in the previous encounters; now they quarrel (*va-yarev*) with him, setting the stage for a far more angry and hostile confrontation.[4]

70

The situation is much more difficult for the Israelites at Rephidim. There was water at Marah, but because the water was bitter, they could not drink it. By contrast, when the people encamp at Rephidim, there is no water at all (17:1). As a result, the people's feelings are much more intense: They thirst for water (17:3).[5] When there is no water, and they begin to experience real thirst, they complain to Moses in harsher terms: "Why did you bring us up from Egypt, to kill us and our children and our livestock?" (17:3).[6]

There is no water (*ayn mayyim*) for the people to drink (17:1). The word *ayn* conjures up "nothingness," *ayin*, a total void of all, a vacuum filled with the people's doubt and anger.[7] Instead of finding a well, an *ayin* (spelled in Hebrew with an *ayin*) at Rephidim, they find nothing to quench their thirst and sustain them. What they experience at Marah—the transformation of bitter waters into sweet waters—is absent from Rephidim, weakening (*rafah*) their spirit and connection with the Divine.[8]

Their complaint is directed squarely at Moses. As soon as they realize that there is no water to drink, they begin to quarrel with Moses, demanding, "Give [*t'nu*] us water to drink" (17:2), and they continue to voice their anger against him (17:3). Although the verb they use, *t'nu* (give), is in the plural form and can include his brother, Aaron, who is his spokesperson, the tradition singles out Moses, their leader, as the object of the people's frustration and anger.[9] Though Moses is God's messenger, simply following God's commands,[10] he is perceived both as responsible for determining the direction they follow on their desert journey and for providing them with the necessary sustenance to survive. It is he who can and must give them the water they crave. And their negativity, bordering on contempt, is evident in the impersonal manner in which they address him: "Why did this one [*zeh*] bring us up from Egypt, to kill us, our children and our livestock with thirst?" (17:3). There is no concern for his stature or the honor he deserves.[11] It is purely a case of what he can do to alleviate their suffering. He even believes they were capable of killing him! (17:4). Such is the fate suffered by many leaders: They have enabled their followers to thrive in the past, but strategies that brought success before are no longer working. They then become the objects upon whom the people cast all their fears, doubts, and eventually their anger.

Moses seems absolutely baffled by the people's challenge to him, saying, "Why do you quarrel with me?" (17:2), and later crying out to God, "What shall I do with this people?" (17:4). Yet he realizes that underlying their derision of him is a testing of the Divine. He adds, in this regard, "Why do you try the Lord?" (17:2).[12] Just as their belief in God translates directly into their faith in their leader Moses (14:31), so, too, their doubting of Moses's leadership reflects a deeper problem: They seem to question God's presence, which they eventually articulate with the powerful phrase: "Is God in our midst or not [*ayin*]?" (17:7). This will not be the last time they test God during their wilderness journey; they are chastised for testing the Divine no fewer than ten times (Numbers 14:22). Though they have experienced God's miracles in the place of nothingness (*ayin*), that is, the wilderness, they still are not sure that God is among them, that there is more than nothingness (*ayin*), void in their lives.[13] Often, when individuals challenge the authority and/or the ability of their leader, it is a reflection of the group's uncertainty about the direction in which the leader is taking them.

Alternative names used to describe the place (Rephidim) where Israel tests God and also quarrels with Moses are *Massah u'Meribah* (17:7), which describes the actions of the Israelites as Moses confronts them: "Why do you quarrel (*t'rivun*) with me? Why do you test (*t'nassun*) the Lord?" (17:2). Massah-Meribah becomes shorthand for Israel's rebelliousness and disloyalty,[14] and these names are even cited in a number of biblical texts.[15] The Israelites' quarreling with Moses is directly related to their testing of the Divine: Either the people don't have water and argue with Moses or they test God to see if the Divine will provide it for them.[16]

MOSES'S REACTION TO THE PEOPLE

As we have seen, this is not the first time that the people quarrel with Moses or even denigrate his leadership, yet his reaction this time is quite different. Challenged by the people at the Red Sea (14:11–12), and at Marah (15:24), and the target of their ongoing bitter complaints, Moses does not respond to them directly, but prays to God to intervene. At Rephidim, by contrast, Moses reacts in an extremely human and personal manner. He cannot tolerate their chastisement, and his personal pain is clearly evident when he says, "Why do you quarrel with me?" (17:2), as if to say, "Why do you find fault with me, when you know I do not do anything without God?"[17] At the root of Moses's angst is his divided allegiance: His authority comes from the people's recognition of him as their leader and from the Divine. He must be responsive to both God and to the Israelites, and he is truly caught in the middle, wondering how he can find the strength to enable the people to survive their journey. Like many leaders, Moses is beset by constant challenges to his leadership ability and authority. He must endure criticism from his followers and persevere in a time of crisis—despite a direct and angry personal challenge—while carrying out the orders of his superiors.

Colleagues of Ernest Shackleton cite as one of his greatest qualities a deep reservoir of personal strength that sustained him through his most trying struggles. He kept things in perspective, remaining calm and collected no matter what happened. He never overreacted in the face of crisis; he always maintained a positive outlook.[18]

Moses is tired of the Israelites' complaints and seems vulnerable for the very first time. He is caught between their anger and God's desire that he shepherd them through the desert, ever protecting them.[19] Moses cries out to God, but he doesn't sound like a leader praying on behalf of his people, as he does at the sea and at Marah, and when he defends them after the building of the Golden Calf (32:11–14). In an acutely angry outburst, he says, "What shall I do with this people? A little more and they will stone me" (17:4). Moses's anger is taking its toll on him. He doesn't sound like the caring leader we would expect. He does not use the personal and affectionate term "my people," but rather distances himself from them by referring to them as "this people."[20] He cannot relate to them as "his people" when they continue to challenge him directly in spite of everything he has done for them. In addition, they seem incapable of understanding God's plan for them, even after directly experiencing the power of the Divine. As a result, he

Elaine Frankowski, a biochemist at Cray Research, a supercomputer company, once publicly lambasted its CEO, John Rollwagen, but she was amazed that he actually heard what she had said and noted her point to a group of employees with whom he spoke several days later. She knew that in most companies, a top manager would never even have listened to her, let alone responded in a constructive manner.[21]

can't see himself as a part of the people. For a leader, it takes strength of character and a commitment to the long-term vision to be able to listen to the people, especially when they voice a strong challenge to his leadership. It is difficult not to take it personally and not to respond in a defensive and angry way. All leaders must strive to maintain control of their emotions and not lash out when they're attacked personally. We all are human and our instinct is to respond in kind. Yet this one challenge goes to the very core of leadership.

God then offers Moses a way of venting the frustration and anger he feels toward the Israelites, even after the miraculous events at the Red Sea and Marah. God directs him to take the very rod he used to strike the Nile, and hit the rock at Horeb and water will issue from it (17:5–6). Moses releases his pent-up anger and water is released from the rock, quenching the people's seemingly unbearable thirst. At Marah, in the face of the people's grumbling, Moses remains in control of his emotions; here at Rephidim, his emotions get the better of him, and God has to find a way for him to release his anger, while producing water for the people.

It is said that not only was Sir Winston Churchill quick to apologize for any outbursts of anger he directed toward his staff or political opponents, but he was also an exceptionally forgiving individual, who did not harbor any malice even when he was attacked personally.[22]

GOD FORCES MOSES TO ENGAGE THE PEOPLE

In response to Moses's withdrawal from the people and his fear that they are about to kill him, God insists that he "pass [*avor*] before the people" (17:5). Instead of giving in to his own frailty and very human fears for his own safety, Moses is directed to walk among the people, to be part of them. By mingling with them, he not only will be seen as asserting his rightful authority,[23] but he will also see that they are not about to stone him.[24] The only way for leaders to deal effectively with followers whom they perceive as threatening is to confront them. Often, the leader discovers that the criticism is not meant personally.

Leaders must overcome the impulse to shy away from those who challenge them as well as their ideas or programs.

As Moses passes among the people, all the Israelites stand up and show him the greatest respect and reverence. God then says to him, "How often have I told you not to be harsh with them, but rather to lead

It is reported by those close to Ernest Shackleton that he maintained his authority over his men and headed off mutiny on their voyages because he went against every human instinct to avoid confrontation and to fight those who challenged his leadership. He actually arranged to bunk with the very members of his crew who were the most difficult and disagreeable.[25]

them as a shepherd leads his flock. Remember, it was for their sake that I brought you out of Egypt and it is on account of them that you are honored."[26] Moses's leadership is grounded in the people, so he needs to better understand them.

By walking among the people, Moses comes to see more clearly what they are experiencing. As individuals and families, they are suffering great thirst that endangers their lives and their livestock, as evident in their very personal and passionate statement: "Why did this one bring us up from Egypt, to kill me and my children and my livestock with thirst?" (17:3). The switch of the object from plural (us) to singular (me) underscores the personal pain experienced by every individual Israelite and the need for Moses to hear and respond.[27] The challenge of every leader, then, is to identify with the people.

Charles Pollard, longtime CEO of ServiceMaster, emphasized that, too often, leaders sit in large offices and think they know the concerns of the people they lead. Leaders must get out among their people, to listen and learn from them. They have to avoid the trap into which so many so-called leaders fall—the arrogance of ignorance.[28]

The journey from Egyptian slavery through the desert to Sinai and then on to the Promised Land is extremely difficult and fraught with obstacles and severe challenges both for Moses and for each and every Israelite. The people have to grow and mature on their journey through the desert of their lives in stages, as the biblical text intimates, "From the wilderness of Zin, the entire Israelite community continued on through their stages [*l'mas'ei-hem*] as the Lord would command" (17:1). The verse does not say "continued on in stages," but emphasizes that the stages are the points of their growth—"they journeyed, matured in their stages."

Once Moses understands the slow journey of maturation of his people—what they are going through at each stage and the pain that each of them feels—he is able to understand the source of their anger and demands. God, therefore, commands him to "pass [*avor*] before the people" (17:5) in order to connect with them. In doing so, he is able to forgive them for the recriminations directed against him. Notice that the verb *avar*, which is used here, can also mean "transgress" or "forgive." Moses is asked to "pass by," meaning to "overlook" the people's transgressions.[29] Part of Moses's own maturation as a leader involves learning when to push and challenge the people, and when to be understanding.

EVERY LEADER NEEDS HELP AND SUPPORT; MOSES IS NO EXCEPTION

Moses does indeed seem lost in the face of the people's attacks upon him and their accusation that they will die in the desert because of him. And as it was at Marah, when confronted by the people's complaints, here at Rephidim he immediately cries out to God, not to ask God to punish the people, but rather to seek God's help in responding to their needs.[30] Like all leaders, Moses cannot succeed on his own; he can only move the people forward if he has support from others. So when God directs him to pass among the people, he is also commanded to bring along with him some of the elders of Israel. For the first time, Moses is urged to take advantage of the support of the leaders of the tribes, those who are closer to the people. They serve as witnesses to his ability to provide the water from the rock to quench the people's thirst (17:5)—lest the people think that the water flows on its own from natural springs. This bolsters the people's faith in his leadership.[31] All leaders must draw on support from their counterparts in other constituencies in the group, and involve those second-tier leaders, keeping the group focused on the mission.

Larry Bossidy, the former CEO of Allied Signal, realized the importance of involving others as partners in the work of the company. In his view, you've got to make sure your employees understand how important they are. As a CEO, he understood that he needed their support more than they needed his.[32]

In the end, Moses's core support comes through God's Presence. In anticipation of the people's doubts that God is truly present among them (17:7), God guarantees Moses that the Divine Presence will be with him. The Rabbis even extend what is written in the biblical text, stressing that every place where human beings are present, God is there with them.[33]

How ironic, then, that in order to quench the people's thirst, God commands Moses to return to Horeb, the place where he first encounters God's presence, and the Divine will be standing on a rock that he should strike with his rod (17:6). The first thing to be noted is that the Israelites do not take a direct route through the desert to the Land of Canaan. Occasionally, it appears as if God has them marching in circles in order to protract the journey through the desert. Second, Moses returns to the place in which God was revealed to him—Horeb—in order once again to draw sustenance for himself and for his people. Finally, God, often referred to as "The Rock" in both the Bible and rabbinic literature,[34] directs Moses to "the rock" that will be the source of life-giving water for the Israelites. One rabbinic tradition emphasizes that, metaphorically at least, the rock that gushes forth with water when Moses hits it with the rod is the very same one that Moses strikes thirty-eight years later at Kadesh, after Miriam dies, to provide the people with sustenance (Numbers 20).[35] In effect, God is always there, as symbolized by the rock, and all Moses has to do is to act. In this regard, one midrash stresses that the Israelites have their choice of rocks: Whichever they choose, water will come forth for them.[36]

God's omnipresence ensures that water is potentially available everywhere. And by appearing to Moses on the rock at Horeb— thought to be identical with Rephidim, the place where he first experiences the Divine Presence, the call to leadership, and the promise of Israel's redemption—God assures Moses of continued divine protection and the people's survival in the aridity of the desert.[37] Moses strikes the rock with his rod and water miraculously flows. Moses has at his disposal the rod, the instrument with which he performed the miracles in Egypt, including striking the Nile and thereby depriving the Egyptians of drinking water (the first plague in Exodus 7:17–24). By contrast, at Rephidim the same rod serves to satisfy Israel's need for water.[38] The very object that was an instrument of affliction for the Egyptians here produces blessing for the Israelites.[39] So lest we think that the rock produces the water by itself at Rephidim, the text reminds us that Moses has to use the rod and strike the rock for water to issue forth from it (17:6). Leaders have to learn that they have in their grasp the tools to ensure their people's survival and growth. But simply possessing the knowledge, insight, ability, and skills is not enough. They also have to draw on these qualities. They have to act to the best of their ability, if these tools are to be effective.

8
The Leader
Needs Support
Exodus 17:8–16

Rephidim, the place where Israel quarrels with God, is also known as
Massah and Meribah, names that describe the people's lack of faith.
After experiencing God's redemptive power on a number of occasions, they still doubt God's presence among them. The Israelites are,
in a sense, in a state of *rephidim,* from the two Hebrew words *rafeh
yadayim,* meaning "weak hands." They lack faith and, as a result, are
cut off from the Divine.[1]

WHO ARE THE AMALEKITES?

Right after the Israelites angrily question whether God has abandoned them in the wilderness, saying, "Is the Lord among us, or
not?" (Exodus 17:7), the Amalekites come and attack them at
Rephidim (17:8). The attack is the direct result of the people's blas-
phemy, which makes them vulnerable.[2] The Rabbis liken this to the
parable of a man who carries his child on his shoulders on a long
journey; a number of times the child sees things he wants and asks his
father for them, and each time the father gives the child what he
requests. The child lacks for nothing. Along the way, they encounter
a passerby, and the child asks him, "Have you seen my father?" The
father then says, "You are riding on my shoulders all this time and yet

you inquire of my whereabouts? Don't you know who has been carrying you?" And with that, the father rudely puts the son down and leaves. Immediately, a wild dog attacks the vulnerable child.[3] So, too, Israel is attacked right after questioning God's presence.

According to most biblical scholars, the Amalekites were a nomadic tribe that lived in the Negev and Sinai Peninsula, south of the Land of Canaan. They most probably interpreted the sudden appearance of the Israelites in this region as a direct threat to their territory and their control of the oases and trading routes.[4]

Because the Amalekites are described as attacking Israel from the rear, preying on the weakest and most tired among them, we are urged to remember what Amalek did to us and to blot out any memory of Amalek from beneath the heaven (Deuteronomy 25:17–19). Therefore, Amalek is understood in the Jewish tradition as the embodiment of evil, and the battle against the Amalekites is part of the ongoing struggle against the *yetzer ha-ra,* the evil urge that is ubiquitous.[5]

God will always do battle against Amalek, as the text here states, "God will be at war [*milhamah l'Adonai*] with Amalek throughout the ages" (17:16). However, if we were to read the verse literally, it would suggest that we fight the battle against Amalek for God (*l'Adonai*) in every generation. We, in effect, are destined to be God's instruments in the battle against evil, and each of us must understand our role. Deliverance from the Amalekites does not come solely through God's intervention, but also through the actions of flesh and blood

Dave Quade accepted the job as vice president of the Foster Products Division of the H. B. Fuller Company because he wanted to be with an organization that put a premium on shared decision making and shared leadership. To him, it "was like coming to heaven." He vowed to continue the company's belief in and empowerment of people.[7]

human beings who are not schooled in war.[6] The Israelites now have the responsibility of confronting their enemy, relying on their own ability as well as God's power.

EMPOWERING OTHERS TO ACT

The battle against Amalek is fought not by God, but by the Israelites themselves. Ironically, however, Moses, the people's leader, does not lead the Israelites in battle. Moses moves beyond the notion that he alone is capable of leading the People of Israel, commanding Joshua, the son of Nun, to choose men to fight the Amalekites (17:9). But in so doing, Moses seems to use a superfluous phrase, "Choose for us [*lanu*] men," when all he has to say to Joshua is, "Choose men and go out and do battle against Amalek."[8] From this choice of words, the Rabbis deduce that Moses sees Joshua, his disciple, as his partner and equal.[9] One of Moses's exceptional leadership qualities is his willingness to trust others to share the burden of leading the people. This is captured in Joshua's own words in the Midrash: "How many notables there are in this generation ... yet Moses enjoined no one except me. And he [believed] that Amalek would fall by my hand."[10] Thus Moses empowers Joshua to lead the Israelites in battle.

In commanding Joshua to "Go out [*tzay*] and do battle" (17:9), Moses understands that Joshua will have to be willing to leave the Israelite camp,[11] which is protected by the omnipresent cloud symbolizing God's Presence.[12] So in order to step up to his new leadership role, Joshua will have to risk his life in ways

One major factor in the successful expeditions led by Ernest Shackleton was his uncanny ability to choose the right men to join his crews. Using somewhat unconventional methods of interviewing and then selecting his crew, which included asking seemingly inconsequential questions such as whether the men could sing, he wanted to see if they would be part of a team. Shackleton found reliable men who shared his vision and dedication to the mission, each one suited to the role he had to play. Shackleton never misled those who applied for work on his crews, spelling out in his recruitment advertisements the real dangers of polar exploration.[13]

that he never dreamed of before. He has to go out and lead the people of Israel in battle, bearing the consequences of every decision he makes. It all starts with the need for Joshua to choose the right men to take on the Amalekites. According to the tradition, these warriors not only have to be brave men, but they must be individuals of impeccable faith, who have never complained against God.[14] A leader must recognize the talents of her followers and place the right people in the right positions to get the job done. This is a key test of leadership.

Like Larry Bossidy, Jack Welch, and other excellent CEOs, Roberto Goizueta, the CEO of Coca-Cola, saw succession as the logical culmination of a program he designed to develop talented individuals. In his view, delegating authority was one of his crucial responsibilities, and training a successor was the ultimate act of delegating authority.[16]

Leading the Israelites in battle is Josha's first step toward his ultimate role as Moses's successor. This is not only his biblical debut, but it is his first opportunity to exercise leadership in the context of battle, a role he will eventually play when he leads the people across the Jordan River to conquer the Land of Canaan.[15] Moses prepares Joshua for the future by placing him in a position to begin to learn what will be demanded of him as he leads the People of Israel into the Promised Land. Appointing one's successor and helping to develop his skills and ability are the responsibility of every good leader.

MOSES CONTINUES TO INSPIRE THE PEOPLE

Though Moses commands Joshua to lead the Israelites in battle, Moses himself continues to be the vehicle through which God's presence inspires the Israelites to confront and defeat Amalek. At the outset of the battle, Moses positions himself on the top of the nearest hill with the rod of God in his hand (17:9), so that it is visible to both the Israelites and the Amalekites. Moses holds aloft the rod with which the Divine ensured Israel's redemption from Egypt and passage through the Red Sea. And now, just as in the past, God will perform miracles for them.[17]

The rod represents a kind of battle flag, from which soldiers in battle draw strength. In seeing their ensign raised, the Israelites are encouraged, knowing that they will prevail, since God is with them.[18] The rod is a symbol of God's power: Moses, in a sense, impersonates the Divine, with his arm raised to strike the foe.[19] When Moses raises his arm, which holds the rod, Israel prevails against the Amalekites, but when he lowers his arm, Amalek gets the upper hand (17:11).

It is not clear whether Moses raises one or both of his hands, since not only are there some biblical manuscripts and translations in which the plural "his hands" (*yadav*) is used,[20] but the very next verse states that "Moses's hands [plural] grew heavy" (17:12). This textual confusion gives rise to several implications for the significance of Moses's gestures in the sight of the Israelites during the battle. Why does he suddenly seem to use both his hands, instead of merely holding up the rod with one?

The tradition emphasizes that it is not literally Moses's hands that determine the outcome of the battle with the Amalekites. The position of his hands cannot ensure Israel's victory. But in raising his hands toward the heavens, Moses is reminding his people of the One who appointed Moses as leader and who has always been their source of strength and redemption. They, then, believe that the same God will empower them to overcome Amalek.[21]

The gesture of raising hands heavenward is also a sign of supplication and prayer. In battle it serves as a symbol—the hands pointing to the real power in the universe. Moses therefore can be seen as praying to God for divine protection.[22] He stands on the top of the hill so that all Israel will see him praying to God and thereby gain encouragement in battle. They, too, may have lifted up their eyes toward the heavens and prayed for God's protection.[23] Once again, however, without Moses raising his hands, Israel seemingly would not have been delivered. Just as he has to raise his hand to hold the rod over the waters of the Red Sea so that they will part, so, too, when he raises his hand with the rod, Israel prevails (17:11). The actions of the leader have an impact on the destiny of his people. By virtue of their willingness to act, leaders bring about particular outcomes. Their actions

inspire similar acts of courage in their followers, and reinforce everyone's belief in the mission.

Sometimes, however, the reverse is true: The people through
their actions bolster their leaders. One tradition asks, in this regard,
why Moses lowers his hands, since he realizes that it will be harmful to the people. This is not a voluntary act on Moses's part. For when the Israelites pray with sincerity, it gives Moses the strength to hold his hands high and his prayers are answered. But when Israel does not direct their thoughts

Patricia Carrigan, first female assembly plant manager in the history of GE, faced some extraordinary problems that tested her courage to act. She believed that if a leader expected an organization to take risks, the leader had to show the willingness to act in the face of adversity. In acting fearlessly, she could inspire others.[24]

to God, Moses no longer possesses the power to hold his hands
aloft.[25] Moses's prayers and actions have to be mirrored by the
people, through their faith and willingness to act, if they are to be
successful.[26]

MOSES, LIKE EVERY LEADER, NEEDS SUPPORT

Since the Bible goes out of its way to emphasize that Moses's hands
are not static—they are raised and lowered at different times—we
have a picture not of a godlike leader's hands, ever outstretched, but
rather those of a flesh-and-blood human being straining to overcome
gravity and occasionally being overcome by it. His are human hands,
which grow weary due to the effort of trying to stay aloft in a posture
of supplication.[27] His hands become heavy (*kevaydim*), weighed
down by the burden of leadership, and he desperately needs help to
complete the mission.

For the first time at Rephidim (*rafad* can mean both "chair" and
"support"), Moses's strength flags and he needs the support of Aaron
and Hur, who place a rock under him and at the same time, hold up
his hands, one on each side (17:12). Not only does Moses need

Joshua to lead the people in battle against Amalek, but his brother and nephew (Hur is Miriam's son, according to the rabbinic tradition) play key supportive roles as well. This is one of Moses's most important legacies as a leader—his recognition that he cannot succeed by acting alone. Like all leaders, he has no choice but to involve others in varying supportive roles.[28]

Aaron and Hur are particularly powerful individuals to cite here as supporting Moses. On the one hand, it is as if Moses's two siblings were c____ upon to support ____er brother in ____ lead the ____ ur is ____ m's ____ and ____ pany ____ unt Sinai ____ Torah (24:14).[30] On the other hand, placing Aaron and Hur ____ mountaintop with Moses emphasizes that Moses is supported by two symbols of power—Aaron representing the priesthood, and Hur from the line of the Davidic monarchy.[31] Thus, support for the leader emanates from key constituents among the people.

Phil Jackson's remarkable success as coach of the Chicago Bulls basketball team stemmed from how he transformed a group of mediocre players with one superstar, Michael Jordan, into a championship team where everyone had a key role to play. Even the substitutes who played only a few minutes a game knew the importance of ensuring the team's success.[29]

The first thing that Aaron and Hur do is to place a rock (*even*) under Moses so he can sit down. The tradition metaphorically identifies the rock with the leaders of the past, the patriarchs and matriarchs, the example of whose lives gives Moses strength to lead the Jewish people on the next stage of their journey and to uphold the divine vision.[32] Yet we cannot help but associate God with the rock, since God is usually referred to as "The Rock" in the Bible, and Moses's greatest support comes from God. When traditional commentators ask why Aaron and Hur place a hard, uncomfortable stone under Moses, they usually emphasize that he refuses to sit on anything else because he wants to identify with his people. When the people suffer—in this case, the Israelites are engaged in battle with the Amalekites—the leader needs to suffer with them.[33] The leader cannot disassociate herself from them. Leaders must be perceived as being one of the people, in Hebrew, *ahad ha-am*.

As a result of the support he receives, Moses's hands remain steady (*yadav emunah*) throughout the battle. The use of the word *emunah* is odd here, since it usually means "faith." Perhaps the point being made is that, because Moses himself is supported by Aaron, Hur, and even Joshua, his own faith is bolstered, even in the face of the enemy. All leaders need support to face and overcome challenges, and that support may reinforce their own resolve. So, too, the very steadiness of Moses's hands boosts the Israelites' faith in God's protective presence.[34] And their faith will lead to their ultimate redemption, symbolized perhaps by the rest of the biblical phrase: "Thus his hands remained steady until the sun sets [*bi'at ha-shemesh*]" (17:12), the Hebrew literally meaning "the coming of the sun."

GOD'S STEADFAST PRESENCE AND PROTECTION IN THE BATTLE AGAINST AMALEK

Though it seems as if Moses's faith in God led to their victory over the Amalekites, Moses wants to make sure that the Israelites understand that it was not the rod nor his actions, but God's presence that ensured the defeat of the enemy. Therefore, following Joshua's rout of the forces of Amalek, Moses erects an altar upon which to give thanks to God and names it *Adonai nissi,* God is my banner, or, perhaps, [the source of] my miracle (*nes*) (17:15). Though the banner as well as the rod can be seen as extensions of his arm and symbols of Moses's power,[35] they are both signs of God's arm and might. It is God who is the ultimate source of their victory and salvation.[36]

The altar, according to Moses, indicates that a "hand is upon the throne of God" (17:16). Throughout the generations, commentators have tried to understand to whose hand the text alludes, generally agreeing that the notion of a "hand on the throne" implies the taking of an oath. Most feel that it is God's hand and oath to which the Bible refers, which is consistent with the previous verse—God's banner will be continually raised, and God guarantees Israel's victory over Amalek for all future times.[37] Yet, victory also comes because Moses raises his hands and extends the rod.

The battle against Amalek is ongoing; God will be at war with Amalek, the embodiment of evil, throughout the generations, *midor dor* (17:16), until even the memory of the Amalekites is blotted out (17:14). The irony is that we are commanded never to forget what the Amalekites did to our Israelite forebears (Deuteronomy 25:17–19), even as we pray in every generation that their memory will be erased. We, then, are asked to be vigilant from one generation to the next, tracking (*medarder*), in a sense, Amalek and his actions.[38]

For until Amalek is totally obliterated—that is, until evil is eradicated from the world—the Godhead can never be whole; the world cannot come to fruition. God's throne, referred to by the shortened form *keis Yah* instead of the expected full form *kissay Adonai,* cannot be complete—neither the throne, the place of God's presence, nor the Divine self—until Amalek is no more.[39] Moses, as the leader of Israel, with the support of those closest to him and empowering Israel to fight the battle against Amalek, teaches us the ultimate leadership lesson—that leadership is not simply about effecting change or leading people to a different place. It also requires leaders to envision a better destination to which they will lead their followers. All change demands time, energy, and some degree of risk, so the goal in the leader's mind must be worthwhile and consonant with the group's highest values, mission, and destiny.

9

A Key to Leadership: Empowerment

Exodus 18:13–27

The burden of the leadership roles that Moses plays is made clear when Jethro, Moses's father-in-law, who has just arrived in the Israelite camp, notes incredulously: "You represent the people before God, you bring their petitions before God, enjoin upon [the people] the laws and teachings, and make known to them the way they are to go and the practices they are to follow" (Exodus 18:19–20).

FEELING THE BURDEN OF LEADERSHIP

Because of Moses's diverse responsibilities and the enormity of the task of judging the cases brought by the entire nation, the people cannot gain access to Moses when they need him. Though he sits in judgment of the people from morning to night (18:13), litigants have to wait endlessly to have their cases heard.[1] As a result, most Israelites give up the hope of receiving a hearing from Moses and choose to tolerate the situations in which they find themselves, even if it places them in harm's way.[2] To Jethro, it seems intolerable for the people to suffer so. Somehow, as in many organizations, a structural change has to be made that can help Moses shoulder his myriad responsibilities without collapsing.

The Rabbis highlight Moses's inability to respond to the Israelites' legal needs by pointing out that the Bible describes Samuel as taking the trouble of traveling from village to village to judge the people in order to meet their needs. Samuel knows how burdensome it is for the people,[3] and his actions stand in stark contrast to those of Moses, who is not available for everyone who needs him.

Larry Bossidy, the former CEO of Allied Signal, understood that he could not know or do everything: "[Being a leader] is a humbling job. The more you search, the more you recognize ... that there is an awful lot more to do all the time." He learned that it reaches a point at which it is impossible for the leader to act on his own. His approach was shaped by a former boss who taught him that success can only come when the leader realizes that others have to share the load.[4]

Even Moses suffers because of the impossible situation in which he finds himself, as we see from the poignant language of the biblical text: "Moses sat judging the people, while the people stood [*omeid*] over him from morning to evening" (18:13). The burden Moses feels is underscored when Jethro confronts his son-in-law over the situation: "Why do you sit [act] alone, while all the people stand [*nitzav*] over you?" (18:14). The use of the forceful verb *natzav* (steadfast), instead of *amad* (stand), highlights how the people loom over their leader, and we, the readers, sense the imposing burden placed on Moses. How in the world can Moses do it all?

MOSES'S EGO PREVENTS HIM FROM UNDERSTANDING WHAT IS DEMANDED OF HIM

It takes the appearance of Moses's father-in-law, Jethro, for him to figure out what is necessary to lead the people effectively. As soon as Jethro arrives in the Israelite camp, together with Moses's wife and two sons,[5] Jethro sees (*va-yar*) everything that Moses is doing to the people (18:13–14). As an objective observer, one who cares for his daughter's husband and for the People of Israel, Jethro understands the consequences of Moses's actions. Therefore he confronts Moses, saying: "What is this ... that you are doing to the people? Why do you act [judge] alone, while all the people stand over you?" (18:14).

What does Jethro see? According to the tradition, he sees that Moses is acting like a king, who sits on his throne while the people stand around him the entire day.[6] Perhaps it is even worse, since the biblical text describes the people standing over him, literally from "morning [*haboker*] to evening [*ha-erev*]," the very words used to describe the period of *Ma'asei Bereshit*, God's creative acts (Genesis 1). Moses appears almost godlike in his actions; in judging his people, he considers himself as uniquely qualified to judge the people because he is God's partner.[7] Jethro finds it difficult to tolerate Moses's treatment of his fellow Israelites. By making the people stand around the entire day, he denigrates their honor. He does not show them the kind of respect that any leader should.[8] This is especially true if we read the biblical text literally here—Moses makes *all* the people stand, even those who are not being judged.[9]

In response to Moses's actions, Jethro criticizes his son-in-law in no uncertain terms, asking him why he is behaving in such a supercilious manner. Moses himself surely understands the terrible burden he is placing on the people, and the burden he himself feels, as he attempts to judge all the cases by himself. Jethro's concerns, which are so fundamental, must have occurred to Moses.[10]

Herb Kelleher of Southwest Airlines emphasized that leaders have to subordinate their own egos to the needs of the business and their employees and customers. The cause that must be served is far greater than any one leader or individual.[12]

However, Moses is convinced that only he can play all the major roles, as we see in his reply to his father-in-law: "It is because the people come to me to inquire of God. When they have a dispute, it [necessarily] comes before me, and I decide between an individual and his neighbor, and I make known the laws and teachings of God" (18:15–16). The haughty tone of Moses's reply betrays his sense that only he can judge, teach, and lead the People of Israel, and surely only he is uniquely qualified to intercede on behalf of the people before God.[11] It is as if Moses were saying to

Jethro: "I realize that you are concerned because I have undertaken a dual responsibility, both to judge and to teach. You feel that it would be prudent to appoint other judges. But how can I do so? When people have a dispute, an ordinary judge will have no way to determine who is speaking the truth. Only I can do that through my prophetic powers."[13] Moses's ego truly gets in the way of recognizing what is in the best interests of his people and their future. Leaders must acknowledge that they cannot control and run everything. What ultimately makes leaders successful, among many crucial traits, is their humility, even as they embody the highest ideals and standards of the group.

JETHRO CONFRONTS MOSES

Moses finds it difficult to recognize that he cannot do it all alone. If he is to succeed, he must take a step back and listen to the more objective voice of his father-in-law, who tells Moses directly, "Now listen to me. I will give you counsel" (18:19). Hearing Moses's strong claim that only he can judge, Jethro responds with utter simplicity: "That which you are doing is not good" (18:17). He resolutely holds his ground in the face of Moses's self-aggrandizing words,[14] and his simple words undercut Moses's haughtiness. The words of Moses and those of Jethro stand in sharp contrast.

Jethro's criticism of Moses is done with great sensitivity and delicacy, so Moses can hear his advice without becoming defensive. He does not tell Moses that what he is doing is bad or evil, but chooses to phrase it as "not good." Quietly, yet with great resolve,[15] Jethro attempts to show Moses the impact that his actions are having on the people and on himself.

Jethro warns Moses: "You will surely wear yourself out [*navol tibol*], and these people as well who are with you" (18:17). That is, Moses will burn out and be unable to function. He will become confused (*nitbalbel*) and find it impossible to respond.[16] He will fade "like the leaves falling [*nibol k'nvol*] from the vine" (Isaiah 34:4).[17] The people will also suffer, those who wait all day for their cases to be heard.

The Rabbis view Jethro's critique as implying much more, however, since the root *nabal* can also mean "disgrace" and "curse" on occasion. What Moses is told is that not only is it irresponsible of him to act in such a manner, but it is forbidden for him to cause the people to suffer so.[18] The Israelites will wind up cursing their leader.[19] Simply put: It is disgraceful in God's eyes for Moses to act alone.

According to Jethro, it was not simply expedient to involve others in the process of rendering judgment, it is what God wants. Jethro communicates this to Moses in a very pointed manner: "If you will do this, this is what God commands you!" (18:23). It is nothing less than a holy act to share the burden of leadership and empower others.

LEADERSHIP DEMANDS EMPOWERING OTHERS

Jethro realizes that there are many roles only Moses can play as the leader of the People of Israel. He notes, "You represent the people before God: you bring their petitions before God. You enjoin upon them the laws and the teachings, and make known to them the way in which they must walk and the practices they are to follow" (18:18–20). However, the greater part of the judicial duties you must entrust to others.[20] The task of judging the people is too arduous for you. Jethro explains, according to the rabbis: Observe a beam when it is still fresh and moist, even two or three people cannot support it. But four or five people can get under it and lift it.[21] Moses, "you need to make it easier on yourself!" (18:22). And that will make it much easier for the people to have their cases heard continuously, as indicated by Jethro's advice: "Let [others] judge the people at all times" (18:22). If there are many judges available, they can judge the people "at all times."[22] Empowering others and sharing leadership authority should be a basic part of the playbook of every leader. This comes through when Jethro urges Moses to "seek out [teheze] from among the people capa-

Those who sailed with Ernest Shackleton understood that his vision of leadership involved sharing with his men much of the responsibility on their voyages, and even giving them some measure of independence. That is what set him apart from others, including one of his mentors, the renowned explorer Robert Scott.[23]

ble individuals" (18:21). The verb *teheze* not only means "to see," but also "to have vision" and even "to prophesy." So Jethro indicates by his choice of words that he sees this selection of judges as a part of leadership vision, which can even be understood as the product of divine inspiration.[24]

In empowering others to share the burden of leadership, the leader must recognize that people can play very different kinds of roles. Not every potential leader is equipped to fulfill every role; choices must be made based on the individual's skills and talents. This is evident in the clear directive which Moses is given by Jethro: "Set these [leaders] over them as chiefs of thousands, hundreds, fifties and tens" (18:21). Moses learns that there are indeed different levels of leadership, and each person can play a role for which she is uniquely suited. All leaders must recognize the importance of what is called "distributed leadership."[25]

However, no matter what kind of role particular individuals are expected to play, Jethro outlines for Moses four basic characteristics that all potential leaders should possess. He suggests that Moses search for individuals who are strong (*anshei hayyil*), who believe in God (*yir'ei Elohim*), who are truthful (*anshei emet*), and who are not enamored of material gain (*son'ei vatzah*) (18:21).[27] According to the tradition, these are the very qualities inherent in Moses, and it is very difficult for him to find people who combine all of them.[28] This is especially true of the first—*anshei hayyil*—strong individuals, people of valor, who have the strength and patience to lead a large nation and bear up under all challenges.[29] To the qualities mentioned by Jethro, the Rabbis add one more crucial characteristic, an absolute essential

The Boston Celtics of the National Basketball Association had great success in the 1960s because, while the Celtics had several stars who led the team, others played crucial supportive roles. The Celtics coach, Red Auerbach, noted, "How you select people is more important than how you manage them." The mix of role players determines the nature of the team as a whole and how it will function.[26]

Winston Churchill often spoke of the qualities he sought in leaders. He looked for strength of character and courage, the ability and willingness to stand up to power, trustworthiness, moral vision, and individuals of substance. He understood the supreme importance of choosing the right people.[31] from the perspective of rabbinic Judaism: All judges, and all leaders of the People of Israel, must themselves be immersed in Torah study if they are to teach and interpret God's words.[30] The biblical text and the Rabbis' commentaries on it give modern readers a significant portrait of leadership for the modern Jewish community—and even the secular community—in broad outline. Imagine if every synagogue, communal organizational, or educational institution's board demanded that all who aspired to leadership in their communities had the following characteristics:

- Strength
- Patience
- Faith in God
- High ethical standards
- The willingness to stand on principle and act on it in the face of aggressive opposition
- A sense that life should not be solely dedicated to acquiring material wealth
- Dedication to Torah (or Bible) study

The qualities highlighted by Jethro apply across the board: They are excellent criteria for all leaders, both secular and religious.

DELEGATING AUTHORITY

Leaders, in sharing authority with others, face the essential challenge of determining exactly which responsibilities to delegate to other members of the group and which to retain for themselves. Throughout the entire tradition, from Josephus to the later Rabbis,[32]

Jethro's advice—that every major dispute (*davar gadol*) should come before Moses, but all minor disputes (*davar katan*) should be decided by others (18:22)—resonates in some way. In every generation, the Rabbis struggle to understand exactly what cases should be delegated to others. Does *davar gadol* mean that important or perhaps difficult cases should remain the prerogative of Moses, while simpler, less important disputes could be assigned to others? Or does *davar gadol* imply that matters involving the *gedolim,* the wealthy and powerful in the community, are to be decided by Moses, while matters involving people of lesser standing can be handled by others?[33] Whatever Jethro's intent, his message to Moses is clear: One person can neither judge every case nor lead the people alone. Leaders must share the burden and the responsibility of leadership. Groups only function well when leaders delegate tasks and authority.

All too often, leaders fail to realize the importance of sharing power and delegating authority to others. They don't understand that by empowering others, they themselves will gain. And even if they understand this in the abstract, they do not take the next step to establish criteria for delegating authority. Jethro makes it clear to his son-in-law what will happen if he heeds his advice: "If you do this—and God has so commanded you—you will be able to bear up [*a'mod,* literally "stand"] and all these people will return to their place in *shalom*" (18:23). Sharing power is what God wants and what God expects. It is truly a holy act, and if you achieve it, God will be with you (18:19) and ensure your success.[35] Not only is it easier for leaders if they delegate authority to others, but they themselves, by

Bill O'Brien, CEO of the Hanover Insurance Company, one of the most powerful insurance companies in the country, realized that if he wanted to succeed, members of his leadership team had to be empowered to make increasingly complex decisions. He said that "the fullest development of people [who share authority] ... will ensure financial success."[34] Giving up some of his power meant that the company would ultimately benefit.

sacrificing some of their power to empower others, will actually increase in stature in the process. Just listen to Jethro's choice of words: "If you [delegate authority to others], you will *a'mod*—be able to stand." The image of Moses standing after empowering others contrasts sharply with the opening scene in the narrative, in which Moses is sitting (*yosheiv*) and the entire people are standing (*ya'amod*) over him from morning to evening (18:13–15). Now, Moses is able to stand—to rise up—symbolizing his increased stature and strength. This is the result of his ability to share power. It has even been suggested that Moses's standing here anticipates the entire nation eventually "standing at Mount Sinai." Moses's increased stature enables him to lead them to Sinai where they

Jack Strack, head of the Springfield Remanufacturing Corporation, knew that sharing power with others would solidify his own authority and strengthen the company in the process. He said metaphorically: "I didn't want to be alone. I was going to be leading the charge up the hill. I wanted to make sure that when I got to the top of the hill and turned around, there was a bunch of people coming up with me. It's easy to stop one guy, but it's pretty hard to stop a hundred." To achieve this goal, he made sure to impart all his financial knowledge to his top managers.[37]

themselves will be ready to stand before God and receive the Torah.[36] Counterintuitively, leaders who empower others increase their own power and standing among their people!

The people, too, ultimately benefit from the leader's sharing authority. As Jethro emphasizes, the Israelites will experience *shalom* (wholeness, peace) in the end. But it is not simply that they will return to their homes unwearied, because they will not have to wait forever to have their cases heard by Moses. The entire people will gain a sense of greater wholeness because of their inclusion in the process of leadership and proximity to Moses.

In the end, realizing the wisdom of Jethro's words, Moses truly hears and internalizes his message: "Moses heard Jethro [*va-yishma*

... *lekol Yitro*] and did just as he said" (18:24). Moses literally "hears Jethro's voice"; that is, he understands the nuances and import of his advice and is sensitive to the emotion with which he speaks. Moses has the wisdom to take the advice of those who care about him and his success.[38] His future as well as that of his people depends on his empowering others and delegating authority to those who are capable of sharing leadership.

10
The Leader's Vision

Exodus 19

While tending to his father-in-law Jethro's flocks, Moses experiences God's presence at the mountain called Horeb, which many scholars view as Mount Sinai. The episode at Horeb is inextricably bound up with the events that will take place later at Sinai, as the text intimates: "This shall be a sign for you ... that you shall worship God at this place" (Exodus 3:12).[1] Again, God appears to Moses in the midst of fire, but the difference is that now God's presence is manifest to the entire people, not just to their leader.[2]

The nature of God's revelation at Sinai also anticipates the way the Israelites will experience the Divine Presence throughout their journey through the desert. Both Mount Sinai and the Mishkan, the wilderness tabernacle, have gradations of access to the Divine. For example, just as Moses alone can ascend to the mountain's summit, so all but one are barred from the inner sanctum of the tabernacle, the so-called Holy of Holies.[3]

MOSES'S ASCENT UP THE MOUNTAIN

When the people camp at the foot of Mount Sinai, Moses ascends the mountain, apparently before God has even called to him, as we see from the sequence in the biblical text: "Moses went up to God. The

Lord called to him from the mountain" (19:3). Why does Moses ascend without waiting for God to beckon to him? Perhaps Moses simply takes the initiative to fulfill God's command given at the Burning Bush, in anticipation of the people's return to the mountain; he is told that they will eventually worship God at this place.[4] Based on past experience, Moses knows what must be done and he does not hesitate to act.

Once Moses is on the mountain, God calls to him. He shows God that he is ready to carry out whatever tasks God has in store for him, having prepared himself for the encounter and having drawn as close to

One of Winston Churchill's greatest qualities was his relentless drive to take the initiative in every ministry that he led. As he once wrote, he "refused to be the passive matrix upon which others imposed their plans." He never wanted to fritter away an opportunity, especially when it could involve much-needed monumental change.[5]

God as he can. Once on the mountain, even though he ascends only part of the way, he is now worthy of God's calling him and allowing him to climb even higher.[6] Moses is now positioned to hear God's address clearly. Moses alone can ascend the mountain when God's presence rests there because he has attained a level of spirituality that is much higher than that of all the other people, as evidenced by his initial encounter with the Divine at the Burning Bush as well as in Egypt.[7] In the end, God, having descended onto the top of Mount Sinai, beckons Moses alone to ascend to the summit (19:20). His brother Aaron, who also hears the words of the Divine in Egypt, is allowed to ascend only part of the way (19:24). The rest of the people, including Aaron's sons, are not allowed to set foot on the mountain. So when Moses takes even one step up the mountain on the way to his encounter with God, he is separated from the people. Moses is actually pictured as ascending and descending Mount Sinai three times (19:3, 14, 20–21, 24–25), which is troublesome to both rabbinic commentators and modern biblical critics because it seems to them an impossible task. However, when approaching the Divine, the journey is different each time—not a peak experience every time. So Moses only ascends to the top of Mount Sinai once—after being summoned by God; the other times he only goes partway up.[8] Like all leaders, no matter how many times Moses is forced to backtrack, he has to persevere and stay the course. Leadership requires us to accept that the leader cannot always reach the heights.

GOD BUTTRESSES MOSES'S AUTHORITY

Why does God summon Moses to the top of the mountain, only to send him back down again to warn the people not to break through and touch the mountain in order to gaze upon the Divine (19:20–21)? Could God not have given him this commandment while he was still down below? God perhaps calls Moses to ascend Mount Sinai several times in order to strengthen his authority in the eyes of the people. Each time they see that they have to remain below, confined to their camps, while only their leader is given permission to go up and down, speaking to God in God's own place.[9]

God makes it clear that the intent is to bolster Moses's power in the eyes of the Israelites when the Divine actually says to Moses, "I will come to you in a thick cloud, in order that the people may hear when I speak with you and as a result will trust you forever" (19:9). The people seemingly are privy in some way to the conversation between God and Moses and thus witness firsthand God's empowerment of him with knowledge from and access to the Divine. From that moment on, the people will recognize and acknowledge Moses's prophetic stature.[10] Later, amid the fire and smoke on the mountain and the blare of the shofar, which grows louder and louder, Moses, standing below with the people gathered at the foot of Mount Sinai, speaks to God. It is only then that God responds to him (19:18–19). It appears that God only speaks once Moses initiates the conversation. All this to further enhance Moses's authority and the respect paid to him by the people.[11] This, in turn, reassures the people as they stand near the mountain, which shakes violently, fire and smoke bellowing from its molten core. Often, the faith that people place in their leader is the only thing that sustains them in the midst of their fears and doubts.

Though the text only says here that "Moses spoke" (19:19), we assume it means that he speaks to God, since it then adds, "God answered him *ba-kol*." But it is conceivable that at that moment Moses actually speaks to Israel. In addition, most translations understand the term *ba-kol* to mean "in thunder" (*kolot*, plural, means "thunder"). However, if *ba-kol* is taken to mean "in the voice," then it is possible to interpret the whole verse as some commentators do: "When Moses spoke, [conveying the commandments to Israel], God strengthened his voice [*kol*], making it more effective so the people would listen to him." The presumption in this tradition is that Moses conveys all the commandments except for the first two, which underscore God's unique existence.[13] Again, by being privy to Moses's conversations with God, Israel's belief and trust in Moses is strengthened. All this is done by God to further enhance Moses's position and authority among his people.

O n their dangerous expeditions to the Antarctic, when they were caught in the grip of acute fear for their lives, the men of Ernest Shackleton's crews were sustained by the faith and trust they placed in their leader. Shackleton was a tower of strength from which the crew drew in every challenging moment.[12]

MOSES AND THE PEOPLE

Having arrived at Mount Sinai, the question is whether the People of Israel are ready for divine revelation. Traveling (*va-yis'u*) from Rephidim, where they rebelled against God, showing their lack of faith, they enter the wilderness and camp (*va-yahanu*) there. The use of the two plural verbs shows that they are not a united people. There is much internal turmoil and dissension. Yet when they arrive at the mountain, the Bible says, "Israel camped (*va-yihan*) in front of the mountain" (19:2), indicating that finally they have drawn together as a people, perhaps in anticipation of God's revealing of the Divine Self to them. They have finally become one people, responding with one heart, and as such they are worthy of the revelation.[14] Then, when

Moses puts all the words that God commands him before the people, they agree as one: "All the people answered as one [*yachdav,* literally, "together"], saying, 'All that the Lord has spoken we will do and we will obey'" (19:8). They are finally united as God's people.[15]

While Israel stands as one before its God, experiencing redemption as a united people, each individual experiences the moment in particular ways, and each one of them has to be addressed personally if the laws are to become meaningful to them. Each individual Israelite is unique and important. Thus the Bible emphasizes that "God was revealed in the sight of all the people" (19:11), meaning that if only one Israelite were missing, they would not have been given the Torah.[16] Furthermore, Moses is instructed to address each Israelite individu-

The wisest leaders—from FDR with his "fireside chats" to Hal Rosenbluth of the giant travel agency that bears his name with his "Hal hotline"—know that it is imperative for each person to have a direct connection with and communication from their leader. FDR's radio "chats" made each of his listeners feel as though they were being addressed personally—a crucial element of leadership, especially at a time of drastic challenges and change.[18]

ally, as indicated by God's instructions to him, "You shall say [*tomar*] to the house of Jacob and declare [*tageid*] to the Children of Israel" (19:3). The use of two different words associated with two separate objects—the house of Jacob and the Children of Israel—is understood as referring to each and every Israelite.[17] Everything has changed for the Israelites—they are now expected to live by God's commandments, so each and every Israelite has to understand and internalize these commandments. Thus, when the task is to adapt the organization to a radically new reality, every leader must recognize that each member must be engaged in the mission.

The tradition consistently interprets the "house of Jacob" (*Beit Ya'akov*) and the "Children of Israel (*Bnai Yisrael*) as references to the women and the men, respectively. *Bnai Yisrael* (the children of

Israel), if read literally, is a masculine reference—*banim* means "sons." *Beit,* the short form of *bayit,* means "house," and is always seen as alluding to women. The men and women are therefore seen as being addressed in very different manners: Moses speaks to the women in very gentle tones, while he addresses the men in very harsh, strict tones.[19]

Since, according to the Rabbis, men are obligated to observe the words of Torah in ways that the women aren't, Moses has to use harsh words to spell out the punishments if they do not observe the commandments. Moses had to "declare [*tageid*]" the words to the people: *Tageid* resonates with the Hebrew word *gid,* meaning "sinew," but also "wormwood," an herb as bitter as oleander![20] One rabbinic tradition holds that women are to receive only the outline of God's revelation, in accordance with their limited understanding, while men are taught all the intricate details.[21] Although we may not endorse the obvious misogyny evident in the Rabbis' reading of this biblical text, it is instructive in showing us the importance of the choice of language and tone with which the leader addresses all the people. Leaders have to select the words and tone that will be most effective in addressing the needs and dispositions of every individual in their organization. Just as at Mount Sinai, the vision of God's presence and the content of revelation are transmitted in ways that every individual can hear and understand, it is imperative for leaders to communicate the common vision in distinctive ways that speak to each one.

Although Moses is told to descend and speak directly with the house of Jacob and the Children of Israel, the first thing that he does is summon the *zekeinim,* the elders of the people, to tell them what God has commanded (19:7). Why does Moses convey God's words to the elders first? Is it only a matter of honoring the recognized leaders of the people?[22] Moses, it seems, intentionally uses the elders, who share with him the task of relaying God's revelation to the rest of the Israelites.[23] Once the elders accept God's commandments, and then in turn speak to the people, those who recognize the elders as their leaders are bound to embrace the Divine's words.[24] Moses understands how to build consensus in stages. Conveying God's revelation to the people directly would not succeed. Co-opting the elders into the process gives Moses the leverage he needs to bring the people along. In modern leadership theory, this is known as a *cascading vision*.

Moses's strategy seems to be working—the people immediately answer in unison, "All that God has spoken we will do" (19:8). They do not hesitate to accept God's words. Yet when it comes time to lead the people to the mountain to experience God's presence firsthand, to hear the commanding voice of the Divine, they are deathly afraid. They tremble at the sight and sounds of the thunder and lightning. The Bible goes out of its way to emphasize that Moses has to lead (*va-yotzei*) the people to the foot of Mount Sinai, implying that they are not able to move on their own (19:17). He literally has to force them out of the camp in order to meet (*likrat*) their God.[26] Just as he leads them out of Egypt, he now leads them from the oppressive narrowness of the camp to the Divine Presence.[27] Leaders like Moses are called on to support their followers on their journey, sometimes even to force them to overcome their innate fears, for the sake of their own growth. Moses is pictured by the Rabbis as arousing the Israelites from their slumber and leading them toward the Divine.[28] One crucial role of the leader is directing followers toward a specific goal that will ultimately benefit them.

Winston Churchill was an excellent model of a leader who understood the importance of preparing the leaders under him with the information and decisions that had to be eventually conveyed to the group as a whole. He noted in a memorandum to his subordinate executives, "It is essential that you should beforehand give the decisions which will allow your lieutenants to act effectively."[25]

SETTING BOUNDARIES, PREPARING THE PEOPLE, AND CONVEYING GOD'S WORDS

Once the Israelites arrive at the foot of the mountain, Moses is told by God to set clear boundaries to prevent the people from ascending Mount Sinai, or even touching it (19:12). His role is to spell out for the people God's instructions. They need structure so they can recognize their human limitations, the distinctions and distances that characterize the human world.[29]

Lest they think that because they will hear the Divine's voice on the mountain, they are capable of ascending to the position of Moses,[30] Moses is told to warn the people not to draw too close (19:21). Not even the priests are allowed on the mountain during the moment of revelation. Only Aaron and Hur are permitted to ascend with Moses (24:14), and even Aaron is limited in how far up he can climb (19:24). As noted earlier, there are distinct areas on the mountain indicating levels of holiness and access to God.[31]

Moses has to descend from the mountain not only to warn the People of Israel that they must stay pure if they are to be ready to experience Divine revelation (19:14–15), but also to urge them to stay within the set boundaries at the foot of Mount Sinai. Moses responds to God by pointing out that he has already warned them about remaining pure and not approaching the mountain (19:10ff), so why must he again descend and warn them a second time? They are already in a state of purity for three days in preparation for the big moment! According to the Rabbis, the Divine acknowledges Moses's argument, but adds, "Still, I want you to go down and warn the people a second time. It is good to give a warning before action is required and then when it is required. You must tell the people that now they must be careful to heed the prior warning, since the time is at hand."[32]

In order for Moses to adequately prepare the People of Israel for the revelation, he has to be down below with them. If he remains on the top of the mountain in God's presence, there will be no one to set boundaries for them, warn them about their behavior, and sanctify them in God's sight.

In this process, God demonstrates to Moses that the people have to be prepared if they are going to understand God's words and embrace them. When they first arrive at Mount Sinai, the Israelites are not ready to hear God's words because of their exhaustion from the desert journey.[33] Then, they first have to hear God speaking to Moses, in order to trust him (19:9); purify themselves for three days in preparation for the moment of revelation on the third day (19:10–14); and then witness Moses addressing God directly and God answering him, so as to overcome the overwhelming fear they experience standing at the foot of the mountain amid the thunder, lightning, and blasts of the shofar (19:18–19). It is only then that God comes down on Mount Sinai and calls Moses to the top. Clearly, the Israelites have to be prepared in stages if they are going to be able to hear and respond to God's presence. Sometimes leaders fail to grasp that their followers cannot embrace their vision or understand everything that is expected of them at the very outset. Their challenge is both to be patient and to bring their followers along in a realistic manner. Most of us who are committed to the ideals and to the institutions to which we have devoted our lives want to accomplish all our goals as quickly as possible, and we tend to forget that we are dealing with individuals who have not heard the same "call" as we have.

God wants the people to obey the laws and keep the covenant, but to achieve this goal, the Israelites will have to be brought along in stages, as the Rabbis' interpretation of the biblical text, "If you will truly obey Me faithfully [*shamo'a tishm'u*]" (19:5), indicates. When the people first arrive at the mountain, they are commanded to hear (*shama*), that is, internalize and obey God's words. But the Rabbis point out that by doubling the root word *shama—shamo'a tishm'a—* the text underscores that they will have to hear—be taught—God's words in stages. Once they hear one command, they can hear others.[34]

In addition, if Moses is to be successful in conveying God's words to Israel in a manner in which they could understand and accept them, then both the tone and form in which he speaks are crucial. When God says to him, "Thus shall you say [*koh tomar*] to the house of Jacob and the Children of Israel" (19:3), the tradition stresses that God wants Moses to repeat the exact tone, form, and content that the Divine has used with him when he communicates the laws to the people.[35] The very voice or tone (*kol*) that God uses in instructing Moses is the tone in which he has to speak.[36]

MOSES SUPPORTS AND DEFENDS THE PEOPLE

As Moses himself matures, he develops a very realistic picture of the people and their ability, and as their leader does not hesitate to communicate that directly to God. He recognizes their limitations and expects of them only what they are capable of doing. He knows that they need boundaries so they will not ascend the mountain against God's will and draw closer to the Divine, as he reminds God, "The people cannot come up to Mount Sinai" (19:23). He, therefore, will have to serve as their intermediary before the Divine, conveying God's words to them and their words to the Divine.[37]

When Moses brings the people's words back to God (19:8), the Rabbis stress that Moses reviews their words so that he understands their deeper significance and can convey that to God.[38] Like all great leaders, he sees his task as truly understanding his followers and representing their real needs.

Looking closely at the biblical text, it seems redundant: Moses reports the people's response to God twice. First, we are told that he "brought [*va-yashev*] back the people's words" (19:8), and in the very next verse, we read, "Then Moses reported [*va-yageid*] the people's words" (19:9). Playing on this seeming repetition, though focusing on the use of two distinct verbs, the Rabbis emphasize two different points. On the one hand, Moses reports to God the Israelites' commitment to God: They will do all that God commands (19:8). All previous doubts about the people's belief seem to have disappeared, and Moses, overwhelmed by the people's response, assures God of their fidelity.[39]

Yet Moses senses that the people, deep inside, are still afraid and they may have some lingering doubts, which will not be overcome by simply hearing God's words from him. He intuits that the Israelites need two things: to hear the commandments directly from the Divine and to be worthy of experiencing God's presence, that is, of seeing God.[40] Moses not only reports their words to God, but brings back much more: He conveys a clear sense of what the People of Israel desperately need. And God accedes to both requests. First, God promises, "The people will hear when I speak with you" (19:9), and then God adds, "On the third day, the Lord will come down in the sight of all the people" (19:11).[41] Every leader must truly hear his followers, understand their individual concerns, and then try to respond to them. More than the willingness to open himself to the people and listen to them, a leader must convey their concerns to those who can respond in a serious way to the issues troubling them.

Moses is devoted to the People of Israel, and they are the sole focus of his life and mission: We recognize this when the text says, "Moses came down from the mountain to the people and warned the people to stay pure" (19:14). The words "to the people" (*el ha-am*) seem superfluous. All we need to know is that "Moses came down ... and warned the people." However, the added reference that he comes directly to the people is picked up in a variety of midrashim, in which the Rabbis note that, instead of attending to his own personal needs after the experience with the Divine on the mountain, Moses immediately turns to his people. He rushes to tell them of God's words and directives.[43] And this is not merely the case when the Torah is about to be given; it occurs on every occasion in which God communicates something to Moses.[44] Moses's authority depends on fulfilling his mission for the People of Israel.

A contemporary leader who possesses exceptional listening skills is Kermit Campbell, the CEO of the furniture giant, Herman Miller. Campbell vowed to meet and listen to every one of his five thousand employees, and to try to understand their concerns on the deepest levels. He did this by making round-the-clock visits to every workstation. And then he pledged to respond to them.[42]

Moses's place is with his people down below, not standing on top of the mountain far removed from them. Like all leaders, he must be with his followers to carry out his mission. So when God is about to give the commandments to the people, God demands that Moses descend to warn the people not to ascend the mountain (19:21–22). But Moses isn't leaving God's presence so fast! He argues that the people have already been warned, so there is no need for him to return to them (19:23). At that point God reiterates that he must descend (*lech reid*), this time ostensibly to bring Aaron up with him. In the end Moses goes down to the people (19:24–25).

According to the Rabbis, God will give the Commandments to the People of Israel only if Moses is below with them, and the Divine needs to find a way to force Moses to descend.[45] To what may this be compared? ask the Rabbis. To a king who wishes to pass laws without consulting the lieutenant-governor. When the king says to him, "Do this thing," the reply is, "It is already done!" The king tries once again: "Go and call this counselor that he may come with you," and when the lieutenant-governor leaves, the king then carries out his wish and enacts the laws. In effect, God has to lure Moses to the bottom of the mountain, for it is

Fred Smith, CEO of FedEx, runs his company by the watchwords *People, Service, Profit*. The order is important, for the *Manager's Guide* of the company states: "Take care of our people; they, in turn, will deliver the impeccable service demanded of our customers who will reward us with the profitability necessary to secure our future."[47]

God's intention for Moses to be with his people when the Ten Commandments are given.[46] At the moment in which God seals the covenant with Israel, Moses has to stand with the people at the foot of the mountain. He is one of them and, as such, is as much subject to the commandments conveyed to them as the lowliest of Israelites. Leaders get into trouble when they set themselves apart from the people whom they serve and see themselves as different, even better. Their leadership role depends on the people and their needs, and it has little to do with their own intrinsic value. If only many of today's CEOs understood this very basic notion, rather than holding themselves above the corporations that they serve, even above the laws of the land. They feel that they are solely responsible for the success of their companies. How misguided! If only they could learn the lesson that Moses himself did: Success can come only when you stand with the people at the foot of the mountain.

11
In the Face of Challenge and Rejection
Exodus 32

Moses spends forty days on Mount Sinai in the Divine Presence, receiving God's laws, which he will subsequently convey to the People of Israel. The grandeur of this encounter stands in sharp contrast to the feelings of abandonment that the Israelites experience at the foot of the mountain, bereft of their leader.[1] "The people saw [*va-yar*] that Moses delayed [*boshesh*] in coming down from the mountain" (Exodus 32:1). After everything they have experienced, all the people can see is that Moses is late in returning. As a result, they are greatly dismayed (*boshesh* comes from the root *boosh*) and anxious, not knowing what has happened to him.[2] Meanwhile Moses is receiving God's law, which will ultimately change humanity for all eternity.[3] Leaders need to adopt a long-term perspective as they act on behalf of their followers. They cannot be caught up in the moment. But the people, sensing a growing distance between themselves and their leader, may find that distance a terrible burden to bear.

BEING TOO DEPENDENT ON THE LEADER

Because they feel abandoned by Moses, the people gather around Aaron, his surrogate, and clearly voice their concern: "That man

Moses, who brought us from the land of Egypt—we do not know what has happened to him" (32:1). The redundant emphasis on Moses and the stress upon his role—he led them from Egypt into the desert—indicates that they want a substitute for Moses who will continue to lead them at God's bidding. They want another leader to ensure that they will survive the desert journey.[4]

Their actual request makes this clear: "Come, make us *elohim* [usually understood as 'God'] who shall go before us" (32:1). They do not ask for a god whom they can worship, but rather a leader or leaders (we can translate *elohim* as "judges," as we see in many places in the Bible, including Exodus 22) who will assume Moses's role.[5] They do not reject their God; all they want is a replacement for Moses, who has disappeared.

They ask Aaron to provide them with "gods" (plural) who will show them the way in the desert. Perhaps they simply harken back to their experience in Egypt, in which they witnessed the worship of a multitude of tangible objects. Waiting at the foot of Sinai for Moses to bring the tablets sealing their covenant with God and panicked that they have lost their leader, they regress perhaps to that earlier time: They need an object to worship, like all the other nations.[6] Their need for a godlike leader, akin to the Pharaoh (*par'oh*), comes through later when Moses describes the people as being *paru'ah*, out of control (32:25). In a sense, they have not as yet weaned themselves from their attachment to Egypt, which they still carry with them.[7]

For the Israelites, Moses has become too much of a focus of power and authority. It is he who brought them out of Egypt, divided the waters of the Red Sea, and miraculously provided them with sustenance in the desert. Their idolatry, so to speak, begins long before the building of the Golden Calf—Moses himself has become an object of reverence for them, upon whom they are pathologically dependent. We can imagine Moses's words to them: "Am I so holy that in my absence you had to make a Golden Calf? Heaven forbid! I am only human like you. God's laws do not depend on me."[8] Like all groups of people, the Israelites have to learn that they can survive on their own.

AARON BUILDS THE GOLDEN CALF

Instead of appointing a leader in Moses's place or assuming the role himself, Aaron fashions a calf in response to the people who have gathered around him, clamoring for "*elohim*" to lead them. Perhaps Aaron is afraid that if he appointed someone, the Israelites might not want to abandon their new leader when Moses eventually returned, and civil strife would ensue. Aaron therefore creates a symbol of leadership.[9]

Yet, according to the predominant rabbinic tradition, this is not the reason why Aaron builds the calf. Angered and dismayed at Moses's protracted stay on the mountain, the people first approach the elders, those who are closer to them, and request a leader. Because the elders rebuke the people for provoking the Divine after witnessing all the miracles God has wrought, the people kill them. They then turn to Hur, Miriam's son and Moses's nephew, with the same request. Hur also courageously refuses even though he would meet the same fate.[10] Leaders possessing courage can face any circumstance. Courage is crucial in establishing and maintaining leadership authority.[11]

W inston Churchill was known as a take-charge person who was also willing to assume responsibility for whatever events he set in motion. Churchill once asserted: "If someone has to take responsibility. I will do so."[13]

So why is it that Aaron gives in to the people's demands? Is it, as the Bible intimates, that "Aaron saw" [*va-yar*] (32:5) that he is next and that he does not possess the inner strength to refuse? Is it that Aaron, a peacemaker at heart, is incapable of making hard, unpopular decisions that leaders must inevitably make?[12] Even Moses seems to chastise his brother for not taking responsibility and lacking the ability to control the people (32:25). He is afraid (*yi'rah*) and capitulates to their demands.

Perhaps, however, what Aaron fears are the consequences of Israel's actions: If they kill him, after killing Hur, they surely will deserve to be punished with exile from their land.[14] He therefore takes it upon himself to build the calf, in hopes that Israel can avert God's wrath. By fashioning the calf himself, by asking the people to gather the women's jewelry, and then working as slowly as he can, he thinks he can forestall the completion of the idol until Moses's return. Furthermore, he builds an altar by himself before the calf, and then insists that everyone wait until the next day to celebrate, delaying even further. Finally, he is willing to take the onus for erecting the calf on himself, thereby preventing Israel's punishment: He will be responsible.[15]

We should note that, in response to the people's expressed need for something concrete to lead them through the desert, Aaron has the wisdom to channel their impulse toward the Divine. In declaring a holiday after fashioning the calf and erecting the altar, Aaron declares: "Tomorrow shall be a festival to *Adonai*" (32:5). Like all great leaders, Aaron chooses to meet the people where they are, affirming their basic impulses, but then directing them to something higher.[16]

MOSES'S STATURE DEPENDS ON HIS PEOPLE

The Israelites are certainly in a very different place than Moses. Not only have they been complaining and rebelling ever since they left Egypt, but while they are standing at the foot of Mount Sinai, they already are turning toward idolatry. In the midst of the revelation of God's laws, having exclaimed, "We will do and we will obey" (19:8), they clamor for Aaron to make them a god.[17] Seeing the calf below, God tells Moses that the people have rushed to turn aside (*saru*) from the divine path (32:8). How ironic a choice of words: The people are quick to turn aside (based on the verb *sur*) from the chosen path, while Moses on Horeb is described as "turning aside" (*sar*) from the path to see the Burning Bush, to witness God's presence (3:4). Moses rushes to embrace the Divine while the people are turning away.

Because the people have sinned, God commands Moses, "Immediately descend [from the Mountain] because your people [God does not say 'My people'] whom you have brought up from Egypt have gone astray" (32:7). When the people of Israel sin, they are identified with Moses ("*your* people"), prompting the Rabbis to stress that Moses is forced to descend from his lofty position with the

Divine on the mountain, to forfeit his greatness, because he is only elevated on account of the People of Israel.[18] Moses's stature is totally dependent on the people and their needs; he does not ascend the mountain for his own glory, but rather for theirs.[19] His authority, in part, comes from them. As quickly (*maher*) as they turn aside from God's path, just as quickly (*maher*) he has to descend from Sinai (Deuteronomy 9:12). When they are to be elevated, so is he; when they fall from the path, his stature diminishes.[20]

Even though God threatens to destroy Israel, the Divine also pledges to Moses that he will become a great nation of his own accord. Moses responds by imploring God to not to be angry at the people (32:10). It is as if Moses replied to God, "For the sake of my own name and success, should I abandon Israel? I cannot live without them!"[21] Moses as the shepherd can only fulfill his role in this world if his flock is kept alive.[22]

MOSES DEFENDS THE PEOPLE

When God tells Moses that the people have made a golden calf and are sacrificing to it, saying, "This is your god, O Israel, who brought you out of the land of Egypt" (32:8), Moses responds with utter shock. Listening in amazement, he is unable to utter a single word. God is then forced to break the silence, "saying further to Moses, 'I see that this is a stiff-necked people'" (32:9).[23] Moses's spirits have been broken and his strength has given out at that moment.[24] How difficult it is for any leader to confront and then deal with a recalcitrant group of followers, especially when they reject essential values of the group.

No matter how deflated and powerless Moses feels, he realizes that there is a kernel of doubt in God's mind regarding the destruction of the People of Israel. The hint of God's equivocation comes when the Divine requests of Moses, "Now, let Me be [*haniha li*] so that My anger may blaze forth against them and that I may destroy them" (32:10). In seemingly asking for Moses's permission to destroy them, God offers an opening for Moses to intercede on Israel's behalf.[25] To what may this be compared? To a king who is angry at his son, and when the son is brought into the chamber and is about to be beaten, the king cries: "Leave me alone, that I may smite him."

Now, the tutor of the son happens to be standing outside and he thinks to himself: "If only the king and the son are in the chamber, then why does the king say, 'Leave me alone'? To whom is he speaking? It must be that the king is crying out because he really does *not* want to be alone! He indeed desires that I should entreat him on his son's behalf."[26] In some rabbinic interpretations, the Rabbis go even further, suggesting that Moses actually seizes hold of God, like a person who grabs his fellow by his garment, and says to God, "I will not let You go until You forgive and pardon them." Moses understands that God is giving him a chance to act on behalf of his people. Their future depends on him; he must intervene. Without hesitation, he implores God to withhold his anger.[27] Like all great leaders at critical turning points, he cannot afford to hesitate.

Moses feels empowered to influence God's decisions through his own actions, and act he does. When God says to him, "Let Me be [*haniha li*]," he implores God to renounce (*hinahem*) the punishment meant for the people.[28] No matter how angry Moses himself might be or the feelings of personal rejection he might harbor, his role as a prophet as well as the leader of the people is to intercede on their behalf. He does so by attempting to convince God in a number of ways why the Divine should not destroy this fledging people.

Moses implores (*va-yehal*) God, "Let not Your anger destroy Your people whom You delivered from Egypt" (32:11). What Moses is saying to God is that the Divine cannot disown them; they will always be God's people, in contrast to God's claim to Moses that he should descend from the mountain because his (Moses's) people have gone astray. Moses chastises God: "When Israel had not yet sinned, You did call them 'My people' (7:4). Now that they have sinned, You say to me that they are my people? They are Your people; Your inheritance forever. You must become reconciled to them, for they are Your children."[29] Playing on the word *va-yehal* (Moses implored), the Rabbis claim that Moses chides God, saying, "It is a travesty for You (*Halilah lecha*) to act this way and destroy this people," echoing Abraham's denunciation of God's desire to destroy the people of Sodom and Gemorrah (Genesis 18:25).[30]

How can God destroy this people, whom the Divine has delivered out of Egyptian slavery? God has already done so much for them, having pledged to the patriarchs to make their offspring as numerous as the stars in heaven and to bring them to their ancestral homeland (32:13). Moses asks God to remember the long-term commitment made to the People of Israel and to see their sinfulness as just one moment in a long chain of events that links past, present, and future. God has to fulfill the divine pledge no matter how His children have acted.

When Moses urges God not to "let Your anger blaze forth against Your people," he notes that God has delivered the people from the land of Egypt (32:11), as if to remind God that they came from the land of idolatry to the holy mountain. Moses further defends his people by emphasizing that they have simply fallen back to old habits learned in Egypt and that God should have reasonable expectations of them.[31] This is compared by the Rabbis to a wise man who opens a perfumery shop for his son on a street frequented by harlots. The street, the work, and the son's youth all conspire to lead the young man into evil ways. When the father catches him with a prostitute, he begins to shout, "I will slay you!" But the father's friend is there and he says, "You were the means of destroying the character of this youth."[32] What is implied by this analogy is that God is partly responsible for Israel's sins, having placed them in Egypt. They have never cleansed themselves of the Egyptian experience, which they still carry with them.[33] Leaders need to recognize their followers' potential as well as the reality of their lives, and what can be realistically expected of them at any given moment.

Moses recognizes that his people have strayed a mere forty days after receiving God's revelation, with the commandment "Thou shalt have no other gods but Me" still ringing in their ears. They have demanded that Aaron provide them with another god to lead them.[34] Israel is young and cannot be expected to act in any other way. They are like a vineyard with precious vines, which, after the first year of being tended, produce sour grapes. The owner wants to destroy the vineyard, but a knowledgeable gardener assures him that the quality of the grapes will improve over time. All it will take is patience.[35] Leaders need to have patience with their followers, understanding that they have the potential to grow with the necessary nurturing. But sometimes, when followers take actions contrary to everything the leader stands for, mustering the requisite patience may be extremely difficult.

MOSES RESPONDS IN A VERY HUMAN WAY

Having convinced God to relinquish the punishment intended for Israel, Moses descends from the mountain with the two tablets of the covenant. Though God has told him of Israel's building of the calf, and though he has also heard the tumult below as he descends (32:17–18), he cannot anticipate how he will react when confronted by the ugly scene of the Israelites reveling in their sinfulness. Seeing Israel dancing around the calf, he cannot believe his own eyes, and he, like God, becomes enraged (32:19).[36] Though he has defended them before God, witnessing the scene himself is the tipping point for Moses. But it isn't just seeing the Golden Calf that causes him to despair of ever being able to remedy the situation. Israel will never be worthy of the tablets if they can exhibit such unadulterated joy as they dance around the idol![37]

Churchill's colleagues and friends always marveled at how calm he stayed amid the most trying of circumstances. In part, his ability to deal with the stress of adversity was a function of his courage and fearlessness.[41]

From the top of the mountain, as he defends his people, Moses can view the calf as being sheer farce, telling God that it lacks all power and is not real.[38] But standing below, Moses senses the power and vitality that Israel imputes to the calf, and he can't help but become infuriated.[39] The sight of the calf literally makes him sick (*holeh*), as the Rabbis sense from Moses imploring (*va-yehal*) God to release the anger directed against the people. Just as God's anger blazes against the Israelites because of their sin, though Moses implores God to renounce that anger, when Moses himself sees the Israelites rejoicing around the calf, his own anger blazes forth to the point where he becomes ill.[40]

Moses loses all patience with the Israelites, who are unworthy of God's commandments. By their behavior, they have broken their covenant with God, and, as a result, he hurls the tablets down, shattering them. Just as the tablets are broken, so is Moses. He now seems all alone, cut off from the very people he is charged with leading to the Promised Land, thus fulfilling God's promise. An impassable gulf seems to stretch between the leader and his people.[42] It is almost impossible for leaders to maintain their calm and objectivity in the face of stress brought on by disappointment, challenge, and personal rejection.

Yet there are Rabbis in the tradition who assert that Moses breaks the tablets deliberately to protect his people. Some reason that if Moses breaks them, Israel cannot be held accountable, since they neither know the commandments nor the punishment that awaits them if they sin.[43] Others feel that Moses breaks the tablets in the sight of the people to awaken them to what they have done and move them to immediately reject the calf and repent.[44] Another point of view holds that by breaking the tablets, Moses links himself with his followers: Even as they sin in worshiping the calf, he sins in breaking the tablets. Moses, the leader, is forced to identify with his people even in their breaking of the covenant with God.[45] Leaders realize that they share the very same faults and weaknesses as their people, and protect the people in every way.

MOSES CONTINUES TO LEAD
IN THE FACE OF ADVERSITY

In spite of feelings of rejection and disappointment in the people, Moses resumes his leadership role. Though he realizes that the people are out of control (32:25), he both curbs his own anger and maintains some degree of faith in them. Having initially been successful in his prayer to God not to destroy the people, he doesn't give up the hope that God will also forgive those who were not involved in the building of the calf. Here Moses demonstrates the essence of leadership—the ability to continue to lead and to galvanize followers, even in the face of failure, disappointment, frustration, and even anger. This may be his finest hour as a leader.[46] It is one thing to encourage and support followers when things are going well. However, it takes even more fortitude and commitment for a leader to press forward with the mission in the face of extreme adversity.[47]

His first act upon witnessing the revelry around the calf is to cry out: "*Mi l'Adonai Alai*—Whoever is for Adonai, come to me"

(32:26). In intoning the cry that will be used by Judah Maccabee generations later, Moses immediately sets out to solidify his base of support so he can build Israel's future as a people. As the Levites rally around him and dedicate themselves to God and the people as God's chosen ones, he himself becomes strengthened. Though he doesn't minimize their sin, he is again willing to ascend the mountain to defend them to God and to ask divine forgiveness for them (32:30–31).

Then comes his courageous ultimatum to God: "If You will forgive their sin [all well and good]; but if not, erase me from the book You have written" (32:32). Moses is willing to sacrifice his very life for the people whom he leads,[48] and, therefore, God is correct in telling him: "Your people have gone astray" (32:7). They indeed are his people, and he is the leader devoted to them. Whether Moses means that God should remove his name from the entire Torah,[49] or from the record of all of Israel's leaders,[50] or even from the Book of Life,[51] Moses emphasizes to God that he cannot continue to live, let alone serve as their leader without them. Moses would rather die than witness their punishment and suffering.[52]

Moses can resume the mantle of leadership because he is willing to put his life on the line for the People of Israel. God instructs him to "Go now, lead [*nehai*] the people where I told you" (32:34), which resonates in Hebrew with his willingness to give his life for them. This notion echoes Moses's challenge to God: "Erase me [*mehaini*] from Your book" (32:32).

And part of his leadership was to punish those who clamored for the building of the calf. Whether it was only the mixed multitude (the *erev rav*) who joined them in the Exodus from Egypt,[53] or a group of indigenous Israelites, or the entire people, because they stood by without protesting,[54] Moses understands that severe punishment has to be meted out if the people are to continue as God's partner in covenant. Moses also has to be willing to demand that his brother account for his actions, and he does not shy away from asking Aaron, "What did this people do to you that you have brought such a great sin upon them?" (32: 21). Even Aaron, whom he empowers to watch over the people, must accept responsibility for his actions, even if his intentions were pure,[55] as he claims. Leadership must demand accountability if the goals and mission of the people are to be fulfilled, and at times that may be difficult to do if the leader is especially close to those who serve on the leadership team.

In contrast to Aaron, Joshua, the future leader of the nation, stays at the foot of the mountain, far from the Israelite camp. Joshua seems completely oblivious to what has transpired in Moses's absence, being pictured as naively saying to Moses, after his descent with the tablets, "There is a cry of war in the camp" (32:17). Surprisingly, Moses responds that it is the sound of singing that they hear (32:18). Though Moses knows the reason for the tumult emanating from the Israelite camp, he deliberately refrains from conveying to Joshua the unvarnished truth. Moses does not want to disparage Israel in the eyes of the one who will take up the mantle of leadership once he is gone.[56] Preparing the next generation of leadership is a crucial element of the leader's responsibility, as we shall see toward the end of Moses's life.

12
Hearing Criticism: Knowing How to Respond
Numbers 12

Continuing their wanderings in the desert, the people once again complain to Moses about the lack of sustenance and Moses, in turn, complains to God: "Why have You dealt ill with Your servant ... You have laid the burden of all this people upon me? Where am I to get the meat to give to this people when they whine before me, 'Give us meat to eat.' I cannot bear all this by myself, for it is too much for me. If You would deal thus with me, kill me rather, I beg You, and let me no longer see my wretchedness!" (Numbers 11:11–5). Not only does Moses seem extremely vulnerable at this point, but he no longer feels capable of leading the Children of Israel. Feeling overburdened by the people, he begins to distance himself from them in order to protect himself.

It appears as if Moses's power is ebbing in certain ways and that he is out of touch with the people. As a result, even Miriam and Aaron begin to criticize their younger brother.[1]

WHO IS THE CUSHITE WOMAN AND WHAT WERE MIRIAM AND AARON'S CONCERNS?

Chapter 12 in the book of Numbers begins with the words, "Miriam and Aaron spoke [*va-tedabber*] against Moses because of the Cushite

[Ethiopian] woman he had married; for he had married a Cushite woman" (12:1). This opening verse is highly problematic. First, it is not clear who is doing the talking, since the verb used—*tedabber*—is third person feminine singular. If read literally, this can imply that only Miriam is speaking and Aaron is simply present. It is therefore not surprising that later on only Miriam is punished (11:10). Miriam seems from this perspective to be the principal instigator of the gossip against their brother.[2]

This is complicated, however, by the fact that the next word is in the plural, "They [both Miriam and Aaron] said, 'Has the Lord only spoken through Moses?'" (12:2). Perhaps, even though Aaron listens silently to Miriam's opening comment about Moses's Cushite wife, he not only is an accessory to the gossipmongering, but tacitly agrees with what she has to say.[3] Yet the phrasing could also mean that Miriam speaks first, though Aaron himself also articulates the same concern about Moses's wife.[4] Indeed, most rabbinic traditions acknowledge that both siblings speak against their younger brother.[5]

No matter how the Rabbis understand who was speaking or what is said, it is clear that the statement is harsh and offensive to the leader of the people. The term *dabber b ...,* in contrast to the term *dabber al ...,* clearly should be translated as "to speak against" and not "to speak about," thus indicating their disrespect for Moses because of the woman he has married.[6] This point is hammered home by the unnecessary repetition in the biblical text that he married a Cushite.

In fact, even claiming that Moses married a Cushite woman is problematic. There is a fanciful early tradition that claims that Moses, having fled Egypt for Ethiopia to the south following the killing of the taskmaster, rises to the rank of commander of the Ethiopian army and, as a reward for defending Ethiopia, is given the princess as a wife.[7] However, Ethiopia is far removed from Moses's activity as described in the Bible, and his sole wife is Tzipporah, who is a Midianite. Most other midrashic traditions and commentators therefore identify the Cushite with Tzipporah by either placing Cush in the wider Midianite territory or understanding Cush as a physical reference, implying that Tzipporah is dark-skinned or perhaps beautiful like women of Ethiopia.[8]

If we are to assume that the biblical text is referring to his marriage to the non-Israelite Tzipporah, why should this marriage now create such a stir, having been consummated prior to the Exodus from Egypt? Is it because she only joins her husband following Sinai (Exodus 18), and it is only recently that the people have met her?[9] Compounding the problem, we are not told what Miriam (and Aaron) say regarding Moses's choice of wife, since, as we wait with baited breath to hear the substance of their concern, we immediately are told, "They said, 'Has the Lord spoken only through Moses? Has [God] not spoken through us as well?'" (Numbers 12:2). There seems to be an apparent disconnect in the biblical narrative, with two different literary strands juxtaposed,[10] contributing to the lack of clarity about their claim.

THE SIBLINGS' CLAIM ABOUT RECEIVING REVELATION

Since the two traditions are joined in the text—that of Miriam and Aaron's concern about Moses's marriage to a Cushite and the fact that God also speaks to Moses's two siblings—the Rabbis try to understand what the connection between them can teach us. On the surface, this looks like jealousy on the part of Moses's two older siblings, directed at their brother who is the recognized leader, even though they themselves play significant roles in the community— Miriam as the prophetess who leads the women in song, and Aaron, the high priest. Like all leaders, Moses is forced to confront the challenge of maintaining his leadership position while being ensconced within a hierarchy—in this case, a family hierarchy. This is especially difficult for leaders who are younger siblings.

Miriam and Aaron's jealousy is obviously connected to the issue of divine revelation, the very source of power and authority. They claim that God speaks to them as well as Moses, and since they married Israelites, while he married a Midianite, they ask why Moses is thought to be so special. They project their jealousy of him onto the fact of his marriage to the Midianite Tzipporah, which gives the Rabbis the opportunity to figure out the connection between the two claims. Miriam says, "I received God's word, but did not refrain from sexual relations with my husband." Aaron likewise says, "I received God's word, and also did not stay away from my wife. And the word came to our forebears and they fulfilled their conjugal obligations."[11] And more—God appears to us first, even prior to Moses's birth![12] Their claim is that Moses has not fulfilled his conjugal obligations to Tzipporah, having separated himself from her from the moment he hears God's words.[13]

How did Miriam and Aaron know that Moses had refrained from sexual relations? Some texts posit that it is because Miriam sees that Tzipporah neglects her personal appearance, telling Miriam that Moses never looks at her;[14] others note that when, according to some rabbinic sources, the wives of the seventy elders are elated that their husbands have the Holy Spirit rest upon them (11:17), Tzipporah indicates that they will be deprived of any conjugal happiness;[15] and there are some texts in which Tzipporah reacts in the very same manner to the wives of Eldad and Medad when they hear that their husbands also begin to prophesy[16] (11:27).

> Winston Churchill's success as a leader in wartime was dependent in part on his ability to take charge and assume full responsibility for all that might occur, even while decentralizing power at the top. People felt that they were given power to act, but everyone knew who was in command.[18]

So it is not surprising that Miriam and Aaron summon the courage to challenge Moses's leadership. Unlike the seventy elders, Eldad and Medad receive their prophetic calling directly from God and not from Moses. So, too, Moses's siblings prophesy independent of their brother.[17] Therefore, God has to underscore the uniqueness of Moses's prophecy: God speaks directly only with him, mouth to mouth, and only he is capable of beholding God's likeness (12:8). While often surrounded by individuals who play important leadership roles, it is crucial for the top leader's distinctiveness to be recognized by all. Each person's contribution should be valued, of course, but when confronted by those who think that they can take charge in the same way the leader can, the leader needs to demonstrate the qualities that distinguish him as a leader.

Though Miriam challenges Moses, some texts emphasize that her intentions are noble and never meant to hurt her brother. That is why she never speaks directly to him about his relationship with his wife and only focuses on the issue of their receiving revelation. As a woman, she indeed reacts strongly to Tzipporah's plight and simply wants to get Moses to return to his wife.[19]

The tradition generally holds that Miriam and Aaron, in chastising Moses's withdrawal sexually from Tzipporah, view him as being too prideful. By withdrawing from domestic life, Moses comes to be considered a leader who is concerned neither about his wife nor about Jewish survival. He is simply isolated from the people, even those close to him, and too caught up in himself.[20] Some even indicate that Miriam and Aaron are merely expressing many of the complaints that the Israelites themselves harbor.[21] Theirs is a challenge to Moses's very leadership model. They see him as someone more comfortable on the top of the mountain than down below with the people.

MOSES: THE EMBODIMENT OF HUMILITY AND FAITHFULNESS

In response to Miriam and Aaron's criticism that Moses is out of touch, God immediately comes to Moses's defense, declaring that "Moses was a very humble [*anav*] man, more so than any other person" (12:3). Moses is neither isolated nor removed from his family or the people, but rather concerned about them and responsive to their needs, a point based on the linguistic resonance between *anav* (humble) and *anah* (respond).[22] Through his humility, he makes God's presence manifest in the world.[23]

Perhaps Miriam, Aaron, and the people simply have the wrong impression of Moses; they see him as withdrawn, while he is becoming more and more preoccupied by the challenges he faces in leading them. Therefore, it is Moses's humility—not standoffishness—that is expressed through his lack of response to the critical comments of

Miriam and Aaron, of which, according to the tradition, he is well aware. God hears what they say, and Moses does as well. The text in Numbers—*va-yishma Adonai . . . Va-ha-ish Moshe anav*—is understood by the Rabbis as, "And God heard ... as did Moses, who most humbly [did not respond]."[25] As hurtful as Miriam's remarks are to Moses, he restrains himself. Occasionally, as we have seen, he does respond angrily when Israel challenges him. But Aaron and Miriam are his brother and sister, whom he loves, and he is sensitive to the people's perception of them.[26] God also responds rather leniently to Miriam and Aaron's remarks, as seen in the Divine's first words of chastisement: "Hear, I pray you [*na*], my words" (12:6). The simple word *na* (please) ostensibly bears the meaning of a request.[27]

Patrick Lencioni, a noted management consultant, stressed that even though leaders need to be charismatic in order to succeed, they must also be humble. In his view, humility means that leaders know that they are inherently no better than the people they lead and must not distance themselves from them.[24]

Furthermore, Moses is described as the Divine's faithful servant in God's household (12:7), so to challenge Moses is to challenge the Divine.[28] Even though Moses has been perceived as aloof from the people and self-consumed and rigid, this perception is in error. God would never have trusted him to be the people's leader if that were the case. Moses is described as being *anav*, humble, which, as noted previously, resonates with the Hebrew root *anah*, respond. He truly cares about his siblings and his people. And, like all leaders, he is responsive to and engaged with the people.

Ernest Shackleton learned from his earliest days at sea that he needed to gain the trust and respect of everyone. What didn't work was leadership that was rigid, remote, and disinterested.[29]

METING OUT PUNISHMENT

Although God responds to the criticism leveled against Moses rather leniently, and Moses himself does not respond at all to Miriam and Aaron's words, Miriam indeed is punished, being stricken with some form of skin disease (*tzara'at*) (12:10). It appears, at least to her brother Aaron, that her skin is eaten away, almost like a corpse (12:12). The metaphor is powerful: When we sin, we indeed diminish the life force in us. (Remember, the Rabbis said that to sin against Moses is tantamount to sinning against the Divine!) So when we commit a sin, we diminish God's presence in us and in the world.

But, the Rabbis ask, why should only Miriam be punished? Is not Aaron also culpable in some way, since he is mentioned as being party to the disparaging remarks about Moses? Interestingly, a number of rabbinic texts assert that Aaron is punished as well, having been stricken like his sister. Whether Aaron is pictured as joining in the criticism of Moses,[30] echoing her sentiments once she starts to gossip about their brother, [31] or he is merely guilty of complicity in his silence,[32] God becomes angry not only at Miriam but also at Aaron: "And God was incensed with [both of] them and departed" (12:9). But since Aaron's role is secondary, his skin disease heals immediately.[33]

Aaron's sense of guilt comes through in his own confession to Moses: "O my lord, account not to us the sin which we committed in our folly" (12:11). He clearly includes himself in the sin, and perhaps, according to the Rabbis, even wants to take more of the responsibility himself, since he begins his remarks to his brother with the pointed words, "O my lord," in Hebrew, *Bi Adoni,* which literally means "Upon me, O lord."[34]

Nevertheless, Aaron clearly states that neither he nor Miriam intended to hurt Moses; their actions are merely the result of a momentary folly. According to one tradition, Aaron attempts to reconcile with Moses by saying, "Moses, my brother, have we ever done evil to anyone in the world?" "No," answers Moses. "If we have done no evil to others in the world," says Aaron, "how could we think of doing evil to you who art our brother? But what am I to do? It was simply an error on our part: We neglected the covenant between us and you. Because of the covenant which we neglected, shall we lose our sister?"[35]

He tries to convince Moses to intercede on their sister's behalf by claiming that they simply acted foolishly. The irony, of course, is that at the very moment that he refers to Moses as *Adoni*, My master, Aaron demonstrates his solidarity with their sister Miriam. Both find themselves in the same position: siblings who have to get along with a younger brother, who is the leader of their people—a leader whom they have challenged. As a result, Aaron feels close to Miriam and will do whatever it takes to protect her, almost like a husband.[36]

MOSES'S INTERCESSION ON MIRIAM'S BEHALF

Moses does not need to be cajoled by Aaron into intervening on his sister's behalf before God. Even though he is probably hurt by her (their) words, he immediately cries out to God (12:13).[37] Ostensibly, he shares her pain (*tza'ar*) and understands the suffering that she is enduring, for he knows what it is like to suffer from the very same kind of skin disease (*tzara'at*—thought to be akin to leprosy), having experienced it in Egypt (Exodus 4:6).[38]

As a result, he bursts forth in desperation: "Please, O God, please heal her" (12:13). Though some argue that Moses's terse prayer shows that he is bereft of any emotion toward her,[39] the very nature of his brief but powerful outburst reveals the depth of his emotions. It is his sister who is suffering, and he wants God to act immediately.[40] He cares deeply about Miriam and will do anything to protect and heal her. This kind of total commitment to one's followers and peers, even in the face of jealousy, conflict, and challenge, characterizes all successful leaders. To succeed, leaders must be able to overcome personal hurt and rejection, and continue to act on behalf of all their followers, even those who have injured them.

Shackleton's commitment to his men was unparalleled, according to those who sailed with him. He was totally supportive, even when tensions and disagreements erupted. He would do anything to protect them from harm, which enabled him to build loyalty in the long run.[41]

Moses not only intercedes on his sister Miriam's behalf, but demands that God heal her. According to the rabbinic tradition, he draws a small circle around himself and declares that he will not move from the spot until God acts. And if God does not act, he, himself will do so![42] Based on the seeming redundancy in the text, when it says that "Moses cried out to God, saying (*leimor*)" (12:13), the Rabbis add that Moses also demands that God respond to him directly concerning his request and indicate that she will be healed. In essence, Moses forces God to heal Miriam.[43]

Though he is hurt by his siblings' comments, he moves beyond any feelings of animosity and not only prays on their behalf, but forgives them. His plea to God to intervene indicates that he holds no grudge, nor does he see them as being anything but righteous.[44]

As a result of Moses's intervention, Miriam is

Another leader who understands that compassion and a forgiving attitude to those who work for you are essential to the success of the company or group is Tim Smucker, head of the Smucker's jam and jelly company. Even when Smucker's was in a difficult contract dispute with its union employees, Tim went out of his way to support those very employees who had personal needs.[45]

only quarantined, or shut out of the Israelite camp, for seven days due to her leprosy. She is healed much more quickly than expected. Nevertheless, because of the manner in which she speaks about Moses, talking behind his back to Aaron instead of confronting him directly, and because she puts herself on a par with her brother who enjoys a unique status in God's eyes, she is isolated from the people. When leaders act inappropriately, they do not deserve to maintain a position of leadership.

Even though Miriam is punished for her behavior, this occasion serves to demonstrate how important she is and the significant role she plays during the desert journey. When the people are breaking camp to resume their march, they realize that neither Moses nor Aaron are ready to leave, nor is there any trace of the well that continuously accompanies them on their journey. Even the pillar of cloud, symbolizing God's immanent presence, is missing. So the people come to understand that they have not been permitted to proceed on the journey because of the absence of the prophetess Miriam (12:15). The rabbis understand that this is a kind of measure for measure: Just as Miriam waits on the shore of the Nile to ensure Moses's survival, the entire people have to wait for her to recover and rejoin them.[46] People are human and occasionally act inappropriately; they can even be hurtful. Nevertheless, they can still fulfill their roles as part of the group, if they are given a chance. Like Moses, all leaders must find ways to continue to engage and work with others to enable them to make the contributions of which they are capable. What helps leaders do this is remembering that they, too, are human, and can make mistakes.

13
Making Tough Decisions; Meeting Challenges
Numbers 16, 17:1–6

The challenge that Moses faces from his siblings regarding the Cushite woman pales in comparison to the rebellion led by Korah, Dathan, and Abiram and their supporters (Numbers 16). What makes this more difficult for Moses to handle is the realization that this is the most egregious of a series of incidents in which the Israelites try to undermine his leadership. Here, Moses faces the most essential test of his leadership: Can he withstand a serious challenge from within that threatens to galvanize mass popular support and mushroom out of control? His ability to lead depends on whether he can marshal the strength and the tact to respond successfully to this threat, which emanates from other recognized forces within the community. At one point or another, every leader faces a moment like this, which tests his courage.

The Bible pictures the Levite Korah, as well as Dathan, Abiram, and others including On, son of Pelet, from the tribe of Reuben—along with 250 leaders of the people—rising up against (va-yakumu lifnei) Moses (16:1–2), the most serious example of the Israelites confronting their leader.[1] The Rabbis note that this is the fourth serious challenge to Moses's mission and God's plan for the People of Israel over a very short period. The others are the building of the Golden Calf (Exodus 32); the Israelites complaining about the manna, which

God provided for them when they craved the delicacies they had in Egypt (Numbers 11); and their response to the report of the majority of those who spied out the Land of Canaan in which they claimed that the Land was unconquerable and that they would die (Numbers 13–14).[2]

THE COALESCING OF OPPOSITION GROUPS WITH DIFFERENT AGENDAS

What makes this rebellion more threatening, however, is that it involves many factions joined together under the banner of their opposition to Moses's and Aaron's leadership. Modern scholars note that three different literary traditions are knitted together in this narrative, each focusing on different oppositional leaders or groups: First, the description of Korah, a spokesperson for Levitical opposition; second, 250 "well-known men" who later join Korah; and finally, rebels from the tribe of Reuben, called Dathan and Abiram. In addition, the various rebel groups have their own claims and reproaches, sometimes directed against Aaron and Moses together, sometimes alone. And these different factions also focus on the source of Moses's and Aaron's authority, and the lack of success of their leadership in general.[3]

The motives of these rebellious factions fall into one of two categories. First, there is generalized opposition to the denial of the rights of the firstborn to serve in the Tabernacle and eventually in the Temple and the ceding of that prerogative to the tribe of Levi. They want their honor restored, and feel slighted by Moses who gives it to his family and, in particular, makes Aaron and his descendants the high priests. They stress that all of Israel is holy (16:3), and God has already sanctified the firstborn (Exodus 13:2). In addition, the tribe of Joseph had supplanted the rightful first tribe, Reuben, and Moses's choice of Joshua, a member of that tribe, as his second in command may have exacerbated their feelings. The second motive may be Korah's feeling that since he is from the tribe of Levi, he has been passed over in terms of Levitical leadership in favor of the leader's brother, Aaron.[4] In essence, there may have been challenges to both the cultic authority of Aaron and the communal authority of Moses.[5]

If this rebellion against the authority of the leaders, Moses and Aaron, is to succeed, Korah has to attract the support of other recognized leaders among the people, which might generate a groundswell of opposition among the people themselves. Therefore, it is important to note that following the description of Korah, Dathan, and Abiram, and On, the son of Pelet, rising up against Moses at the outset of the narrative, the text adds that 250 leaders, recognized as men of repute, join the gathering against both Moses and Aaron (16:2–3).

This anonymous group of leaders, described as *nesi'ei eida* (chieftains of the community), comprise not only Levites but a cross-section of the tribes.[6] They seem to have joined in the rebellion once Korah and the others have committed themselves to confronting Moses.[7] They present a unified front challenging the existing leadership, and Moses is pictured as responding to "Korah and his congregation [*eida*]" (16:5), knowing that the word *eida* generally is used to refer to the entire people of Israel. Korah seems to have galvanized an entire corps of opposition to Moses and Aaron.[8]

Bill Weiss, the CEO of Ameritech, faced a similar challenge from within when, before his retirement, he attempted to transform the company from a sleepy local phone company into a far-reaching telecommunications conglomerate. Bob Knowling, the powerful general manager of Indiana Bell, opposed any change and created a groundswell of opposition. It took a great deal of courage and savvy for Weiss and his designated successor, Dick Notebaert, to fend off this challenge.[10]

Moses faces an all-out rebellion, as the Bible describes Korah's ability to rally a significant segment of the community to his cause. Several times in the narrative, either Korah is said to have "gathered [*va-yakheil*] the entire community against them" (16:19) or the people are "gathered [*va-yikahalu*] against Moses and Aaron" (16:3).[9] The people seem to agree with the claim that both Moses and Aaron have relegated to themselves too much power and authority, and they stand up as one to denounce them with the words: "You have gone too far [*rav lachem*]; why do you raise yourself above the Lord's congregation?" (16:3) The entire *kahal* (congregation, community) seems to have been caught up in Korah's rebellious acts.[11]

HOW IS THE REBELLION FOMENTED?

Although the rebellion attracts a wide base of support, it is guided by the very personal agenda of a number of individuals and groups, none more important than Korah, whose grandfather, Kohat, is the same as that of Moses and Aaron. According to the Rabbis' reconstruction of the rebellion, Korah maintains that since the sons of Amram, Moses's father, the eldest son of Kohat, assume both the leadership of the people and the office of high priest, the position of head of the Kohatite family should have rightly been given to him. After all, he is the eldest of Kohat's second son, Izhar, and he ostensibly is next in line. Instead, Moses appoints Elizaphan, the firstborn of Uzziel, the youngest of Kohat's four sons (3:30).[12]

According to some traditions, Korah's jealousy is directed against the choice of Aaron as high priest. After all, if the claim is that "the entire community is holy" (16:3), meaning that all heard God's commands at Sinai, then if Moses has assumed power for himself, why doesn't he appoint someone for the priesthood other than his brother?[13]

Korah is overcome by his jealousy of Moses and Aaron, believing that he is due honor because of his status in their Levitical family. A kinsman of the sons of Amram, he also is very wealthy and therefore powerful in his own right, which only enhances his status.[14] To further convince him that he deserves greater status, he learns (probably from a soothsayer) that a long and distinguished progeny will emanate from him, including the judge Samuel, which only proves that his power play is justified. If it weren't, how could he be the father of such a distinguished line?[15]

Korah thinks that he is better than all of them, as noted by the first description of Korah's actions: "He betook himself [*va-yikah*], along with Dathan, Abiram, and On ..." (16:1). The object of the verb (*lakah,* to take) is missing, thus allowing the Rabbis over the centuries to interpret it in a number of ways. Whether understood as Korah "separated himself,"[16] that "he was carried away" by his jealousy and desire for power,[17] or that he "seized power" for himself,[18] it is clear that he is able to attract others to his cause. In fact, the verb *va-yikah* (he took) is occasionally interpreted as his "drawing" the chieftains of Israel to him through his persuasiveness. In effect he wins over their hearts with words.[19] The ability to communicate effectively, thereby convincing others of a desired course of action, is essential if leaders are to succeed.

Among those attracted to Korah's cause are the Reubenites Dathan and Abiram. Not only are the Reubenites neighbors of the Kohatites, both encamped to the south (3:39), but they have similar claims against Moses. Both claim that their status as firstborn has been compromised—Korah by the choice of Elizaphan as head of their Levitical family and the Reubenites whose position is usurped by the tribe of Joseph.[20]

Korah is particularly dangerous because, like all demagogues, he masks his own motives, presenting himself as the guardian of the people's interests, even their freedom.[21] He goes from tribe to tribe,[22] asserting, "Do you suppose that I am working to obtain greatness for myself? I desire that we should all enjoy power and greatness, not like Moses who has appropriated the kingship for himself and the priesthood for his brother!"[23] But he goes even further in his attempt to win the people over to his cause; he claims that Moses has literally hoodwinked them with false promises (the biblical text stresses that the rebels asserted that "they gouged out the people's eyes" [16:14], which is understood in the tradition as the modern idiom, to "pull the wool over one's eyes").[24] And what are the false promises Moses has allegedly made? He has taken them out of the fleshpots of Egypt, promising to bring them into a land flowing with milk and honey, but he has failed.[25] He has guaranteed that they will enjoy the fruits of the land, once they arrive in the Land of Canaan, but Aaron and his family will receive a large percentage of their flocks and produce. The laws of the Torah, rather than being liberating, will be utterly oppressive.[26]

Demoralized by their long sojourn in the wilderness and the many challenges and setbacks they have experienced, the people fall prey to Korah's demagogic arguments.[27] Korah easily capitalizes on the Israelites' intense bitterness, which is evident in the response of Dathan and Abiram to Moses and Aaron: "Is it not enough that you have brought us from a land flowing with milk and honey [how ironic that they now describe Egypt in these terms!] to have us die in the wilderness, but that you would also lord it over us?"(16:13).

At first, only 250 chieftains join with the rebels; most of the people remain loyal to their leaders, Moses and Aaron, who speak in God's name. However, as the sedition grows, the people increasingly respond to Korah; their allegiance can be won over.[28] This is apparent in Korah's ability to "gather the whole community at the entrance to the Tent of Meeting" to see what will come of the sacrificial test that Moses had set up (16:19). Their interest in seeing who will prevail at least reflects their dissatisfaction with Moses and Aaron. However, according to the Rabbis, some of the people are so convinced by Korah that they want to stone Moses![29]

MOSES RESPONDS TO THE REBELS

When first confronted by Korah and his comrades, who have risen up (*va-yakumu*) against his leadership, claiming that he raised himself over the people (16:1–4), Moses falls on his face (16:5). After overcoming so many challenges throughout the journey from Egypt, Moses is devastated by their belief that he has relegated too much power to himself and to Aaron. In an almost naïve manner, Moses turns to God and cries, "I have not wronged any one of them" (16:15). All his actions have been dictated by God and are only meant to serve the people's best interests.[30] Yet he never defends himself against the rebels or against the people, leaving God to respond by making known those who are the divinely chosen leaders (16:5–7). By contrast, when Aaron is challenged directly, Moses comes to his defense: "Who is Aaron that you should rail against him?" (16:11).[31]

Though angered by their words, Moses does not let the strife escalate. He seeks out both Korah and then Dathan and Abiram, in an attempt to overcome their ill feelings. At first, he speaks to Korah gently, saying, "Hear, I pray you [*na*], sons of Levi" (16:8), and then calls on the Reubenites, trying to mollify them as well (16:12).[32] He appeals to Korah and his followers, arguing that it is unreasonable for them to demand greater status than they have already received. Ironically repeating the same phrase Korah uses, Moses says, "It is enough for you [*rav lachem*], sons of Levi" (16:7). They have already been set apart from the rest of the people through their service in the Tabernacle, ministering to the community and serving God; why then are they not satisfied with their position? They already have great responsibility and superior status. If they will only use their reason, they will see that they do not need to demand the high priesthood as well (16:10).[33] According to the tradition, he addresses the 250 chieftains who accompany Korah the same way, stressing that they already are worthy of great honor and have achieved great status.[34] Moses addresses the entire tribe of Levi, along with Korah, not only because Korah attempts to involve all of them in the rebellion, but because Moses hopes that the rest of the members of his tribe will convince Korah of his folly. Perhaps in their presence, Korah is reticent to advance his personal agenda.[35]

In approaching both Korah and his followers (16:5ff),[36] as well as Dathan and Abiram (16:12, 25), Moses hopes that these different rebellious factions will come to their senses and return to the Lord in repentance.[37] He truly believes that he can convince them to accept his leadership and to back away from confrontation. The Rabbis note that in order to do so, Moses puts off till the morning when God will demonstrate who are the Divine's chosen leaders (16:5), thereby giving Korah and his band the opportunity for further reflection and the opportunity to abandon their opposition.[38] One of the traits of successful leaders is the ability to let go of any malice or enmity they might feel toward those who oppose them, recognizing that conciliation better serves the overarching needs of the people.

Despite Moses's efforts at reconciliation, none of the rebels respond to him. Though he comes to Korah and speaks with him directly, Korah does not even acknowledge Moses's pleas; he never utters a word.[40] His silence communicates everything (16:11). He has no intention of hearing him out. Similarly, though Moses sends for Dathan and Abiram, they refuse to meet with him (16:13), openly rejecting his authority. As a result, Moses becomes infuriated (16:15) and utterly dejected. The realization finally sets in that he is facing an outright rebellion that cannot be quelled with conciliatory words or gestures.[41]

MOSES MUST SUPPRESS THE REBELLION

Moses understands that Korah and his followers have to be met head on because their actions constitute not merely a threat to his leadership, but ultimately a rejection of the Divine, as we see from his very direct words to Korah: "Truly it is against God that you and all your company have banded together" (16:11). Both Moses and his brother Aaron have not assumed their positions of authority of their own accord. Had they assumed power on their own, the people could rightly have rejected them. However, all their power comes from God's appointment

Another of the qualities that made Churchill very effective was that he was an exceptionally forgiving individual. In describing himself, he wrote in a letter in 1921: "I do not harbor any malice.... I always forgive political attacks or ill-treatment [by opponents] if it is not directed at my private life." In the context of political struggle, Churchill was able to move beyond the desire for retribution, which ultimately enabled him to win over even his opponents to his side.[39]

of them, as Moses himself underscores: "It was the Lord who sent me and they are not of my own devisings ... and you shall know that these people have spurned the Lord" (16:28–30).[42] Challenging Moses (and Aaron) is tantamount to attempting to overthrow the cultic and religious foundations established at God's command—in effect, to deny the chief tenets communicated on Mount Sinai.[43]

Those who "rose up" (va-yakumu) against Moses have to be stopped at all costs. Moses responds to them in kind, rising up (va-yakom) against them (16:25) and communicating to them that "they have gone too far [rav lachem]" (16:7) in response to their claim against Moses and Aaron that "you have gone too far [rav lachem]" (16:3). He conveys his anger to Korah (16:8–11) and to Dathan and

Abiram, and then, when they do not respond to him, he confronts them in person. Individuals in a group who abuse their power must be stopped, and the leader must have the strength to act because of the seriously deleterious effect such behavior can have on everyone else. This especially applies to influential members of the group.

Moses challenges the rebels, though he doesn't do it alone. He gathers the elders of the tribes with him, as if the People of Israel as a whole support his drive to destroy all those involved in the rebellion.[45]

The rebellion is a disease that threatens the life of the People of Israel, and it has to be wiped out. Only the total excision of the rebels can prevent the rebellion from infecting the whole nation. The disease involves the rejection of the divine nature of Moses's role.[46] God has to demonstrate publicly that all that has transpired is the result of Divine will and that those who challenge it will be utterly destroyed.[47] Not only will they be rejected by God, but their punishment has to be so dramatic that it leaves an indelible impression on the people as a whole. So Moses pleads with God to reject their sacrifices (16:15) and to cut them off completely, even obviating any chance that they might have to repent for what they did.[48] Every leader must realize that there may come a moment when, for the sake of the group, termination is the only option. This is especially difficult when it involves someone who has some authority and status in the eyes of group members, but perhaps even more important.

> Hans Schroeder, who worked for the Kellogg Corporation, was a power-monger. He was overly harsh in his interactions with people with whom he worked, which had disastrous consequences for the individuals and the company. He was abrasive and imperious, lashing out in meetings. In response, Schroeder was summarily fired by Kellogg's CEO.[44]

Following Moses's plea the entire nation knows that those who rebelled were spurned by God. The earth opens and swallows up all of Korah's supporters, their households, and all their possessions, and they go down (*va-yerdu*) alive to the depths of Sheol—the abode of the dead in a region below the earth (16:30–33). They disappear without a trace, since there is no mention in the Bible of the place where the event occurs nor are any traces left behind of the terrible judgment.[50] Those who rose up (*va-yakumu*) (16:2) against Moses, the people who refused to come up (*na-aleh*) to meet Moses (16:12), and all those who complained that "Moses brought us up [*he-elitanu*] from Egypt to die in the desert" (16:13) are now cast down.

Phil Myers, a ServiceMaster account manager, is one leader who understood that even the most powerful executives in the firm must be confronted when their actions undermine the whole team. He followed a three-step process: First, confront the negative behavior directly; second, give the employee a chance to change; and then, ultimately, terminate the individual if there is no improvement.[49]

Moses remains silent as his fellow Israelites are being swallowed up, never arguing that perhaps some innocent individuals are being killed. It is impossible to distinguish between the people who actually are among the rebels and those who are merely supporters of the insurrection in some way and those who are inadvertently in their camp.[51]

But the people do have a chance to separate themselves from the rebels. Moses addresses the entire community, urging them to "move away from the tents of those wicked men and touch nothing that belongs to them, lest you be wiped out for all their sins" (16:26). The people can demonstrate that they do not make common cause with Korah and his band by "withdrawing from the abodes of Korah, Dathan, and Abiram" (16:23).[52] Perhaps only those aho are truly guilty, those who actually are counted among the people who rebelled against Moses and Aaron, will be killed.

THE AFTERMATH: GUARANTEEING THE FUTURE

Unfortunately, the discontent aroused by the rebels does not die with them. The next day the people rail against Moses and Aaron, claiming, "You two have brought death upon the Lord's people!" (17:6) The people are not convinced that Moses and Aaron's sole authority is justified; they still believe that all of Israel is equally holy, picking up Korah's refrain. Such a notion resonates with most of us, who are committed to democratic institutions. Yet we should not ignore the fact that Korah's actions undermine those leaders chosen by God and are insidious to boot. In addition, the people also believe that Moses and Aaron have conspired to kill other Israelites without justification.[53] Because of the rebellious stance of the people, God decides to annihilate the entire nation, except for Moses and Aaron, by bringing upon them a deadly plague (17:10). It is only due to Aaron's intervention through the burning of incense among the

Fred Smith of FedEx faced a judgment call. Confronted by pilots demanding huge raises and lavish benefits at a time when the company was grappling with severe economic hardship, he had the courage to stand firm and not give in to the demands of his employees. He risked a strike, which would have alienated his pilots, because he realized that in the long term his stance would save FedEx from bankruptcy.[55]

people, thereby expiating their sins, that the People of Israel are spared. Yet some 14,700 Israelites die that day (17:11–15). The same fire pans used to bring death to the rebels—those who sought power against God's will—now are utilized to burn incense, thereby averting death, by those who are the authorized leaders of the people.[54]

The rebels' fire pans are hammered into plating to be used in erecting the altar, forever serving as a warning to the People of Israel: No unauthorized leader can ever assume power and authority (17:3–5). At certain times, leaders, like Moses, are justified in wielding their power to quell any rebellion that threatens the survival of their people. Leaders are always challenged to gauge the long-term damage that rebellious actions can have upon the group as a whole against the short-term pain that confronting extreme inappropriate behavior or demands may cause. It all comes down to judgment.

Moses's crushing of Korah and his cohort is not seen in the rabbinic tradition in any kind of negative way. On the contrary, it is deemed a righteous act that saves Israel and its covenant with the Divine.[56] And as such it serves as a model for all leaders; they must learn that the use of force to prevent rebellious acts that might threaten the very existence of the group and its value system is not only justified but demanded.

14

Balancing the Personal and the Professional

Numbers 20:1–13; 21:16–19

As the journey through the desert toward the Land of Israel begins to draw to a close, it is clear that the Israelites' survival depends on the triumvirate of leadership of Moses and his two siblings. As the prophet Micah notes, God places the three children of Amram and Yocheved before the Children of Israel to lead them from Egypt to the Promised Land.[1] And to ensure Israel's survival, God provides the people three sources of redemption during their wanderings, all because of Moses, Aaron, and Miriam: the miraculous manna that provided them with nourishment (Exodus 16), the pillar of cloud representing God's Presence that protected them by day as did the pillar of fire by night (Exodus 13:21), and the well that provides them water throughout their trek. When Aaron dies, the pillar of cloud disappears, and upon her death, Miriam's Well—named for her since she stood by the Nile in order to guarantee Moses's survival after he was placed in the bulrushes—stops flowing.[2]

MIRIAM: THE SOURCE OF ISRAEL'S REDEMPTION

Since Miriam is considered by both the biblical writers and by the Rabbis as equally responsible for Israel's survival in the desert, it is most ironic that when she dies in the wilderness of Zin, her death notice in Numbers 20 is abbreviated. Unlike the descriptions of her brother Aaron's death on Har ha-Hor, at the end of the very same chapter, and that of Moses in Deuteronomy 34, there is barely any marking of the moment. All that we are told is that she dies at a place called Kadesh in the first month, and is buried there (Numbers 20:1). The brevity of her death notice and the lack of the Israelites' response to her death are startling. Yet, the biblical text and the rabbinic tradition are not totally void of information. According to the Rabbis, Miriam dies with a kiss from God, just as her brother Moses does, which indicates her supreme importance. According to the Rabbis, this detail is omitted from the Bible because it would be unbecoming to include it because she was a woman.[3]

But a close reading of the biblical description of Miriam's death offers the reader several important details that spotlight Miriam's crucial redemptive role in the life of the People of Israel. First, her death comes right after the description of the atoning power of the Red Heifer's ashes in Numbers 19, as if to indicate that the death of this righteous leader also has atoning power for the people.[4] The fact that she plays an atoning or redemptive role is also stressed in the timing of her death. We are told that she dies in "the first month" when the people arrive in the wilderness of Zin, which is Nissan, the month in which we celebrate Passover, the holiday of liberation. Since the Bible does not usually indicate when the people arrive at particular desert encampments, this only serves to enhance the notion that her life and death are sources of redemption for her people. The tradition stresses that she dies at the outset of this time of liberation, on the first day of Nissan.[5] Finally, we are told that she dies and is buried at a place called Kadesh (20:1). Though there is more than one biblical site with this name,[6] most commentators and modern scholars believe that the Israelites camp at Kadesh in the last year of their sojourn.[7] Miriam indeed dies in a place of holiness (*kodesh–Kadesh*) because her entire life embodies the potential not only for Israel's survival, but indeed its life as God's holy, covenanted partner.

The most important fact is that, following her death, the people have no water (20:2). Hardly has Miriam expired than a dearth of water sets in, thus indicating that the supply of water upon which they depend during their journey through the desert is due to the piety of Miriam.[8] As we have noted, the Rabbis speak of Miriam's Well, which accompanies the people during their forty years in the desert. It was created during the Six Days of Creation when God created all the necessary vehicles for ultimate redemption.[9] The well serves the People of Israel as a source of redemption in every generation; each generation's leaders were able to draw from it. The loss of the water symbolizes the loss of the people's leader, the one who ensures their survival.[10]

MOSES'S AND AARON'S REACTION TO THE ISRAELITES' COMPLAINT

Moses and Aaron immediately begin to mourn for their older sibling, upon whom they, as well as the people, depend. Immersed in their own grief, they are unaware of the disappearance of the well that has sustained them on their journey from Egypt. Seeing the people gathering (*va-yikahalu*) around their tent, Aaron assumes that as a community (*kahal*) the Israelites have come to comfort them in their loss. Moses knows better, however, realizing that the people are approaching in a moblike fashion. They literally "gathered upon [*va-yikahalu al*] Moses and Aaron," as opposed to "gathering about" or "in front of them" (20:2). They have not come to pay their respects to the brothers nor to Miriam, but rather to complain about the lack of water.[11] The Rabbis envision them quarreling with Moses, "How long must you sit here and weep?" Moses answers, "Shall I not weep for my sister, who has died?" They reply, "While you are weeping for one soul, weep at the same time for all of us who are about to die for want of water!" God is even described in some traditions as chastising Moses for mourning while Israel is dying.[12]

We, the readers, must simply stop and experience the moment from Moses's and Aaron's perspective. They are mourners who have just lost their older sister and now, once again, the people are quarreling with them—this time about the seeming lack of water: "Why did you bring us into the wilderness to die? Why did you force us to leave Egypt and bring us to this wretched place ... where there is not even water to drink?" They not only see the desert, where they finally experience freedom, as a place of death, but they remember Egypt only as a luxuriant place filled with grain, figs, vines, and pomegranates (20:3–5). After a journey of almost forty years in which they have repeatedly witnessed God's redemptive hand, have they not internalized anything about God's power and their leadership? Has surviving all the travails of the journey through the wilderness not taught them any-thing? And have they not come to appreciate all that Moses, Aaron, and Miriam have done for them? Now that Miriam has died, how can they not reach out to her brothers in their time of need? How are Moses and Aaron to respond to the people, after suffering

Those who served with Ernest Shackleton on his voyages cited his remarkable inner strength, which seemed almost superhuman. It enabled him to keep things that were the most personally difficult in perspective and sustained him in times of crisis.[13]

through the myriad of complaints all these years and having just experienced the loss of their sister? How can these two leaders bear the people's tirade one more time, especially in their fragile emotional state? All leaders must find the strength to weather personal attacks and continue to help their followers grow and realize their potential, even when they, the leaders, are suffering their own personal crisis, and even grief.

Hearing the people's demand for water and witnessing again their lack of faith, the two leaders move away from the congregation toward the Tent of Meeting and there fall on their faces (20:6). They literally are sapped of their strength, having finally lost their patience and perhaps even their resolve. They flee from the people and break down in tears in the sanctuary of the Tabernacle.[14] Their impulse is to hide from the Israelites and their complaints so they can now mourn their sister's death.

This may really be the sin for which the brothers are punished by not being allowed to enter the Promised Land. Up to this point, they have been resolute in their commitment to lead the Israelites through the wilderness. Now they appear to have lost their faith in the People of Israel and in their own ability to lead.[15] They can no longer effectively lead the people into the land and provide the needed leadership for the next stage of the people's journey in covenant with God.

But God does not allow them the luxury of abandoning their leadership responsibilities, even in the face of their own pain. The Divine commands them to assemble (*hak'el*) the people in order to provide water for their sustenance, the very people who themselves had gathered (*va-yikahalu*) against them (20:8). Leaders cannot desist from their mission under any circumstance, even when they feel personally compromised.

Moses and Aaron's role is to produce water for the Israelites, even though the people challenge them as leaders and God's providence as well. In some traditional sources, the Israelites add insult to injury by continuing to challenge Moses and Aaron's ability to lead by demanding that they draw water from a specific rock that they have chosen. They believe that as a shepherd, Moses will know whence to draw water. Their real expectation is that he will provide the source of sustenance in a miraculous fashion![17]

Winston Churchill was the embodiment of the genuine leader who, from time to time, and especially in a crisis, must simply summon up his willfulness, refusing to give in. Churchill's most famous lyric of resolve was "Never, never, never give in." Though Churchill was facing an external enemy, not internal dissension, the strength he showed under the most trying circumstances, even when he doubted himself, is a model for all leaders in all contexts.[16]

DRAWING WATER FROM THE ROCK

God commands Moses and Aaron to take up the rod, the symbol of God's presence and the vehicle through which redemptive miracles occur, and assemble the people (20:8).[18] They, too, need to demonstrate their continued faith that God will deliver them, as God has done before. The rod was in the possession of leaders in every previous generation, and they have to continue to hold fast to it regardless of their personal doubt, pain, and hurt.[19]

At Rephidim, near the outset of their desert journey (Exodus 17) and in a similar circumstance, God commands Moses to strike the rock with the rod in order to produce life-giving water for the People of Israel. Perhaps, by directing Moses to take hold of the rod again, God is intimating that the same scenario will be repeated—Moses once again will strike the rock and water will gush forth.[21]

However, here at Kadesh, God commands them to "speak [*dibartem*] to the rock in the presence of the people" (20:8). The tradition wonders why God commands Moses to speak to the rock at Kadesh, toward the end of the journey, while at Rephidim, striking the rock is the way to draw water.[22] The Rabbis themselves answer the question by stressing that forty years into the desert journey, the people as well as their leaders have matured spiritually and now, following the revelation at Mount Sinai and the receipt of God's words (*devarim*), the use of force is no longer appropriate.[23]

Herb Kelleher of Southwest Airlines was a true believer in the concept of servant leadership, in which the best leaders are seen as good followers as well. He stressed that at times the leader has to be willing to subject her own ego to the fulfillment of the group's mission, which can be very difficult.[20]

Moses therefore takes the rod, as God has commanded, he and Aaron assemble the people in front of the rock, and Moses says to them, "Listen, you rebels [*morim*], shall we get water for you from the rock?" (20:10). Up to this point in the desert journey, each time Moses and Aaron are confronted by the people demanding sustenance from God, they are able to hold back any anger they feel toward their quarrelsome followers.[24] However, suffering from the death of their sister, Miriam, and being unable to mourn for her, and having lost patience with his followers, Moses lashes out at the people as a whole, referring to them as "*morim*."[25] Understood either as "rebels" or, more generally, "fools,"[26] the choice of words is not unintentional. Written defectively in Hebrew as *m'rim*, the word has the same consonantal structure as Miriam's name, underscoring very poignantly that Moses is projecting onto the Israelites all his frustration and anger because of Miriam's death, of which they are oblivious. Moses is unable to control his emotions, and, as a result, though he is told to speak to the rock, he raises the rod and strikes it not once, but twice (20:11). As he strikes the rock, the reader can feel his anger. He doesn't raise his hand and the rod prayerfully to God, but instead releases all his rage. Leaders must strive to control their emotions, despite what they may be feeling in order to continue to fulfill their larger roles. However, being able to refrain from carrying over feelings from the personal to the professional domain is an especially difficult challenge.

Ernest Shackleton exemplified the leader who was able to control his emotions. He always responded to his crew in a balanced and positive manner, regardless of what he might have been feeling. He was unfailingly optimistic and never showed a long face.[27]

However, though the water came forth as a result of Moses's actions, both he and Aaron are chastised by God: "Because you did not ... affirm My sanctity in the sight of the Children of Israel, therefore you will not lead this congregation into the land" (20:12). Even in the eyes of most of the rabbinic commentators, it is not clear what exactly is considered to be Moses's sin.[28] For most, it was not even the fact that Moses strikes the rock with the rod, contrary to God's directive. However, some stress that he probably should have tried at least to speak to it first.[29]

So why is Moses, who has led his people in their forty-year journey from Egypt through the wilderness, forbidden from fulfilling his mission? What has he done that is so terrible that he does not deserve to enter the land with his people?

First, Moses acts contrary to God's command in the sight of the entire people. Moses surely has expressed doubts to God before (for example, Numbers 11:22), but these doubts are expressed privately. By contrast, here Moses's actions are witnessed by all, and this could have caused irreparable damage to God's relationship with Israel.[30] If Moses can challenge and reject God's words, so, too, can each and every Israelite. All leaders must realize that every one of their public actions must be seriously weighed because of how it can affect their followers. Leaders are considered exemplars, and everything that they do is scrutinized by their followers. That is why it is so important for Moses to control his own emotions and to follow God's directive. Leaders must not only weigh their actions carefully, but even their words. Some rabbinic sources stress that Moses's sin is denouncing the Israelites as *morim,* rebels or fools. He inappropriately vents his anger against the people, who do not deserve this calumny.[31] Another text pictures the following conversation when Moses and Aaron flee into the Tabernacle: "God says to Moses, 'What ails you?' and Moses replies, 'O Lord of the world. Your children want to stone me, and had I not escaped, they would have stoned me by now.' God says, 'Moses, how much longer will you continue to denounce My people?'"[32] Every single word uttered by Moses and Aaron, let alone any of their individual acts, has the potential to either enhance God's sanctity in the eyes of the people or diminish the Divine Presence. Leaders must learn the importance of all that they do. Everything has perceived meaning in the eyes of their followers, if not real influence.

Adversity energizes and motivates courageous and capable leaders, but quickly "quenches the passion and fire" of those who are burned out and unable to summon the necessary courage. One such leader was Eric Schmidt of Novell, who knew that when you are faced with severe challenges and a downturn, you have to have the strength to fight the instinct to either be overly cautious or succumb to the fear. Confronting a $20 million loss for the first quarter when he took over, he did not back off in any way, but rather took immediate measures to develop new products, thereby setting a new course for the company.[33]

In the end, the core reason why Moses is forbidden to lead the people of Israel into the land promised to their forebears is that he demonstrates that he no longer has the ability to do so. His capacity to lead is diminished, along with his authority.

In claiming that Moses has not sanctified (*l'hakdish*) God in the eyes of the people, what the Bible is saying is that his own actions are not suffused with holiness (*kedushah*): He does not model the highest values to which every Israelite should aspire. In losing control and being swept away by his anger over his personal circumstance, he can no longer serve as an exemplar for his flock.[34] The test of Moses's ability to continue to lead is whether he can summon the patience, stamina, and courage to tolerate severe adversity. Unfortunately, at this stage in the people's journey through the desert, confronted one more time by their neediness and complaints, Moses fails. He has grown too weary to face obstacles and challenges.

OVERCOMING THE WATERS OF MERIBAH; DRAWING WATER AT BE'ER

The place where all this transpires is named Kadesh, the Holy Place. However, it becomes forever signified by the water that flowed there from the rock that Moses strikes, which is branded in this biblical story as *Mei Meribah*, Waters of Meribah—Waters of Contention (20:13). It is here that not only does Moses act in a way that causes his downfall as a leader, but the people once again are seen as quarreling not merely with Moses, but also with God. It is in this place, one of potential holiness (*Kadesh*), that Israel contends with God and that Moses fails to sanctify (*l'hakdish*) the Divine Presence. Yet the text goes on to say that "[God] affirmed the Divine's sanctity (*va'yekadeish*) through them." God's holiness is affirmed irrespective of the people's actions. There is a power in the universe that makes for wholeness, that brings ultimate redemption, whether or not human beings recognize it.

It is not clear, however, how God affirms divine holiness here, and most scholars find the text, especially its plural ending, to be problematic. What does the phrase "[God] affirmed the Divine's sanctity through *them*" (*bam*) mean?[35] There are several possibilities proffered in the tradition, but the chief among them is the notion that it refers to Moses and Aaron, who are the previous subjects mentioned. The Rabbis point out that God's justice is affirmed through the punishment of the two leaders: God judges all people evenhandedly; even Moses does not receive special treatment when he acts in a sinful manner.[36] Sometimes it is difficult for both the leader and her followers to be mindful that the leader is human and simply one of the people—no better or worse. Everyone must be held to the same standards. In the end, all are accountable for their actions, even the most powerful leaders of the generation.

For Israel, at this point in its journey, having suffered the death of Miriam, the imminent death of Aaron, and the first inkling that Moses will not lead them into the Promised Land, there is a real question of whether they can survive. Can they find a way of continuing to draw forth water in the wilderness of their lives without Miriam's Well and Moses's rod?

Leaving Kadesh and crossing the Arnon, a wadi (river valley) on the border of the Plains of Moab,[37] the Israelites come to a place ironically named Be'er (well) (21:13–16). The issue is this: Can Israel draw water from Be'er on its own? And in an astonishing fashion, what takes place seems not only to atone for Israel's sins at Meribah, but also to directly parallel what happened almost forty years before as Israel passed through the life-giving waters of the Red Sea.[38] God directs Moses to "gather the people so that I may give them water" (21:16), and at that moment, Israel breaks out in song: *Az yashir Yisrael et ha-shirah ha-zot* (21:17), "then Israel sang this song," the exact same words used in Exodus 15:1 to describe Moses's Song at the Sea (*az yashir Moshe*), in which Israel only played a minor role. Then the Israelites were just a young, fledgling people, who could at best merely repeat Moses's words. Now, after the travails of their forty-year trek through the wilderness, a mature Israel is ready to sing on its own (*az yashir Yisrael*). Moses has no part in this iteration of the song of praise; the Israelites themselves have learned to sing.[39]

But there is more. The words they sing accentuate the message that they feel empowered to sing without their leaders: "Arise O well—sing (*enu*) to it." The word for singing, *enu*, is the very verb (*anah*) used to describe Miriam's song at the conclusion of the Song at the Sea—*ve-ta'an lahem Miriam*, "And Miriam sang/responded to them" (Exodus 15:21).[40] Not only do the people internalize Moses's song—the singular, individual song of the male leader—but they also emulate Miriam's song of response to her sisters and to the nature that enveloped them. The true test of leadership is to empower others to find their own voices, to recognize their own ability to act in the world. Over time, Moses and Miriam, despite all their own shortcomings, have taught their followers that they themselves have the wherewithal to ensure their own survival by recognizing God's presence in the world. How many leaders never learn that theirs is not the only voice to be heard, that each one of us has the ability to give voice to our own individual song?

The well, the source of redemption in the desert, is not only accessible to the Israelites at that moment at Be'er, but the text asserts that it is "a well dug by all the princes and unearthed by the nobles" (21:18). Every generation of leaders and their followers can access the well to survive their own journey. Metaphorically, the well is given (*nittenah*) to all of us.[41] It is a perennial gift (*mattanah*) to those in the desert, as underscored by the Rabbis' interpretation of the very next verse describing the next stage of the Israelites' journey: "[And Israel went] from Midbar [Desert] to Mattanah" (21:18). Of course they were in the desert, but they were actually pictured as being at Be'er, so what is the intent of this description of their continuing itinerary? God has given them a *mattanah*, a gift, *mei'Midbar*, from the desert.[42] The Be'er (the Well) is the gift from the desert experience, one bequeathed by Miriam (and Moses).

We, too, can draw water from Miram's well. But where can it be found? The tradition suggests that for those searching near the Mediterranean Sea, the well is located in the sieve-like rocks near Mt. Carmel (perhaps the underwater caves at Rosh ha-Niqra); and for those looking near the Kinneret, the Sea of Galilee, the well can be found in the hot springs there.[43] So where is Miram's well? It seems the Rabbis are telling us that it is everywhere—it is all around us, if only we can open our eyes and see it.

The lesson is clear: All of us can find a way of drawing on the resources we possess, not merely to survive the aridity and heat of our journeys through our own wildernesses, but to eventually reach the Promised Land, that place of fulfillment and wholeness. At times it may be difficult for us to see it, to recognize the strength we each possess; we find it hard to believe that it is even there. But it is possible to draw water from our own wells because we are taught and touched by models of leaders in our lives.

15

Leaders Struggle with Their Mortality

Deuteronomy 3:23–28

The Israelites' journey from Kadesh and Be'er leads them to the shore of the Jordan River, just east of the Land of Canaan. But before they can cross the Jordan, they have to defeat the Amorite kings, Sihon, the king of Heshbon, and Og, the king of Bashan. Once those battles are over, Moses and his people control the territory on the east side of the Jordan, from the Wadi of Arnon, near the Dead Sea, to Mount Hermon far to the north (Deuteronomy 3:8). With the defeat of the Amorites and the division of the land among the tribes of Reuben, Gad, and half the tribe of Menasseh (3:12–13), Moses and the Children of Israel are poised to enter the land about which they have dreamt for forty years during their trek through the desert.

MOSES'S DESPERATION TO ENTER THE LAND

Moses's unbounded desire to cross over the Jordan with his people is evident in his own words: "I pleaded with *Adonai*…. Let me, I pray, cross over and see the good land on the other side of the Jordan, that good hill country, and the Lebanon" (3:23–25). The phrases, "the good land" and "that good hill country" make tangible Moses's longing for the Promised Land, especially the phrase, "the good land," which God uses in his first words to Moses in which the promise is made to bring Israel there (Exodus 3:8). Moses's efforts during the forty years since God's revelation to him at the Burning Bush are directed toward their reaching their destination.[1]

Moses has endured so much during the forty years in the desert for God's sake, especially the Israelites' constant quarreling with him. Now he wishes to complete the task he has been given: to bring them into the land of Israel.[2] This is highlighted when he refers to himself as God's servant: "You let Your servant [*avdekha*] see the first works of Your greatness" (3:24). Not unlike many leaders, he feels that he is due his reward for his struggles and all that he has had to suffer to bring Israel to the shore of the Jordan River.[3]

As a result, he gives vent to strong emotion, saying: "I pleaded (*ve-ethanan*) with *Adonai*" (3:23). And even if he doesn't deserve to lead the people into the Promised Land, he calls on God to have mercy (*hayn*) on him. He addresses God with the divine attribute of compassion (*middat ha-rahamim,* which is represented by the name *Adonai,* as opposed to *Elohim*) and begs to enter the land.[4] The depth of his desperation comes through when he pleads, "Let me please [*na*] cross over" (3:25). Yet he believes that God's decree that he not lead the people into the Land of Israel (Numbers 20:12) and God's anger are the result of Israel's complaints at Kadesh. He tells the Israelites, "God was angry at me on your account [*le-ma'anchem*]" (Deuteronomy 3:26).[5] Moses feels that he is not being punished for anything he has done, a point made in Psalm 106:32: "And they provoked God at the Waters of Meribah and [God] did evil to Moses on their account." Therefore, he feels totally justified in asking God to allow him to cross over the Jordan with his people.

Deserving or not, Moses, who has experienced God's redemptive power on a number of occasions and witnessed God's greatness, simply wants to continue in his role serving the Divine. Even with all that God has done for the People of Israel while Moses has been their leader, he feels there is so much more to come; he has only begun his work (3:24).[6] Most leaders find it difficult to accept that their role has run its course and that they will not accomplish all their goals. How can Moses accept the fact that he won't enter the land and be able to fulfill the very commandments associated with the land itself, which he himself has conveyed to his people?[7] And he demands that God respond to his request, saying: "Master of the Universe, give me an answer to my words, whether I am to enter the land or not."[8]

THE TIMING OF MOSES'S PLEA TO GOD

If Moses knows at Kadesh that he will not lead his people into the Promised Land, why does he wait so long to plead his case? Why does he wait until he has conquered the Amorite kings and divided their land among the 2½ tribes, and designated Joshua to take his place (Deuteronomy 2–3)? It would have made more sense for Moses to have prayed for himself as soon as God was angry with him and issued the divine decree.[9]

Perhaps the Bible emphasizes that Moses entreats God "at that time" (3:23) because he is prompted by the defeat of Sihon and Og, whose lands are apportioned to the Israelites. After all, God has allowed him to enter the land on the east side of the Jordan, and because he subdues the Amorites, God might then annul the original decree. It isn't as if God had not been entreated by Moses to change divine decrees before.[10] Should Moses, therefore, not have been confident that God would accept his pleas regarding himself?[11]

Not only does he defeat the two Amorite kings "at that time," but he also reiterates that Joshua will lead the people as they cross the Jordan, and God will be with Joshua in battle, as the Divine has been with him (3:21–22). It may have occurred to Moses at that moment that even if he weren't to lead the Israelites into the land, there was no decree against him simply entering the land, just like any other Israelite. So, after he himself has said, "I commanded Joshua" (3:21), which means that he acknowledges handing the mantle of leadership over to his disciple, he feels that he can beg to be permitted to merely cross the Jordan and enter the Promised Land.[12]

Perhaps Moses pleads with God at the moment when Israel is ready to cross the Jordan because he realizes that his fate is tied to that of the entire generation that came out of Egypt and was destined to die in the desert. As a result of their sinfulness and, more importantly, their faithlessness, which reached a climax when they railed against Moses and Aaron upon hearing the frightening report of the men who had spied out the Land of Canaan (Numbers 14), God decrees that all who have witnessed the miracles in Egypt will die in the wilderness except Caleb and Joshua, who felt that the land was fertile and Israel should not fear the inhabitants (14:5–9, 30).

And now, when they had all died, Moses can no longer feel confident about himself and, as a result, he begins to entreat God.[13] His time has truly come—his service is coming to an end, and he has to make peace with the fact that Joshua will succeed him.[14] This can be compared to a king who has a favorite, who is given the power by the king to appoint generals, governors, and commanders-in-chief, and now in vain begs the gatekeeper to let him enter the palace, but is not permitted to do so. Everyone is amazed at this, and says, "Yesterday he was appointing generals and governors, and now he begs to enter the palace!" So, too, with Moses, God's trusted servant, who is given the power to lead the people to the shores of the Promised Land. His hour has passed.[15] His plea falls on deaf ears. How difficult it is for leaders to acknowledge when their time has come. Most attempt to hang on to any vestige of power, and often this is simply futile. Letting go of the reins is one of the most difficult tests for every leader.

The antithesis of the leader who refuses to retire was Jack Welch of GE, who promised, "The day I go home, I'll disappear from the place and the person who comes in will do it his or her way."[16]

GOD'S RESPONSE TO MOSES'S PLEA

Nevertheless, Moses desperately wants to cross over the Jordan River with his people. The verb *avar*, pass over, is an oft-repeated theme in chapters 2–3 of Deuteronomy, and Moses uses it in his plea. And God's angry response to his request is derived from a homonym of the same root, "God was wrathful [*va-yit'abber*] with me."[17] God responds directly to Moses and does not listen to anything Moses has to say, cutting him off with the words, "Enough for you [*rav lach*]. Never speak to Me of this matter again!" (3:26). Like a parent reacting to a child who insists on getting what he wants, God impatiently ends the conversation. Moses's death is inevitable and, like most human beings, he feels as if his life's work has failed to reach full fruition.[18]

Perhaps by saying to Moses, "Enough for you," when the word *enough* would have sufficed, God is urging him to recognize just how much he has accomplished in his life. When Moses faces his inability to cross over into the Promised Land and his ultimate demise, God tries to comfort him by pointing up his achievements, and the distinct recognition he had won from both the Divine and his fellow Israelites.[19] Just as he has admonished the Levites to be satisfied with the status they hold (Numbers 16:7),[20] he, too, needs to recognize and be satisfied with his achievements—freeing his people from Egyptian oppression and bringing them through the wilderness to the shores of the Jordan. It is not easy for Moses, as for most leaders, to be satisfied with fulfilling only part of his mission and dream.

Those who knew Ernest Shackleton emphasized that he was proud of what he accomplished on his voyages, despite being disappointed over failing to achieve his dream of crossing the Antarctic. He was able to understand that going as far as he did and bringing his men home alive was enough of a reward.[21]

Perhaps that is why God commands Moses to go up to the top of Pisgah and gaze across the land on the other side of the Jordan, saying, "See it with your own eyes" (3:27). Instead of rubbing salt into the wound of his not being able to cross into the land, God wants Moses to at least see the land to which he led his people. Though God denies his request to enter the land, the Divine fulfills his wish to see the land—Moses has said, "Let me please cross over and see the good land" (3:25). In so doing, God hopes that Moses will recognize just how far he—and the people he led—have come.[22] Standing on Pisgah, all Moses has to do is turn around and gaze at the desert behind them to realize the miraculous nature of their journey.

MOSES AS A PARADIGM FOR ISRAEL

Although God grants him his wish of seeing the land, even if from afar, no matter how minor his sin, Moses has to be punished for his actions. Of course, Moses claims that just as God listened to him when he defended Israel after the incident with the Golden Calf, now God should forgive him for his sin. If God can undo the divine decree regarding the punishment of the people, surely God can forgive the actions of one human being, which pale in significance.[23] Moses even goes as far as to expect the Israelites to pray to God for him, just as he interceded on their behalf.[24]

But Moses's expectations are unfounded. On the one hand, just because God was willing to forgive the People of Israel as a whole, that does not mean that individuals should not be held accountable for their actions. The treatment of the individual has to be different from that of the people and how they act in their covenant with the Divine.[25] Second, Moses is the ultimate exemplar: No one, not even their leader Moses who brought them to the shores of the Promised Land, can escape punishment for his sins. Every one, even the leaders of the people, has to bear responsibility for what they do.[26] Just as Moses cannot cross the Jordan River and experience firsthand the fulfillment of all his dreams, every leader must recognize her limitations. No individual, however powerful, will necessarily complete every task she undertakes. In this world of imperfection and no guarantees, individuals rarely see all their dreams fulfilled. In fact, almost all leaders reach a point at which they can no longer serve their people in the same way as they have done earlier in their careers.[27]

So when Moses tells the Israelites, "Adonai was wrathful to me on your account [*le-ma'anchem*]" (3:26), perhaps it should not be understood as God being angry at Moses because of Israel's actions. Rather, the word *le-ma'anchem* can be translated as "for your sake," implying that it is in the Israelites' best interest for Moses not to cross over with them. If new leadership has to arise for Israel to survive, then Moses's continued presence among them will surely be a severe obstacle. In order to live out God's Torah in the Land of Israel, the people need to move beyond the desert experience, which is synonymous with Moses's leadership.[28]

Moses simply cannot lead the People of Israel in perpetuity. The individual who possesses the ability to lead them from Egypt to the shores of the Jordan is not necessarily the one to be their leader once they settle in the land and begin to establish a community. A different set of skills and a different vision will be necessary for the next stage in their life as a people in their own land. There are limits even to Moses's leadership role.

Dave Ulrich, professor of business administration at the University of Michigan, noted that "when leaders linger, staying on boards, holding offices, consulting ... very often these well-intentioned efforts backfire. CEOs should leave with honor and dignity, transferring 'relational equity' to the new CEO, and then get out of the way."[29]

In addition, Moses has to understand that he is human and not God or even godlike. If he accompanies the Israelites into the Promised Land, then they will face the danger of enshrining him in their midst, rather than observing the laws that he has transmitted to them.[30] This often happens with modern-day charismatic leaders, who are "worshiped" by their followers.

It is significant that Israel is not even instructed to carry Moses's bones into Canaan. Unlike the bones of Joseph, which are transported through the desert and buried in the Promised Land (Genesis 50:25), Moses's remains are buried somewhere on the eastern side of the Jordan River (in present-day Jordan). Perhaps the message is that even his bones should not become holy relics to be venerated by the people.

RECOGNIZING JOSHUA'S SUCCESSION

This new generation of Israelites needs new leadership if they are to conquer Canaan and adapt to their new dwelling place. As God emphasizes, "[Joshua] shall go across at the head of this people and shall allot to them the land" (3:28). Joshua will continue what Moses has begun, fulfilling the leaders' vision of settling in the land of their ancestors.

To facilitate the transition, Moses himself has to prepare Joshua to take his place. God commands Moses first to "instruct Joshua" (3:28), thus giving him insight into the challenges he will face, the individuals with whom he will have to deal, and the lessons he will need to grasp to lead their people.[31] Then God emphasizes that Moses's role is also to encourage and strengthen his disciple. Moses must "imbue him with strength and courage" in order to support him in the future challenges that he will face.[32] If Joshua is to succeed, like anyone who ascends to a position of leadership, he will need the support and guidance of his predecessor, especially one like Moses who is so closely identified with divine power.

Before he stepped down, Roger Enrico, the CEO of PepsiCo, conveyed to all those participating in the company's executive development program that in order for any organization to remain successful over the long term, every leader's legacy must be to groom new leaders who will surpass their predecessors. Preparing a new generation of leaders and passing the baton to them is the measure of all successful leaders.[33]

Some traditions emphasize that Moses, understanding that God has only decreed that he will not lead the people into the Land of Canaan, still believes that he will be allowed to cross over under Joshua's leadership. As simply "one of the people," he will be able to assist Joshua. Some texts in fact stress Moses's willingness to become his protégé's disciple: Joshua will teach the people what God wants and Moses will follow him.[34]

Moses simply cannot live in the Promised Land as a common Israelite. The dangerous implications of this scenario are captured in the following rabbinic conversation: When Moses hears that he must die on the other side of the Jordan, he says that he would rather be Joshua's student as he teaches the People of Israel than die outside the land. God accedes and after they have crossed, Moses goes to Joshua's tent and stands by the door as Joshua is teaching Torah to Israel. When the Israelites see that Moses is standing by the door while Joshua is seated, that is, in the place of honor, they say to Joshua, "What is this? You sit and your teacher, Moses, stands?" When Joshua sees Moses standing there, he tears his garments and weeps, and says, "My Rebbe, my master, teach us Torah." Moses replies, "I am not permitted." All of Israel says, "We will not let you leave." Then a heavenly voice proclaims, "Learn Torah from Joshua!" Moses then says to God, "Master of the World, the time has come; I wish to die."[35] Top leaders are often known for their powerful egos, without which perhaps "things wouldn't get done." As a result, some leaders simply cannot let go of the reins, especially when their successors are inexperienced and somewhat reticent to assert themselves. But as a wise leader matures, the drive that pushes him to achieve gives way to an overarching concern for "generativity"—the nurturing of the next generation of leaders. Organizational survival becomes more important than personal success.[36]

MOSES AS EVERY PERSON:
THE STAGES OF ACCLIMATING TO DEATH

One of Moses's most important acts as a leader is his willingness to facilitate Joshua's takeover as the leader of the People of Israel. He not only prepares Joshua for leadership, but is ready to graciously step away from the seat of power. To do that, Moses has to overcome his fear of death and his longing for immortality. Nothing epitomizes this challenge more for Moses—and, by extension, for every one of us, whether we are an important leader or simply a member of the group—than a touching midrashic recreation of Moses's death scene found in several midrashic compilations. As we listen to Moses's pleas, let us realize that his is the voice of every person who simply wants to remain alive to see the result of the works of his hands. Death does not distinguish between leader and follower:

> "Your Torah is a fraud! This is the reward for the forty years
> of labor and pain, which I have gone through in order for
> Israel to become a faithful and holy people. Master of the
> Universe, the suffering that I have endured in order to bring

the People of Israel to believe in Your name is manifest to You. I really thought that just as I witnessed this people's suffering, so, too, would I witness their success. But now their success has come—they are about to enter the Promised Land, the land about which we have dreamt, and You prevent me from passing over with them?"

Moses, seeing, however, that the decree has been sealed, resolves to withstand God's proclamation. He draws a small circle—a magic, protective ring—around himself and exclaims, "I will not move from here until You annul the decree." He dons sackcloth and ashes, and stands in prayer before the Almighty ... until the heavens and the very order of nature are shaken.

And what does God do? At that hour, God has it proclaimed at every gate of each of the heavens that the angels should not receive Moses's prayers. He commands Achzariel, the Angel of Proclamations, to descend quickly and bolt all the gates, because the sound of Moses's supplications threatens to force its way into heaven.

Then a voice sounds from heaven and says, "Moses, why do you struggle in vain? You have but half an hour more of life in this world!" Moses then says to God, "If you will not bring me into the Promised Land, at least let me live and not die. Let me become like the beasts of the field that eat and drink and live, and enjoy the world." God then answers, "Enough (*rav lecha*)!! Let it suffice. Prepare yourself, for you have but a few moments more to live."

Out of sheer desperation, Moses grabs hold of a scroll, writes God's name on it, and wraps himself in it, hoping to fend off the Angel of Death. But at that very moment, God says to Sammael, the Wicked, "Go forth and bring Moses's soul to me."

Upon seeing the Angel of Death, Moses becomes enraged, and, taking hold of the staff upon which the tetragrammaton, God's four-letter name, is engraved, he assaults Sammael with all his strength until the angel flees from before him ...

In the end, a heavenly voice is heard, declaring, "The end, the moment of your death has come, Moses." Moses implores God, "Please, remember the time when I dwelt upon Mount Sinai for forty days and nights. Please, don't hand me over to the Angel of Death!" Thereupon, a heavenly voice comforts him, saying: "Fear not, Moses, I Myself will attend to you and your burial." Then God descends from the highest heaven to remove Moses's soul, and with God are the three ministering angels: Michael, Gabriel, and Zagzagel. And God kisses Moses and takes away his soul with a kiss of the mouth, and God begins to weep, saying, "Who shall rise up for me against the evildoers?" And the Holy Spirit weeps and says, "And there has not arisen a prophet since in Israel like Moses." And the heavens weep and say, "The godly person has perished from the earth."[37]

This is the story of every human being. It epitomizes the five famous stages of acclimating to death through which human beings pass, as noted by Elisabeth Kübler-Ross in her popular work, *On Death and Dying:* denial, anger, bargaining, despair, and acceptance.[38] Moses teaches all of us about the struggle to accept our mortality, especially when we are cognizant of all that we will miss in the future, both personally and professionally. We who long to see the fulfillment of our visions and efforts, or our children grow and mature, and have their own families and establish their own careers, know Moses's pain. We all must recognize and accept, like it or not, that the world—those we love, and those we serve—must go on without us. Ironically, Moses teaches his people the most important lesson by leaving them. The ultimate goal of the leader is to make herself superfluous.[39]

16
Raising Up the Next Generation of Leaders
Deuteronomy 31

Standing on the Plains of Moab opposite Jericho, the Israelites can see the hill country on the other side of the Jordan River. They are poised to cross over and enter the land about which they have dreamt during the forty-year trek through the desert. But this is also a moment of transition for Israelite leadership. Throughout the desert journey, Moses has begun to prepare Joshua as a leader.[1] He intuits early on that it is the ultimate responsibility of leaders to replace themselves, even though stepping away from power may be difficult for him personally.[2]

MOSES WILL NOT CONTINUE TO LEAD

As the Israelites are about to enter the Promised Land, Moses realizes that his time has come, and he tells the people, "I am now one hundred and twenty years old; I can no longer be active" (Deuteronomy 31:2). He seems to know that he cannot perform the tasks necessary to lead the People of Israel. And even if his physical skills have not diminished significantly, he nevertheless has to relinquish the reins of leadership, since God has told him directly, "You shall not cross this Jordan" (31:2).[3] Every leader must "let go" at some point, ceding leadership to the next generation. Mature leaders realize when the time is near for them to leave the stage, though surrendering power is rarely easy.[4] However, their handing over the mantle in a gracious and supportive manner is crucial for a sense of continuity.

Moses is aware of just how important his actions are at this crucial point in his people's history. Especially now that he is about to die, the people, dependent on him during their entire journey through the desert, may lose their confidence as they prepare to enter into battle in the Land of Canaan. He is needed to secure their future, and he

T hose who sailed with Ernest Shackleton recognized his selflessness. No matter how difficult his own situation or personal circumstances, he was always supremely aware of the needs of others, which often took priority for him. His sailors, his people, were his life.[7]

does so by urging the Israelites and Joshua not to fear the Canaanites. He emphasizes that God is their true ruler; Joshua is God's earthly representative and God's power is demonstrated in their recent victory over Sihon and Og (31:3–6).[5]

Confronted by both the culmination of his forty years of leadership and his impending death, Moses is able to move beyond his own personal anguish and pain, and concern himself with his people's future. The people's needs overshadow his own immediate personal concerns, and this shows him as a true leader—one primarily devoted to his flock.[6]

MOSES'S ATTEMPT TO COMFORT THE PEOPLE

Moses's concerns about the people and their reaction to his impending death are well-founded. They cannot help but be devastated by the void his death will create, and as he approaches his end, their emotion and expressions of grief run very deep.[8] As a result, God warns him that the people's immediate reaction to his death will be to worship foreign gods. As he would soon lie with his ancestors, they would rise up and be led astray (31:16). With Moses's absence, they will feel that God is no longer in their midst. No matter how much Moses stresses that God will always be there for them, they seem to have come to identify the Divine Presence in their midst with Moses (31:17).

Moses knows just how rebellious the Israelites can be, having experienced this rebelliousness firsthand on numerous occasions. He, himself, has lost patience with them and now understands that with his impending death, they surely will react defiantly (31:27). As a result, God impels him to write the song of *Ha'azinu* (Deuteronomy 32), in which heaven and earth will be called to bear witness against the People of Israel when they rebel and break the covenant (31:19).

Nevertheless, even though he has ambivalent feelings toward the people, having person-ally been the target of

In evaluating what made Winston Churchill a highly successful leader in the eyes of the British, most people cite his forcefulness as a leader, especially in times of crisis. He engendered in his followers a sense of confidence in the face of great challenges.[11]

their wrath, he is able to overcome his anger, knowing that his role is to support them. He, therefore, goes forth and speaks to all Israel (*kol Yisrael*), telling them that because of his advanced age (120), he can no longer fulfill his role as their leader (31:1–2). According to the tradition, he goes to every tribe (because the biblical text emphasizes "all Israel") to comfort them over his impending death.[9] He focuses on his age and his inability to be active, so the people will not be over-wrought at the loss of his leadership and the transference of power.[10]

As a way of strengthening their resolve, Moses emphasizes, "God will cross over [the Jordan] before you" (31:3) and then he adds, "Be strong and of great courage; fear not [the enemy whom you will encounter], for Adonai, your God, marches before you and will not fail nor forsake you" (31:6). God is really the force that will lead the people, yet Moses immediately adds that it will be Joshua who will lead them into the Promised Land (31:3). At the end of his life, Moses forcefully exerts his leadership, buttressing the People of Israel in their time of greatest doubt and need.

MOSES'S SUPPORT FOR JOSHUA

To show his support for both the people and for his successor, Moses calls to Joshua in the sight of all the people (31:7). This public act of "calling," in which Moses states that it will be Joshua who will lead the people into the land, is a first step in the passing of the mantle of leadership. Moses's intention is for all of Israel to give Joshua the respect that he himself has been accorded, so he appoints Joshua as the leader in their presence.[12]

Roberto Goizueta, CEO of Coca-Cola, recognized that delegating authority in key areas was crucial to enabling the succession of power. In fact, designating a successor is the ultimate act of delegation. For Goizueta, such an act was the culmination of his program at Coca-Cola to develop and promote talented individuals, challenging them to fulfill key tasks in the organization.[13]

In so doing, he urges Joshua to be strong and courageous, for God will surely be with him as he leads the People of Israel into the land. God will not allow him to fail (31:7–8). Moses gives his disciple as much personal support as he can, including emphasizing that Joshua will play the role that he, Moses, was planning to play for the people—not only leading them into the land of their forebears, but also apportioning the land to each tribe (31:7). A challenge to all leaders is to personally facilitate the transition of leadership by handing over key roles that signify authority.

Though Moses has already called Joshua and indicated that he will lead the people into the land, God then commands Moses to call Joshua once again, so that both of them can enter into the Tabernacle (31:14). It will be in the Tabernacle, in the presence of the entire people,[14] and in the presence of the Shechinah, that the essential transference of leadership to Joshua will take place. With Moses standing beside Joshua, God now instructs him, as he did Moses. Joshua assumes the role of representing God to the people in the holy surroundings of the Tabernacle.[15] It is Moses's role as leader to publicly witness and support Joshua's succession to power.

The smooth transition is subsequently ensured when Moses him-self commands Joshua (*va-yetzav*), in an almost godlike fashion, "Be strong and resolute; for you shall bring the Israelites into the land which I promised them in an oath, and I [*anochi*] will be with you" (31:23). It is almost as if Moses has sworn that the Israelites will inherit the Land of Canaan and that he will always be with them, as if he were still alive. By using the term *anochi*, which is generally used by God in referring to the Divine Self, Moses's speech takes on a superhuman aura, which further buttresses Joshua's leadership.

An excellent example of a modern leader who both groomed his successor over several years and affirmed his role publicly at every turn is Norman Pearlstine, editor-in-chief of Time Inc. The ascension of John Huey, Pearlstine's second in command, was planned and effected by the editor-in-chief, to the point where the transition will be made almost seamlessly.[16]

JOSHUA BEGINS TO ASSUME THE ROLE OF LEADER

Most rabbinic commentators understand verse 31:23 to mean that God, not Moses, commands (*va-yetzav*) Joshua, even though the antecedent in the previous verse is Moses.[17] This then is the first time that God speaks to Joshua directly, thus underscoring his new role and legitimizing his authority.[18] Furthermore, in indicating that Joshua will lead the Israelites into the land (31:23), God tells him to take Moses's staff, the symbol of leadership.[19]

Further demonstrating Joshua's taking Moses's place as leader and prophet, God commands both Joshua and Moses to compose the song of *Ha'azinu* to teach the Israelites what is expected of them when they cross the Jordan River. God uses the plural command *kitvu* (write), thus indicating that Joshua already possesses divine inspiration while Moses is still alive.[20] Like all great leaders, Moses has to continue to mentor Joshua up until his death, sharing with him the process of writing down God's words and communicating these words to their people.

The tradition envisions Joshua beginning to teach the people even in Moses's presence.[22] In one text, a herald is seen passing through the Israelite camp, proclaiming, "Come and hear the words of the new prophet who has arisen for us." All of Israel approaches Joshua to pay honor to him … And Moses bids him to speak to the people.[23]

Moses is even described as serving Joshua in order to enhance the people's recognition of him as their new leader. The time has come for his disciple to become the teacher and leader, and as a result, Moses is portrayed as ministering to all of Joshua's needs: dressing him, cleaning his tent, and then leading him out to teach the people. Though Joshua is ashamed and refuses to have Moses serve him, Moses insists, saying, "With the measure that you meted out to me, do I mete out to you." And Moses places Joshua, in Moses's stead, on the golden throne upon which he sat while teaching God's words.[24]

Kermit Campbell, CEO of Herman Miller, was an excellent example of how to mentor and develop new leaders. By sharing his expertise and involving potential leaders of the company in strategies of leadership, he raised them to a higher level than they ever envisioned achieving.[21]

Moses indeed urges God to let Joshua assume his role, insisting that he call Joshua "My teacher" and accompanying Joshua to the Tabernacle to receive divine inspiration. When the pillar of cloud finally departs, Moses approaches Joshua and asks him, "What was revealed to you?" Joshua replies, "When God's word was revealed to you, Moses, did I know what God spoke to you?" At that moment Moses bitterly exclaims: "Better it is to die a hundred times than to experience envy, even once." Moses loves Joshua, but he is also jealous of him.[25] Even with his death looming, the surrender of power is difficult for Moses, as it is for many leaders.

MOSES'S LEGACY

Even as Moses comforts the People of Israel, stressing that God will be with them and Joshua will lead them into the land, he reminds them of the commandments that he has taught them. He is responsible for the commandments that were conveyed to them (31:5). On the day of his death, Moses's last act is to write down the whole Teaching, the Torah, which he has conveyed to the people, and enjoin them to read it every seven years in the presence of the entire people. The Torah, embodying God's words that Moses taught, should never be forgotten (31:9–11).

According to the Rabbis, Moses actually writes not one but thirteen Torah scrolls, twelve for the twelve tribes, and one to be placed in the Holy Ark, so every Israelite will have direct access to Moses's teaching. Moses also thinks that if anyone wants to change even one iota of the Torah that he has taught them, they can refer to the copy kept safe by the Levites in the ark.[26] Moses's teaching will be preserved forever. So, too, the song of *Ha'azinu,* which Moses also writes, will be read every year by the people (31:21).

Moses occupies himself with the writing of the Torah up to the moment of his death, immersing himself in his people's source of life, perhaps attempting to put off the inevitable. According to a midrashic tradition, he might have thought to himself, "Through busying myself with the Torah, the whole of which is life, the day will set and the decree against me will be nullified."[27] Though the decree has been sealed and Moses will die before the setting of the sun on the seventh day of Adar, it was as if the Rabbis were telling each of us that Moses's immortality, like our own, depends on the extent to which our lives are bound up with God's words. Immersed in Torah and living its teachings, Moses's will live forever, his legacy enduring in the hearts and minds of every future generation. We are all his progeny.

And so, as his final moment in this world approaches, Moses climbs Mount Nebo in the Plain of Moab, opposite Jericho. After being shown by God the entire Land of Israel, which his people will inherit, he dies with a kiss from the Almighty. He lived one hundred and twenty years, yet when his soul leaves him, his eyes are not dimmed, nor is his vigor abated (34:7). His strength endures, just as his teaching lives on after him, as it continues to be a source of our own self-understanding and transformation.

Conclusion

Looking back on Moses's journey as a leader of the People of Israel, we cannot help but marvel at his growth and how much he personally accomplished. When he first encounters the Divine, he is married to the daughter of a Midianite priest, Jethro, and keeper of Jethro's sheep. In experiencing God's call, he is awash in self-doubt as he is told that he will be the one to free the Israelites from Egyptian persecution: His initial response to God's revelation at the Burning Bush epitomizes his humility: "Who am I that I should bring forth the Children of Israel from Egypt?" (Exodus 3:11). Understanding that he will be the leader to confront the Pharaoh, he proclaims to God that he is incapable of speaking: "I am not a person of words; for I suffer from a speech impediment" (Exodus 4:10). There is not a shred of hubris in him.

Yet, over time, this very same reticent, self-deprecating human being becomes the fluent communicator of God's words to his people and the singer of God's songs—*Shirat Ha-Yam* (The Song at the Sea) and *Ha'azinu*. His farewell address fills most of the Book of Deuteronomy.[1] The lonely shepherd who flees Egypt develops into a leader who is capable of navigating the journey through the desert, fraught with internal and external challenges, bringing his people to the mountain and covenant with God, and then to the shores of the Promised Land.

Moses starts out as the iconoclastic leader, challenging the Egyptian establishment, but once his nation is forged at Mount Sinai, his voice mellows into that of the conservative leader who puts down internal challenges to the status quo and demands that the people recognize God's supreme authority.[2]

In one respect, all the leadership roles in the Bible coalesce into one in the person of Moses. He is founder of the nation, a revolutionary, a lawgiver, a priest, a judge, a politician, a teacher, a prophet, a comforter, and a guide—all rolled up into one.[3] He is the paradigm for all subsequent leaders, for all of us, in the different roles we are called on to play. Never again will there be a leader like Moses—one person who will fill such a range of roles for the people. Perhaps giving a single leader such power is perceived as too dangerous, as the people chart their future on the land.[4]

The range of leadership roles and styles assumed by Moses during his life reflects his flexibility—he is able to adapt to the changing needs of his people. The ability to assess any situation and determine the most effective way to handle it is crucial to the success of any leader, and over and over again Moses demonstrates his adaptive capacity.[5]

Moses's life also reflects the mercurial nature of leadership: moments of supreme success followed by unbridled challenges to the leader's authority. Mistakes and disappointments intermingle with moments of joy and uplift. To be sure, Moses teaches all of us that if we choose to don the mantle of leadership, we will not experience unalloyed joy and success.[6]

Even more important is the realization that with all the challenges and disappointments, Moses finds the strength to maintain his leadership role. Perhaps it is because he never loses sight of the vision he possesses from the very beginning, the higher purpose for which he is called—fulfillment of the people's covenant with God. This may be one of the most important lessons that we who aspire to leadership can draw from his life: the need to continually focus on the mission of the group above all else. Despite the people's challenges to his leadership and their outright rejection of his authority, Moses never totally loses hope. If anything, Moses embodies the reality that all leaders must be severely tested by conflict and challenge before they themselves can even discern whether they truly have the ability to lead.[7]

The hardships that Moses faces have an even greater impact on him. His own understanding of the suffering that he goes through personally elicits in him greater empathy for others who suffer.[8] However, Moses's caring and concern for others prompts him to go even further: He is portrayed as always willing to act on those feelings. When he sees a wrong being perpetrated, he is moved by a sense of justice to take action. In key episodes in Exodus, chapters 2–3, Moses does not hesitate to attempt to save those who are victims.[9] Even though Moses sees himself as one of the people (*ahad ha-am*), like every leader, he has to remain somewhat removed from them. He is the one who ascends the mountain to stand with God and transmit divine laws, thus setting himself apart. This is the struggle of every leader: how to walk the fine line between being part of the community, and exercising leadership over that same community.[10] Maintaining an uneasy balance between the two is the only way Moses can mediate between God's absolute power and demands, and the people's human nature.[11] The balance in this ongoing dialectic is what defines Moses's role as the leader of the Jewish people and the preservation of their covenant with God.

At times, Moses is isolated not only from his fellow Israelites, but also from his own family. We see this in Miriam and Aaron's complaints against him—ostensibly involving the Cushite woman he has married (Numbers 12)—as well as in the absence of almost any mention of his wife and sons during the entire journey through the desert. On the one occasion when his wife, Tzipporah, appears at the Israelite camp with their two sons, Gershom and Eliezer, and her father, Jethro (Exodus 18), Moses greets his father-in-law and reviews for him all that has occurred to the people, and Jethro proceeds to instruct Moses on how to delegate power if he is to succeed as their leader. And then, unexpectedly, Moses sends Jethro back to Midian, with not a mention of his wife and sons. It is as if they were not part of Moses's life with the People of Israel. Perhaps Moses, like many leaders, is unable to maintain a relationship with family while fulfilling the demands of leading the people. As successful as he is as the leader of the Jewish people, he seems to have no relationship with his own children. In a powerful midrashic tradition, when Aaron is dying and lamenting his fate, Moses tries to console him by saying that at least his sons will carry on his legacy of the priesthood, while Moses has no sons to follow in his footsteps.[12]

Though Moses occasionally does feel isolated from the very people whom he serves, he is linked to them in a very powerful way, even to the point of realizing that he needs them if he is to succeed. As such, he comes to understand that sharing power and delegating responsibility and the concomitant authority to others will lead to the people's growth and transformation. Only God has absolute power; shared leadership has to be the hallmark of Jewish existence.[13] Yet, whenever Moses acts alone, as is appropriate in certain circumstances, his moral courage and high ideals mark him as a true leader, whose work is aligned with God's greater purposes.[14]

One of the ways to distinguish between managers and leaders is that managers are inherently conservative, while leaders are willing to take bold risks in order to effect change.[15] Moses transforms a group of former slaves into a people with a clear sense of their future. He articulates a vision that both motivates his followers and gives them a sense of the ultimate importance of their lives.[16]

For all these reasons, and many more, not only do the Rabbis model their lives and leadership styles after Moses and his life—he will forever be known as *Moshe Rabbenu*, Moses, our rabbi, our teacher. His life is instructive for every one who aspires to leadership. His legacy endures in both the teaching he transmitted as well as through his own actions and life experiences, which can help us understand our own.[17] More than the words he speaks, Moses's deeds become examples for others to emulate. He becomes a role model not only for future leaders, but for every human being, for every one of us.

So what is Moses's leadership model? What can he teach us about ourselves? Among the myriad of lessons we have drawn from this review of Moses's journey as a leader of his people, let us first consider that a human being who is limited by personal challenges nevertheless is capable of achieving greatness and making an extraordinary contribution. Concomitantly, Moses also teaches us that no leader, no one person, is indispensable. Moses is denied the total fulfillment of his life goal to teach us that each leader, each person, must pass along unfinished work to the next generation. Moses's burial site in the Land of Moab is left unidentified (Deuteronomy 34:6), graphically illustrating the incompleteness of his journey.[18] Though he never fulfills his dream of leading his people into the Land of Israel, he experiences the blessing and satisfaction of seeing with his own eyes the land promised to them by God. We can learn from him that we, too, have the capacity to overcome disappointments and challenges and then experience the satisfaction that Moses feels standing on Mount Nebo, gazing upon the land of promise, and knowing that he has led his people to the shores of a new world.

Notes

INTRODUCTION

1. Chuck Lucier, Rob Schuyt, and Junichi Handa, "CEO Succession 2004: The World's Most Prominent Temp Workers," www.strategy-business.com/press/article/05204.

2. Harvey Cox, *The Secular City* (New York: Macmillan, 1966).

3. This is especially true of our relationships with the others in our lives—parents, children, siblings, spouses, lovers, and friends. See, in this regard, my first book, *Self, Struggle and Change: Family Conflict Stories in Genesis and Their Healing Insights for Our Lives* (Woodstock, Vt.: Jewish Lights Publishing, 1995) and my latest work, *Hineini in Our Lives* (Woodstock, Vt.: Jewish Lights Publishing, 2003).

4. Elie Wiesel, *Messengers of God: Biblical Portraits and Legends* (New York: Random House, 1976), p. 181.

5. For example, Leviticus 8:10–35.

6. Deuteronomy 34:10.

7. Hal Lewis, *Models and Meanings in the History of Jewish Leadership* (Lewiston, Queenston, Lampeter: Edwin Mellen Press, 2004), p. 10.

8. For example, Malachi 3:22.

9. Deuteronomy 34:5.

10. Deuteronomy 34:11.

11. Levi Meier, *Moses: The Prince, the Prophet: His Life, Legend and Message for Our Lives* (Woodstock, Vt.: Jewish Lights Publishing, 1998), p. 4.

12. All translations are drawn from Gunther Plaut's *The Torah: A Modern Commentary* (New York: Union of American Hebrew Congregations, 1981), with occasional slight modifications by the author.

13. Deuteronomy 34:1.

14. Exodus 3:1.

15. See Levi Meier's comments in this regard in his *Moses: The Prince, the Prophet,* p. 4.

CHAPTER 1: SHOWING THE POTENTIAL FOR LEADERSHIP

1. The prophecy of Moses's birth is attributed in the tradition to Miriam. See, for example, *Shemot Rabbah* 1:22. Pharaoh's astrologers had told him that the redeemer of the Hebrews was about to be born, though they did not know if he would be a Hebrew or an Egyptian. Therefore, in the Exodus text, when Pharaoh repeats his decree that the midwives kill every male child born, he uses the nonspecific language, "every boy" (verse 22), thus including both Egyptian and Hebrew children. See, in this regard, B.T. *Sotah* 12a and *Shemot Rabbah* 1:20. It is ironic that Moses, in a sense, carried both identities, having been born to a Hebrew mother, but raised by the princess of Egypt.

2. Exodus 1:16, 22.

3. See Genesis 1:25.

4. In addition, following the creation of humankind, God saw all that had been created as being "very good" (Genesis 1:31). See the comments of Rabbi Levi Meier in this regard, in *Moses: The Prince, the Prophet,* p. 17.

5. *Me'am Loaz* to Exodus 2:10, as well as Amos Hakham, *Sefer Shemot* (Mosad ha-Rav Kook 1991), to Exodus 2:10. Most scholars agree that his name was probably Egyptian, not Hebrew, citing Egyptian sources referring to an early figure with the same name.

6. See, for example, Philo, *De Vita Mosis* 1, 23–24.

7. See Moshe Greenberg, *Understanding Exodus* (New York: Behrman House, Inc, 1969), p. 56, and Nehama Leibowitz, *Studies in Shemot,* vol. 1 (Jerusalem: WZO Department for Torah Education and Culture in the Diaspora, 1978), p. 40.

8. See Rashi's comment on Exodus 2:11, in which he states that Pharaoh even places Moses in charge of his palace, and *Me'am Loaz* to Exodus 2:10–12.

9. Aviva Zornberg, *The Particulars of Rapture: Reflections on Exodus* (New York: Doubleday, 2000), p. 24.

10. The tale of Moses leaving the palace in order to engage the common people conforms to a universal type of folkloristic tale, described in Stith Thompson, *Motif Index to Folk-Literature,* 6 vols. (Bloomington: Indiana University Press, 1955–58), motif P14.19. William H. C. Propp,

The Anchor Bible (New York: Doubleday, 1998) to Exodus 2:11–15a notes the parallelism with the Buddhist figure, Siddhartha, who like Moses leaves the royal estate to view human suffering and subsequently experiences a spiritual transformation.

11. Meier, *Moses: The Prince, the Prophet*, p. 20.

12. For example, *Tanhuma ha-Nidpas, Shemot* 9; and *Midrash ha-Gadol* to Exodus 2:13.

13. Note Elie Wiesel's quote of the Gerer Rebbe in his *Messengers of God*, p. 185.

14. Zornberg, *The Particulars of Rapture*, pp. 24–25.

15. Ramban on Exodus 2:11. See also Rashi on Exodus 2:11.

16. *Midrash Aggadah* to Exodus 2:11 and *Me'am Loaz* to Exodus 2:12.

17. Peter M. Senge, *The Fifth Discipline* (New York: Doubleday, 2006), pp. 129–130.

18. Among several texts, see *Midrash Lekah Tov* and *Midrash Sekhel Tov* to Exodus 2:11.

19. *Shemot Rabbah* 1:27.

20. *Pirkei Avot* 2:5.

21. See, for example, B.T. *Sotah* 11b and *Shemot Rabbah* 1:29, 33.

22. *Vayikra Rabbah* 32:4.

23. Meier, *Moses: The Prince, the Prophet*, p. 21.

24. See *Midrash Aggadah* to Exodus 2:11, which states that Moses killed the Egyptian by actually mentioning the Divine Name.

25. *Mekhilta d'Rabbi Ishmael, Massekhta d'Shirta, parashah* 1; and *Midrash Tanhuma ha-Nidpas, Shofetim* 5 et al.

26. Lorin Woolfe, *Leadership Secrets from the Bible* (New York: MJF Books, 2002), p. 64. Most of the quotes on leadership drawn from other sources in this book are taken from Woolfe's notes. See, in this regard, Warren Blank, *The 108 Natural Born Leaders* (New York: AMACOM, 2001), p. 62.

27. Wiesel, *Messengers of God*, p. 186.

28. "The Business Case against Revolution: An Interview with Nestlé's Peter Brabeck," *Harvard Business Review* (February 2001): 118.

29. See the emphasis on the superfluousness of the word *ish* and the notion that Moses was approximately twenty years old at this point in the narrative in such sources as *Midrash Tanhuma ha-Nidpas, Shemot* 9; *Shemot Rabbah* 1:30; and *Yalkut Shimoni*, vol. 1, *remez* 167.

30. See Rashi's commentary to Exodus 2:14 and *Shemot Rabbah* 1:20.

31. See *Pirkei d'Rabbi Eliezer*, chapter 48; and *Yalkut Shimoni*, vol. 1, *remez* 167.

32. Leibowitz, *Studies in Shemot*, p. 41; and Meier, *Moses: The Prince, the Prophet*, p. 24.

33. This is underscored by the contrast with the manner in which Jethro's daughters describe to their father what had occurred: "An Egyptian rescued us [*hitzilanu,* not *hoshiainu*] from the shepherds" (verse 19). Robert Altar points this out in his book, *The Art of Biblical Narrative* (New York: Basic Books, Inc., 1981), p. 57.

34. Philo, *De Vita Mosis* 1:60.

35. *The Anchor Bible* to Exodus 2:11–15a.

36. Ibid., 2:15b–23a.

37. Greenberg, *Understanding Exodus*, p. 59.

38. Brent Bowers and Deidre Leipziger, eds., *The New York Times Management Reader* (New York: Times Books, 2001), pp. 186–187.

39. Wiesel, *Messengers of God*, p. 87.

40. *The Anchor Bible* to Exodus 2:15b–23a.

CHAPTER 2: THE CALLING—OVERCOMING SELF-DOUBT

1. *The Anchor Bible* to Exodus 3.

2. Ibid. See also Philo, *De Vita Mosis* 1:60.

3. For example, *Meam Lo'az* and *Midrash Lekah Tov* to Exodus 3:1.

4. This designation is frequently found in the Zohar.

5. See, among many sources, *Shemot Rabbah* 2:2; *Me'am Lo'az* to Exodus 3:11; and *Sefer ha-Yashar* to *Shemot*.

6. Richard Deft, *Leadership: Theory and Practice* (Fort Worth: Dryden Press, 1999), p. 352.

7. *Midrash Tanhuma Buber,* Shemot 12.

8. Meier, *Moses: The Prince, the Prophet*, p. 31.

9. See *Shemot Rabbah* 3:2 and *Midrash Ha-Gadol* to Exodus 3:3.

10. Note Shadal's comment on Exodus 3:1 as well as that of *Tzena U'Rena*. Josephus, *Antiquities* 2:254 even states that Moses led the flocks to graze on the mountain called Sinai.

11. See, for example, *Midrash Lekah Tov* to Exodus 3:2.

12. Ibid.

13. Rashi on Exodus 3:2.

14. Zornberg, *The Particulars of Rapture*, p. 338.

15. For example, *Midrash Aggadah* to Exodus 3:3.

16. Senge, *The Fifth Discipline*, pp. 60–61.

17. *Midrash Lekah Tov* and *Midrash Sekhel Tov* to Exodus 3:3.
18. *Yalkut Shimoni,* vol. 1, *remez* 167; and Zornberg, *The Particulars of Rapture,* pp. 79–80.
19. Psalm 91:15. This verse is cited in many midrashim, including *Mekhilta d'Rabbi Shimon* to Exodus 3:2, 8.
20. See, among many midrashic parallels, *Mekhilta d'Rabbi Shimon* to Exodus 3:8; *Pirkei d'Rabbi Eliezer,* chapter 40; Rashi's comment on Exodus 3:2; *Midrash Tanhuma ha-Nidpas, Shemot* 14; *Yalkut Shimoni,* vol. 1, *remazim* 167, 169; *Midrash ha-Gadol* to Exodus 3:2; and Keli Yakar's comment on Exodus 3:2.
21. *Shemot Rabbah* 2:5.
22. Philo, *De Vita Mosis* 1:67; *Shemot Rabbah* to Exodus 2:1, 5; and Hizkuni's comment on Exodus 2:2.
23. *Pirkei d'Rabbi Eliezer,* chapter 40; and *Yalkut Shimoni,* vol. 1, *remez* 169.
24. *Mekhilta d'Rabbi Shimon* to Exodus 3:8.
25. *Tzena U'Rena* to Exodus 3:4.
26. *Yalkut Shimoni,* vol. 1, *remez* 168; and *Midrash ha-Gadol* to Exodus 3:4.
27. Patrick Lencioni, "The Trouble with Humility," *Leader to Leader* (Winter, 1999): 44.
28. See, for example, Rashbam to Exodus 3:1.
29. Keli Yakar to Exodus 3:11.
30. Umberto Cassuto, *A Commentary on the Book of Exodus,* translated from the Hebrew by Israel Abrahams (Jerusalem: The Magnes Press, 1967), p. 36; and Rashi to Exodus 3:11.
31. Josephus, *Jewish Antiquities* 2:271, 9 vols., The Loeb Classic Library (Cambridge: Harvard University Press, 1964).
32. *The Anchor Bible* to Exodus 4:10.
33. Neff and Citrin, *Lessons from the Top,* p. 66.
34. *Midrash ha-Gadol* to Exodus 4:10 emphasizes that we pale in comparison to Moses.
35. See *Midrash ha-Gadol* and the comment of the Ramban to Exodus 4:10.
36. Greenberg, *Understanding Exodus,* pp. 92–93.
37. Leibowitz, *Studies in Shemot,* p. 73. Leibowitz bases most of her reading on Rashi's comment to Exodus 3:10, 12.
38. William Propp points out in the *Anchor Bible* to Exodus 1–18, on Exodus 3:12 that the phrase *ehyeh imakh,* "I will be with you," is a recurring

expression of divine reassurance. See, for example, Genesis 26:3, 28:15, and 31:3.

39. Woolfe, *Leadership Secrets from the Bible,* p. 75.

40. See Rashi and Rambam's comments on Exodus 3:12.

41. Greenberg, *Understanding Exodus,* p. 78.

42. Rashi on Exodus 3:14.

43. *The Anchor Bible* to Exodus 3:6.

44. In *Midrash ha-Gadol* to Exodus 3:14, God's name *Ehyeh,* in Gematria, rabbinic numerology, adds up to 21, which is said to match the first letters in the name of Abraham, Isaac, and Jacob, *aleph* (1), *yod* (10), and *yod* (10).

45. This point is also made in many midrashim, including several traditions that note that Moses is instructed to tell the people that "God has surely remembered (*pakod pakad'ti*) you" (3:16), and, as a result, the people will listen to him and follow him (3:18). Why? Because these very words are used by both Jacob and Joseph to announce the approaching redemption, and Moses's use of them indicates his power to make it happen. See the comments of the Ramban to Exodus 3:18 in this regard.

46. Sarna, *JPS Torah Commentary to Exodus* 3:16, p. 18, n.16.

47. Cassuto, *A Commentary on the Book of Exodus,* p. 42.

48. Ibid., p.46.

49. See, for example, *Yalkut Shimoni,* vol. 1, *remez* 170; and *Midrash ha-Gadol* to Exodus 4:17.

50. For example, *Midrash ha-Gadol* to Exodus 4:11.

51. See Philo, *DeVita Mosis* 1:85; and Targum Onkolos to Exodus 4:13, as well as the Ramban's comment on this verse.

52. Morell and Capparell, *Shackleton's Way,* pp. 58–59.

CHAPTER 3: THE VISION OF LEADERSHIP

1. Leibowitz, *Studies in Shemot,* p. 141. See also *Da'at Soferim* to Exodus 6:12.

2. Yehuda Nachshoni, *Studies in the Weekly Parashah,* trans. from the Hebrew by Raphael Blumberg (Jerusalem: Mesorah Publications Ltd., 1989), pp. 371–372.

3. Rashi to Exodus 6:2.

4. *Midrash ha-Gadol* to Exodus 6:2.

5. Greenberg, *Understanding Exodus,* p. 134, and Sarna, *JPS Torah Commentary* to Exodus 6:3.

6. Rashi to Exodus 6:2.

7. *Targum Yonatan* to Exodus 6:2.

8. *Da'at Soferim* to Exodus 6:4–5.

9. Rashi to Exodus 6:2.

10. Jay Conger and Beth Benjamin, *Building Leaders* (San Francisco: Jossey-Bass, 1999), p. 123.

11. Greenberg, *Studies in Exodus,* p. 132.

12. Ibid., p. 133.

13. Leibowitz, *Studies in Shemot,* p. 137. See also *Yalkut Shimoni,* vol. 1, *remez* 176.

14. Zornberg, *The Particulars of Rapture,* p. 82.

15. See, for example, *Da'at Soferim* to Exodus 6:8.

16. Zornberg, *The Particulars of Rapture,* p. 82.

17. Cassuto, *A Commentary on the Book of Exodus,* pp. 81–82.

18. Erich Fromm, *Escape from Freedom* (New York: Holt and Company, 1994), pp. 31–36, 103ff.

19. Greenberg, *Studies in Exodus,* p. 134, and Cassuto, *A Commentary on the Book of Exodus,* p. 80.

20. Geoffrey Colvin, "Larry Bossidy Won't Stop," *Fortune* (January 13, 1997): 135–137.

21. Note, for example, P.T. *Pesahim* 10a and *Shemot Rabbah* 6:4.

22. *Me'am Lo'az* to Exodus 6:8, among several sources.

23. See *Shemot Rabbah* 6:4 and *Me'am Loaz* to Exodus 6:8 for examples of this tradition.

24. *Midrash ha-Gadol* to Exodus 6:6.

25. *Sefat Emet* on *Parashat Va'era,* section 634.

26. Nachshoni, *Studies in the Weekly Parashah,* pp. 369–370.

27. Woolfe, *Leadership Secrets from the Bible,* p. 30, citing J. Kermit Campbell, CEO of Herman Miller.

28. Meier, *Moses: The Prince, the Prophet,* p. 61.

29. Sforno on Exodus 6:9; *Me'am Lo'az* to Exodus 6:13; *Da'at Soferim* to Exodus 6:9; and Sarna, *JPS Torah Commentary to Exodus* 6:2–7:13, p. 30.

30. Note, for example, *Mekhilta d'Rabbi Ishmael, Massekhta d'Pisha, parashah* 5; and *Targum Onkolos* and *Midrash Aggadah* to Exodus 6:6.

31. *Me'am Lo'az* to Exodus 6:9.

32. See how the Rabbis interpret the verse, "And Adonai spoke with Moses and Aaron, commanding the Israelites and Pharaoh, king of Egypt, to deliver the Israelites from the land of Egypt" (Exodus 6:13). God

commands Pharaoh to free the Israelites, but what does God command the Israelites themselves to do? If they are to be redeemed from Egypt, they need to be forced to abandon idol worship. See, in this regard, *Mekhilta d'Rabbi Ishmael, Massekhta d'Pisha, parashah* 5; *Yalkut Shimoni,* vol. 1, *remez* 177; *Midrash ha-Gadol* to Exodus 6:6; and Nachshoni, *Studies in the Weekly Parashah,* p. 372.

33. Cassuto, *A Commentary on the Book of Exodus,* pp. 82–83.

34. *Mekhilta d'Rabbi Shimon* to Exodus 6:2, and the Ramban on Exodus 6:12.

35. Zornberg, *The Particulars of Rapture,* pp. 83–84.

36. *Sefat Emet* to Exodus 6:9, and Nachshoni, *Studies in the Weekly Parashah,* p. 373.

37. *Shemot Rabbah* 7:1; *Midrash ha-Gadol* to Exodus 6:12; Ramban on Exodus 6:13; *Torat Moshe* on Exodus 6:9; and *Da'at Soferim* to Exodus 6:13.

38. Zornberg, *The Particulars of Rapture,* p. 95.

39. *Shemot Rabbah* 7:3; *Yalkut Shimoni* vol. 1, *remez* 177; and *Me'am Lo'az* to Exodus 6:13.

40. Nachshoni, *Studies in the Weekly Parashah,* p. 372.

41. See, among many sources, Rashi, *Midrash Sekhel Tov,* and *Da'at Soferim* to Exodus 6:13.

42. Robert Levering and Milton Moskowitz, *The 100 Best Companies to Work for in America* (New York: Plume/Penguin, 1994), p. 342.

43. Leibowitz, *Studies in Shemot,* p. 146.

CHAPTER 4: WE POSSESS THE POWER AND THE ABILITY

1. Exodus 14:8 describes the Israelites' boldness at the time of their departure with the words *b'yad ramah,* "with upraised hand," which symbolizes the power they felt.

2. Zornberg, *The Particulars of Rapture,* p. 202.

3. *Mekhilta d'Rabbi Ishmael, Massekhta d'Beshallah, parashah* 3.

4. For example, Exodus 3:7.

5. See, for example, the commentary of Isaac Arama, *Akedat Yitzhak* on *parashat Beshallah.*

6. See, for example, Rashi's comment to Exodus 14:10, which parallels numerous other traditions, in which it is emphasized that the Israelites in Egypt follow the example of their forebears in praying to God.

7. Zornberg, *The Particulars of Rapture,* p. 202.

8. See the comment of Nachmanides on Exodus 14:11.

9. Philo, *De Vita Mosis,* vol. 1, pp. 171–172. See also Josephus, *Jewish Antiquities,* vol. 2, pp. 327–328.

10. *The Anchor Bible* to Exodus 14:11, Notes, and Benno Jacob's commentary to Exodus 14:11.

11. Zornberg, *The Particulars of Rapture,* p. 202.

12. *The New Interpreters Bible*'s commentary to Exodus 1–14:31, and Benno Jacob's commentary to Exodus 14:12.

13. Woolfe, *Leadership Secrets from the Bible,* pp. 47–48.

14. For example, Exodus 16:3, 17:3; Numbers 11:4, 14:3, 16:13, 20:3f, and 21:5.

15. Zornberg, *The Particulars of Rapture,* pp. 202–203.

16. See the comments in *Targum Yonatan* to Exodus 14:10–11 and the Ramban's interpretation of Exodus 14:10, as also cited in modern commentaries, such as Benno Jacob on Exodus 14:12 and Nehama Leibowitz, *Studies in Shemot,* pp. 257–258.

17. *Mekhilta d'Rabbi Ishmael, Massekhta d'Beshallah, parashah* 3. See also, among many, *Mekhilta d'Rabbi Shimon* to Exodus 14:14; *Targum Yonatan* and *Targum Yerushalmi* to Exodus 14:13; *Yalkut Shimoni* vol. 1, *remez* 234; *Midrash ha-Gadol* to Exodus 14:14; *Midrash Sekhel Tov* to Exodus 14:14; *Midrash Lekah Tov* to Exodus 14:14, and more modern commentaries, such as Nachshoni, *Studies in the Weekly Parashah,* p. 427.

18. *Mekhilta d'Rabbi Ishmael,* and a more extended rendition of this tradition in *Me'am Lo'az* to Exodus 14:13–14.

19. Neff and Citrin, *Lessons from the Top,* p. 318.

20. *The Anchor Bible* to Exodus 13:17–15:21, Notes, p. 479.

21. Ramban on Exodus 14:15, and Nachshoni, *Studies in the Weekly Parashah,* p. 427.

22. *Yalkut Shimoni,* vol. 1, *remez* 234.

23. *Shemot Rabbah* 21:2.

24. Sforno to Exodus 14:15.

25. Ibid, and Nachshoni, *Studies in the Weekly Parashah,* pp. 427–428.

26. Benno Jacob's commentary to Exodus 14:16.

27. Cassuto to Exodus 14:13.

28. Josephus, *Jewish Antiquities,* vol. 2, pp. 329–333.

29. Among many parallel traditions throughout midrashic literature, see the *Mekhilta d'Rabbi Ishmael; Massekhta d'Beshallah, parashah* 3;

Mekhilta d'Rabbi Shimon to Exodus 14:14; *Yalkut Shimoni*, vol. 1, *remez* 234; and *Midrash ha-Gadol* to Exodus 14:13.

30. Zornberg, *The Particulars of Rapture*, p. 209.

31. "The Business Case against Revolution," *Harvard Business Review* (February 2001): 118.

32. Benno Jacob's commentary to Exodus 14:14.

33. Nachshoni, *Studies in the Weekly Parashah*, p. 427.

34. *Shemot Rabbah* 21:4.

35. See, for example, *Targum Yonatan* and *Targum Onkelos* to Exodus 14:15, and *Pirkei d'Rabbi Eliezer*, chap. 42.

36. *Mekhilta d'Rabbi Ishmael, Massekhta d'Beshallah, parashah* 3, *Mekhilta d'Rabbi Shimon* to Exodus 14:13; *Yalkut Shimoni*, vol 1, *remez* 234; and *Midrash ha-Gadol* to Exodus 14:13.

37. Woolfe, *Leadership Secrets from the Bible*, p. 156.

38. This is a paraphrastic version of the midrashic tradition found in *Mekhilta d'Rabbi Ishmael, Massekhta d'Beshallah, parashah* 6; B.T. *Berachot* 4:18; and B.T. *Sotah* 37a, with a number of other later parallels.

39. Morrell and Capparel, *Shackleton's Way*, p. 147.

40. See Rashi on Exodus 14:15 and Aviva Zornberg's interpretation of it in *The Particulars of Rapture*, p. 203.

41. Steven Hayward, *Churchill on Leadership* (New York: Gramercy Books, 1997), p. 116.

42. See Isaac Arama's commentary *Akeidat Yitzhak* on *Beshallah* in this regard.

43. Jon Carlzon, *Moments of Truth* (New York: Harper and Row, 1987), p. 77.

44. *Torat Moshe*, the commentary of Rabbi Moshe Alshich on the Torah, translated and condensed by Eliyahu Monk, vol. 1 (Jerusalem: Rubin Mass Ltd., 1988), to Exodus 14:15, and *Me'am Lo'az* to Exodus 14:16.

45. *The Anchor Bible* to Exodus, Notes, p. 497.

46. *Shemot Rabbah* 21:6 and *Midrash Va-Yosha*, p. 148.

47. *Vayikra Rabbah* 1:5 and *Midrash ha-Gadol* to Exodus 14:14.

48. Nachshoni, in his *Studies in the Weekly Parashah*, p. 428, quotes the commentary *Meshech Hochmah* in this regard. See also Leibowitz, *Studies in Shemot*, p. 256.

49. *Shemot Rabbah* 21:10.

50. *Shemot Rabbah* 21:8.

51. See, in this regard, *Targum Yonatan* to Exodus 14:15; the *Mekhilta d'Rabbi Ishmael, Massekhta d'Beshallah, parashah* 3; *Mekhilta d'Rabbi*

Shimon, Midrash Lekah Tov, Midrash Sekhel Tov and *Midrash ha-Gadol* to Exodus 14:14; and *Yalkut Shimoni,* vol. 1, *remez* 234.

52. Leibowitz, *Studies in Shemot,* p. 260.

53. Hayward, *Churchill on Leadership,* pp. 9–10

54. *Mekhilta d'Rabbi Ishmael, Massekhta d'Beshallah, parashah* 4.

CHAPTER 5: THE LEADER'S UNIQUE SONG

1. They also emphasize the power signified by God's hand in *Shirat ha-Yam,* the Song at the Sea, itself: "Your right hand, O Lord, glorious in power, Your right hand, O Lord, shatters the foe" (Exodus 15:6).

2. Meier, *Moses: The Prince, the Prophet,* p. 107.

3. Benno Jacob's commentary to Exodus 14:30–31 and *Me'am Lo'az* to Exodus 14:31.

4. Sarna, *JPS Torah Commentary to Exodus* 14:31. He is called the *servant of God* or some version of this over thirty times in the Bible.

5. For example, *Mekhilta d'Rabbi Ishmael, Massekhta d'Beshallah, parashah* 7, *Mekhilta d'Rabbi Shimon* to Exodus 14:31; and *Midrash ha-Gadol* to Exodus 14:31.

6. Among many parallel traditions, see *Mekhilta d'Rabbi Ishmael, Massekhta d'Beshallah,* parashah 7; *Midrash Tanhuma Buber, Beshallah* 11; *Midrash ha-Gadol* to Exodus 14:31; and *Shemot Rabbah* 22:3.

7. In addition to the sources mentioned in note 6, see also *Me'am Lo'az* to Exodus 15:1 and Rabbenu Bahya to Exodus 15:1.

8. Rashi and Ramban to Exodus 15:1, as well as the *Or Hayyim.*

9. Meier, *Moses: The Prince, the Prophet,* p. 108, and Wiesel, *Messengers of God,* p. 193. Wiesel reminds us that while stutterers have difficulty speaking, they have no problems singing.

10. See Josephus, *Jewish Antiquities,* vol. 1, pp. 345–346, and Benno Jacob's commentary to Exodus 15:1.

11. Hayward, *Churchill on Leadership,* pp. 98–99.

12. Zornberg, *The Particulars of Rapture,* pp. 216–17.

13. See, for example, Ramban and Sforno's comments on this passage. See also *Me'am Lo'az* to Exodus 15.

14. Zornberg, *The Particulars of Rapture,* p. 224.

15. See, for example, the classic midrashic interpretation of Exodus 15:1 in *Mekhilta d'Rabbi Ishmael, Messekhta d'Shirta, parashah* 1.

16. For example, *Mekhilta d'Rabbi Ishmael, Massekhta d'Shirta, parashah*; P.T. *Sotah* 23a; and *Me'am Lo'az* to Exodus 15:1.

17. *Shemot Rabbah* 23:12.

18. *Mekhilta d'Rabbi Ishmael, Massekhta d'Shirta, parashah* 1, *Yalkut Shimoni*, vol. 1, *remazim* 241–242; and *Midrash ha-Gadol* and *Midrash Lekah Tov* to Exodus 15:1, among many parallel traditions.

19. *Or Hayyim* and *Me'am Lo'az* to Exodus 15:1.

20. For example, *Mekhilta d'Rabbi Ishmael, Massekhta d'Shirta, parashah* 1; *Yalkut Shimoni*, vol. 1, *remez* 241; and *Midrash ha-Gadol* to Exodus 15:1. See also Moshe Alshich's commentary to Exodus 15:1, in which he emphasizes that the words *va-yomru laimor,* "they said, saying," indicate that the People of Israel are not passive, but rather sing along with Moses.

21. Morrell and Capparell, *Shackleton's Way,* pp. 89–91.

22. *Midrash Va-Yosha.* See a re-creation of this midrash in Ginzberg's *Legends of the Jews,* vol. 3, pp. 33–34.

23. This tradition is cited very early, in *Sotah* 5:4, and is repeated in *Sotah* 6:2–4; P.T. *Sotah* 23c, and B.T. *Sotah* 27b and 30b. It is also found in many midrashic compilations, including *Shemot Rabbah* 23:9. See also Benno Jacob's commentary to Exodus 15:1.

24. See also, among several parallel traditions, *Mekhilta d'Rabbi Ishmael, Massekhta d'Shirta, parashah* 1; *Yalkut Shimoni*, vol. 1, *remez* 241; and *Midrash ha-Gadol* to Exodus 15:1.

25. See my *Self, Struggle and Change,* p. 25.

26. Woolfe, *Leadership Secrets in the Bible,* p. 202.

27. Among many sources, see *Mekhilta d'Rabbi Ishmael, Massekhta d'Shirta, parashah* 1; *Midrash Tanhuma ha-Nidpas Beshallah* 11; *Midrash ha-Gadol* to Exodus 15:1; and *Me'am Lo'az* to Exodus 15:1.

28. Philo, *De Vita Mosis,* 1, 180.

29. Noel Tichy, *The Leadership Engine* (New York: Harper Business, 1997), pp. 41, 85.

30. Note, for example, *Mekhilta d'Rabbi Ishmael, Massekhta d'Shirta, parashah* 10; the *Mekhilta d'Rabbi Shimon* to Exodus 15:21; *Pirkei d'Rabbi Eliezer,* chap. 42; and *Midrash ha-Gadol* to Exodus 15:21. This parallelism may, in part, stem from a literal reading of *Az yashir Moshe u-Venai Yisrael,* in which Bnai Yisrael is understood not as "the Children of Israel," but rather as "the sons of Israel." See also Zornberg, *The Particulars of Rapture,* p. 225; and Burton L. Visotzky, *The Road to Redemption* (New York: Crown Publishers, Inc., 1998), p. 138.

31. Note, among several parallel sources, B.T. *Megillah* 14a and *Sotah* 12b–13a.

32. Visotzky, *The Road to Redemption,* p. 137.

33. The text actually says, *ve-ta'an lehem Miriam,* Miriam responded to them, where the object is masculine, *lahem.* Why it isn't *lahen,* "to them"—the females—is not clear.

34. Benno Jacob's commentary to Exodus 15:21.

35. Sarna, *JPS Torah Commentary to Exodus* 15:20–21, which alludes to such traditions as found in *Sa'adia Gaon's Commentary* to Exodus 15:21; Rabbenu Bahya to Exodus 15:21; and Hizkuni to Exodus 15:21.

36. *Me'am Lo'az* to Exodus 15, 20–21.

37. Among many parallel citations, see *Mekhilta d'Rabbi Ishmael, Massekhta d'Shirta, parashah* 10; *Mekhilta d' Rabbi Shimon* to Exodus 15:20; *Pirkei d'Rabbi Elieizer,* chapter 42; Rashi to Exodus 15:20; and *Yalkut Shimoni,* vol. 1, *remez* 253.

38. Zornberg, *The Particulars of Rapture,* pp. 225–230.

39. B.T. *Ta'anit* 9a and *Bamidbar Rabbah* 1:2 and 19:23. See also Zornberg, *The Particulars of Rapture,* p. 232, concerning this tradition.

40. *Mekhilta d'Rabbi Ishmael, Massekhta d'Vayassa, parashah* 5.

41. See my *Self, Struggle and Change,* p. 25.

CHAPTER 6: WE CAN SURVIVE THE DESERT AND SWEETEN THE WATERS

1. Amos Hakham, *Sefer Shemot,* to Exodus 15:22.

2. Note the debate, which is ongoing, between Rabbi Joshua and Rabbi El'azar in the *Mekhilta d'Rabbi Ishmael, Massekhta d'Va-Yassa, parashah* 1 in this regard, which is quoted in a series of midrashic compilations over the centuries.

3. See, among many parallel texts, *Mekhilta d'Rabbi Shimon* to Exodus 15:22; *Midrash Tanhuma Buber, Beshallah* 16; and *Yalkut Shimoni,* vol. 1, *remez* 254.

4. Morrell and Capparell, *Shackleton's Way,* pp. 191–192.

5. *Mekhilta d'Rabbi Shimon* to Exodus 15:22; *Midrash Tanhuma Buber, Beshallah* 16; Rashi to Exodus 15:22; Keli Yakar to Exodus 15:22; *Midrash ha-Gadol* to Exodus 15:22; *Me'am Lo'az* to Exodus 15:22; and *Tzena U'Rena* to Exodus 15:22, just to mention a few sources.

6. See, for example, *Mekhilta d'Rabbi Ishmael, Massekhta d'Va-Yassa, parashah* 1, and *Shemot Rabbah* 24:2.

7. Hayward, *Churchill on Leadership,* p. 152.

8. The first time Shur is described in this manner appears in *Mekhilta d'Rabbi Issmael, Massekhta d'Va-Yassa, parashah* 1, but it is repeated many times over.

9. Meier, *Moses: The Prince, the Prophet*, p. 117. The notion of "three days" is commonly found in most narratives of the Ancient Near East as a measure of travel and distance, for example, in the Epic of Gilgamesh's story of the journey of Gilgamesh and Enkidu to the Forest of the Cedars. See Cassuto's comments on Exodus 15:22.

10. *Mekhilta d'Rabbi Ishmael, Massekhta d'Va-Yassa, parashah* 1; *Midrash Tanhuma ha-Nidpas, Beshallah* 19; *Yalkut Shimoni*, vol. 1, *remez* 254; and *Me'am Lo'az* to Exodus 15:22, among many parallels.

11. *Mekhilta d'Rabbi Ishmael*, and the *Mekhilta d'Rabbi Shimon* to Exodus 15:22.

12. See the description of the Israelites in Philo's *De Vita Mosis*, vol. 1, pp. 181–183, and in Josephus's *Jewish Antiquities* 3:1–3.

13. Zornberg, *The Particulars of Rapture*, p. 233, quoting *Mei Ha-Shiloach*.

14. "Leader as Social Advocate: Building the Business by Building the Community, An Interview with Anita Roddick," *Leader to Leader* (Summer 2000), p. 21.

15. Cassuto on Exodus 15:23 notes that Marah is identified with *Ein Hawwarah*, a pool of bitter water situated three days' journey from the Bitter Lakes.

16. See, for example, Psalms 78:40 and 107:7.

17. Daniel Boyarin, *Intertextuality and the Reading of Midrash* (Bloomington: Indiana University Press, 1990), pp. 59, 65.

18. Visotzky, *The Road to Redemption*, p. 145.

19. Note this controversy between Rabbi Joshua and Rabbi El'azar in *Mekhilta d'Rabbi Ishmael* as indicated in note 2 above, as well as in many subsequent parallels, including *Mekhilta d'Rabbi Shimon* to Exodus 15:24; *Midrash Tanhuma Buber Beshallah* 18; and *Midrash ha-Gadol* to Exodus 15:24. See also Daniel Boyarin's insightful analysis of this controversy in his *Intertextuality and the Reading of Midrash*, p. 60.

20. Josephus, *Jewish Antiquities*, 3:5–8; *Torat Moshe*, the Commentary of Moses Alshich on the Torah to Exodus 15:22; and Amos Hacham, *Sefer Shemot* to Exodus 15:24.

21. The verb used here is *va-yilonu* (they complained), which has as its root *lun*, which also means to "reside," "dwell," or "rest" in a certain place. The Israelites here "rest" all their burdens on Moses.

22. *Shemot Rabbah* 43:3.

23. Hayward, *Churchill on Leadership*, pp. 121, 129.

24. See *Torat Moshe* to Exodus 15:22. Moses Alshich states that this is the meaning of the seemingly redundant word *leimor*, meaning "saying," in verse 24: "And the people complained to Moses, saying."

25. See, for example, *Mekhilta d'Rabbi Ishmael, Massekhta d'Va-Yassa, parashah* 1.

26. Andrew Grove, "Strategic Inflection Points," *Leader to Leader* (Winter 1999): 17–18.

27. The notion that the waters are only temporarily bitter and can become sweet again accords with the view of Rabbi Joshua in the controversy with Rabbi El'azar in *Mekhilta d'Rabbi Ishmael, Massekhta d'Va-Yassa, parashah* 1, and its later parallels.

28. Morrell and Capparell, *Shackleton's Way*, pp. 191–192.

29. See the same *Mekhilta* passage we've cited with all of its parallels. Note especially, *Me'am Lo'az* to Exodus 15:25.

30. Plaut, *The Torah: A Modern Commentary*, p. 497, note 25.

31. In the *Mekhilta* tradition, it is the *Dorshei Reshumot*, seemingly ancient allegorists, to whom this figurative interpretation is attributed.

32. Throughout the ages, the Rabbis in the Midrash and biblical commentators attempt to identify which laws are actually conveyed to Israel at Marah, beginning in the *Mekhilta* passage that suggests that the *hukkim* are the laws of Shabbat and the *mishpatim* are laws about robbery, fines, and injuries.

33. Neff and Citrin, *Lessons from the Top*, p. 172.

34. See the comments of Rashi; *Me'am Lo'az*; and Amos Hacham, in his *Sefer Shemot*, to Exodus 15:25.

35. Note the discussion in the *Mekhilta d'Rabbi Ishmael* passage to which we have referred and its later parallels, in the name of Rabbi El'azer.

36. See, for example, Josephus, *Jewish Antiquities*, 3:8–12 and *Legends of the Jews*, vol. 3, p. 40.

37. *Mekhilta d'Rabbi Ishmael, Massekhta d'Va-Yassa, parashah* 2; *Midrash Aggadah* to Exodus 15:27; Rashi to Exodus 15:27; and *Tzena U'Rena, Beshallah*, to Exodus 15:27.

38. Philo, *De Vita Mosis*, vol. 1, pp. 188–189, and *Mekhilta d'Rabbi Ishmael*.

39. Nachshoni, *Studies in the Weekly Parashah*, to Exodus 15:27.

CHAPTER 7: THE BURDEN OF LEADERSHIP

1. Wiesel, *Messengers of God*, p. 197.

2. Leibowitz, *Studies in Shemot*, p. 273.

3. Sarna, *JPS Torah Commentary to Exodus* 17.

4. Ibid., 17:25.

5. Leibovitz, *Studies in Shemot*, pp. 273–274.

6. *Me'am Lo'az* to Exodus 17:3.

7. Zornberg, *The Particulars of Rapture,* pp. 236–237.

8. B.T. *Sanhedrin* 106a; *Midrash Lekah Tov* and *Midrash Sekhel Tov* to Exodus 17:1.

9. See, for example, *Yalkut Shimoni,* vol. 1, *remez* 261; Abraham Ibn Ezra to Exodus 17:2; and Hizkuni to Exodus 17:2.

10. Sforno to Exodus 17:2.

11. *Midrash Sekhel Tov* to Exodus 17:2.

12. *Yalkut Shimoni,* vol. 1, *remez* 261, and *Midrash ha-Gadol* to Exodus 17:2.

13. Zornberg, *The Particulars of Rapture,* pp. 237–239.

14. Visotzky, *The Road to Redemption,* p. 157.

15. For example, Deuteronomy 6:16 and 9:22.

16. The use of the two words/verbs—*massah* and *meribah*—indicates to the Rabbis that there were two groups of Israelites being described. See, in this regard, the comment of Abraham Ibn Ezra to Exodus 17:2.

17. Leibowitz, *Studies in Shemot,* p. 276, citing the *Ha'emak Davar.*

18. Morrell and Capparell, *Shackleton's Way,* pp. 186–187.

19. *Yalkut Shimoni,* vol. 1, *remez* 261; *Midrash ha-Gadol, Midrash Lekah Tov,* and *Midrash Sekhel Tov* to Exodus 17:4.

20. Leibovitz, *Studies in Shemot,* p. 278, and Meier, *Moses: The Prince and the Prophet,* p. 120.

21. Levering and Moskowitz, *The 100 Best Companies,* p. 80.

22. Hayward, *Churchill on Leadership,* pp. 117–118.

23. *Midrash Lekah Tov* and *Midrash Sekhel Tov* to Exodus 17:5.

24. Meier, *Moses: The Prince, the Prophet,* p. 120, and *Me'am Lo'az* to Exodus 17:5.

25. Morrell and Capparell, *Shackleton's Way,* p. 140.

26. *Midrash Tanhuma ha-Nidpas, Beshallah* 22.

27. *Or ha-Hayyim* to Exodus 17:5, as cited in Leibowitz, *Studies in Shemot,* p. 280, and the Ramban to Exodus 17:4.

28. Charles Pollard, "The Leader Who Serves," in Francis Hesselbein, Marshall Goldsmith, and Richard Beckhard, eds., *The Leader of the Future* (San Francisco: Jossey-Bass, 1996), pp. 244–248.

29. *Shemot Rabbah* 26:2 and *Midrash ha-Gadol* to Exodus 17:5.

30. *Yalkut Shimoni,* vol. 1, *remez* 261, and *Midrash ha-Gadol* to Exodus 17:4.

31. Rashi to Exodus 17:5, and *Shemot Rabbah* 26:2.

32. Deepak Sethi, "Learning from the Middle," *Leader to Leader* (Summer 2000): 6.

33. *Yalkut Shimoni,* vol. 1, *remez* 262; *Midrash ha-Gadol, Midrash Lekah Tov,* and *Midrash Sekhel Tov* to Exodus 17:6.

34. For example, Deuteronomy 32:18; 2 Samuel 22:3; and *Pirkei d'Rabbi Eliezer,* chap. 43.

35. For example, the Ramban and Rabbenu Bahya ben Asher to Exodus 17:6.

36. *Shemot Rabbah* 26:2.

37. Sarna, *JPS Torah Commentary to Exodus* 17:6.

38. Ibid., 17:5.

39. See, among many sources, Rashi to Exodus 17:5.

CHAPTER 8: THE LEADER NEEDS SUPPORT

1. *Mekhilta d'Rabbi Shimon* to Exodus 17:8; *Pesikta d'Rav Kahana, pisqa* 3:1; *Yalkut Shimoni,* vol. 1, *remez* 263; *Me'am Lo'az* to Exodus 17:8; and Zornberg, *The Particulars of Rapture,* p. 244.

2. This is an example of the rabbinic notion of *semichut,* contiguity means causality: The Israelites' statement of their lack of faith is followed in the very next biblical verse by the attack of the Amalekites. See, in this regard, among many parallel traditions, *Pesikta d'Rav Kahana, pisqa* 3:2; *Midrash Tanhuma ha-Nidpas, Beshallah* 25; *Pirkei d'Rabbi Eliezer,* chap. 44; *Shemot Rabbah* 26:2; and Visotzky, *The Road to Redemption,* p. 172.

3. Rashi to Exodus 17:8; *Shemot Rabbah* 26:2; *Me'am Lo'az* to Exodus 17:8; and Leibowitz, *Studies in Shemot,* p. 287, among many sources.

4. Sarna, *JPS Torah Commentary to Exodus* 17:8–17; Cassuto, *A Commentary on the Book of Exodus* 17:8, p. 204; and Amos Hacham, *Sefer Shemot,* to Exodus 17:8.

5. Moses Alshich's Commentary to Exodus 17:14.

6. See, for example, Ramban to Exodus 17:10, and Nachshoni, *Studies in the Weekly Parashah, Beshallah.*

7. Levering and Moskowitz, *The 100 Best Companies,* p. 138.

8. Visotzky, *The Road to Redemption,* p. 173.

9. Among many parallel traditions, see *Mekhilta d'Rabbi Ishmael, Massekhta d'Amalek, parashah* 1; *Avot d'Rabbi Natan, A,* chap. 27; *Midrash Tanhuma ha-Nidpas, Beshallah* 26; Rashi to Exodus 17:9; *Yalkut Shimoni,* vol.1, *remez* 63; *Midrash ha-Gadol* to Exodus 17:9;

Midrash Lekah Tov and *Midrash Sekhel Tov* to Exodus 17:9; and *Tzena U'Rena* to Exodus 17:9.

10. *Pesikta d'Rav Kahana, pisqa* 3:3.

11. Abraham Ibn Ezra to Exodus 17:9.

12. *Mekhilta d'Rabbi Ishmael, Massekhta d'Amalek, parashah* 1; and *Midrash Ha-Gadol* to Exodus 17:9.

13. Morrell and Capparell, *Shackleton's Way,* pp. 57–65.

14. See Rashi to Exodus 17:9; *Me'am Lo'az* to Exodus 17:9; and Amos Hacham, *Sefer Shemot,* to Exodus 17:9.

15. *Shemot Rabbah* 26:3; Rashi and Abraham Ibn Ezra to Exodus 17:14; and Visotzky, *The Road to Redemption,* pp. 173–174.

16. Dennis Carey and Dayton Ogden, *CEO Succession* (Oxford, UK: Oxford University Press, 2000), p. 15.

17. The *Mekhilta d'Rabbi Ishmael, Massekhta d'Amalek, parashah* 1; *Yalkut Shimoni,* vol. 1, *remez* 264; *Midrash Sekhel Tov* to Exodus 17:9; and Moshe Alshich's Commentary to Exodus 17:9.

18. Rashbam on Exodus 17:9; Nachshoni, *Studies in the Weekly Parashah, Beshallah;* and Sarna, *JPS Torah Commentary to Exodus* 17:11.

19. *The Anchor Bible* to Exodus 17:8–16, comment on Moses's gesture.

20. See *The Anchor Bible* to Exodus 17:11, Textual Notes.

21. These traditions all build on *Mishnah Rosh ha-Shanah* 3:8, and include *Mekhilta d'Rabbi Ishmael, Massekhta d'Amalek, parashah* 1; *Midrash Tanhuma ha-Nidpas, Beshallah* 27; *Yalkut Shimoni,* vol.1, *remez* 264; *Midrash Lekah Tov* and *Midrash Sekhel Tov* to Exodus 17:11; and such modern works as Zornberg, *The Particulars of Rapture,* p. 245, and Meier, *Moses: The Prince, the Prophet,* p. 130.

22. *The Anchor Bible* to Exodus 17:8–16, comment on Moses's gesture.

23. *Pesikta d'Rav Kahana, pisqa* 3:3; Ramban to Exodus 17:9; and *Me'am Lo'az* to Exodus 17:11–12.

24. James Kouzes and Barry Posner, *The Leadership Challenge* (San Francisco: Jossey-Bass, 1995), p. 37.

25. *Me'am Lo'az* to Exodus 17:11.

26. *Mekhilta d'Rabbi Shimon* to Exodus 17:11; *Pirkei d'Rabbi Eliezer,* chap. 44; *Midrash ha-Gadol* to Exodus 17:11; and Moshe Alshich's Commentary to Exodus 17:12.

27. Zornberg, *The Particulars of Rapture,* p. 245.

28. Amos Hacham, *Sefer Shemot,* to Exodus 17:12.

29. Woolfe, *Leadership Secrets from the Bible,* pp. 139–140.

30. Visotzky, *The Road to Redemption,* p. 177.

31. According to the Bible, Hur's lineage is not clear. However, he seems to be from the tribe of Judah, since he is in the line of Bezalel, as noted in Exodus 31:2. Therefore, King David is part of his progeny.

32. For example, *Mekhilta d'Rabbi Shimon* to Exodus 17:12 and *Midrash Tanhuma ha-Nidpas, Beshallah* 26.

33. This is a notion quoted throughout the rabbinic tradition, including *Mekhilta d'Rabbi Shimon* to Exodus 17:12; B.T. *Ta'anit* 11a; Rashi to Exodus 17:12; *Yalkut Shimoni*, vol. 1, *remez* 265; *Midrash ha-Gadol* to Exodus 17:12; *Tzena U'Rena* to Exodus 17:10; and *Me'am Lo'az* to Exodus 17:12.

34. Visotzky, *The Road to Redemption*, p. 177.

35. See, for example, *Mekhilta d'Rabbi Shimon* and *Midrash ha-Gadol* to Exodus 17:15.

36. Cassuto, *A Commentary on the Book of Exodus*, to Exodus 17:15, and *The Anchor Bible* to Exodus 17:14ff, Notes.

37. Among many sources, see Rashbam to Exodus 17:15 and *Me'am Lo'az* to Exodus 17:16.

38. *Pesikta d'Rav Kahana, pisqa* 3:16. Note the play on the odd phrasing of *midor dor*, instead of the expected form *midor ledor*, and therefore the interpretation of the two words (*midor dor*) as one verb, *medarder*.

39. Ramban to Exodus 17:16; *Me'am Lo'az* to Exodus 17:16; and Amos Hacham, *Sefer Shemot*, to the same verse.

CHAPTER 9: A KEY TO LEADERSHIP—EMPOWERMENT

1. Sforno to Exodus 18:14; Hizkuni to Exodus 18:14; and *Me'am Lo'az* to Exodus 18:17 and 22.

2. Ramban to Exodus 18:22.

3. *Midrash Tanhuma ha-Nidpas, Korah* 7; *Midrash Tanhuma Buber, Korah* 19; *Shemot Rabbah* 16:4; and *Bamidbar Rabbah* 18:10.

4. Neff and Citrin, *Lessons from the Top*, p. 66.

5. The biblical text goes out of its way to emphasize that Jethro witnesses Moses judging the people the very next day after his arrival in camp.

6. *Mekhilta d'Rabbi Ishmael, Massekhta d'Amalek, parashah* 4; *Mekhilta d'Rabbi Shimon* to Exodus 18:14; Rashi to Exodus 18:13; *Yalkut Shimoni*, vol. 1, *remez* 270; *Midrash ha-Gadol* to Exodus 18:14; *Midrash Lekah Tov* to Exodus 18:13; and *Me'am Lo'az* to Exodus 18:14.

7. *Mekhilta d'Rabbi Ishmael, Massekhta d'Amalek, parashah* 4; Rashi to Exodus 18:13; and B.T. *Shabbat* 10a.

8. Rashi to Exodus 18:14; Abraham Ibn Ezra to Exodus 18:14; Meier, *Moses: The Prince and the Prophet,* p. 137; and Zornberg, *The Particulars of Rapture,* p. 252.

9. See, most poignantly, *Me'am Lo'az* to Exodus 18:14.

10. See Rabbi Isaac Arama's Commentary, *Akeidat Yitzhak,* to Exodus 18.

11. Rashbam to Exodus 18:15; and Amos Hacham, *Sefer Shemot,* to Exodus 18:15.

12. Neff and Citrin, *Lessons from the Top,* p. 191.

13. *Me'am Lo'az* to Exodus 18:15–16.

14. Amos Hacham, *Sefer Shemot,* to Exodus 18:17.

15. See Josephus's description of Jethro's remarks in his *Antiquities* 3:67.

16. Rashbam to Exodus 18:18 and Hizkuni to Exodus 18:18.

17. *Mekhilta d'Rabbi Ishmael, Massekhta d'Amalek, parashah* 4, among several sources.

18. Rabbenu Bahya's Torah Commentary to Exodus 18:18.

19. *Mekhilta d'Rabbi Shimon* as well as *Midrash ha-Gadol* to Exodus 18:18.

20. Cassuto, *A Commentary on the Book of Exodus,* to Exodus 18:19.

21. *Mekhilta d'Rabbi Ishmael, Massekhta d'Amalek, parashah* 4.

22. Ramban to Exodus 18:22–23 and Amos Hacham, *Sefer Shemo,* to Exodus 18:22.

23. Morrell and Capparell, *Shackleton's Way,* p. 36.

24. Moshe Alshich's Commentary to Exodus 18:19, and, among many midrashic parallels, *Midrash ha-Gadol* to Exodus 18:21.

25. Senge, *The Fifth Discipline,* p. 319.

26. John Maxwell, *Developing the Leaders Around You* (Nashville: Thomas Nelson, 1995), p. 152.

27. Though the description *son'ei vatzah* literally means "those who hate ill-gotten gain," the Rabbis understand it more broadly. See, among many sources, *Mekhilta d'Shimon* to Exodus 18:21; and *Yalkut Shimoni,* vol. 1, *remez* 270.

28. B.T. *Eruvin* 100b; *Devarim Rabbah* 1:10; *Midrash Tannaim* 95; and Amos Hacham, *Sefer Shemot,* to Exodus 18:21.

29. Abraham Ibn Ezra and the Ramban to Exodus 18:21.

30. For example, *Mekhilta d'Rabbi Ishmael, Massekhta d'Amalek, parashah* 4; *Mekhilta d'Shimon* to Exodus 18:22; *Midrash ha-Gadol* to Exodus 18:22; and *Me'am Lo'az* to Exodus 18:21 and 22.

31. Hayward, *Churchill on Leadership,* pp. 62–63, 152–153.

32. Josephus, *Antiquities* 3, 4:1.

33. *Mekhilta d'Rabbi Ishmael, Massekhta d'Amalek, parashah* 4; B.T. *Sanhedrin* 18a; *Yalkut Shimoni,* vol. 1, *remez* 271; and *Midrash ha-Gadol* to Exodus 18:21.

34. Senge, *The Fifth Discipline,* p. 144.

35. See, for example, Ramban to Exodus 18:19; Rabbi Moshe Alshich's Commentary to Exodus 18:19; and *Me'am Lo'az* to Exodus 18:19.

36. Amos Hacham, *Sefer Shemot,* to Exodus 18:23, and Zornberg, *The Particulars of Rapture,* pp. 252–253.

37. *Managing People: 101 Proven Ideas* (Boston: Inc. Magazine, 1992), pp. 141–142.

38. Josephus, *Antiquities* 3, 73.

CHAPTER 10: THE LEADER'S VISION

1. Meier, *Moses: The Prince, the Prophet,* p. 140.

2. Ibid., p. 144.

3. Sarna, *JPS Torah Commentary to Exodus* 12:25.

4. Hizkuni to Exodus 19:3, and Amos Hacham, *Sefer Shemot,* to Exodus 19:3.

5. Hayward, *Churchill on Leadership,* pp. 25–26.

6. *Me'am Lo'az* to Exodus 19:3.

7. Rabbi Moshe Alshich's Commentary to Exodus 19:3.

8. Benno Jacob's Commentary on Exodus 19:3. The Rabbis emphasize that Moses is rewarded for every ascent and descent. See *Mekhilta d'Rabbi Ishmael, Massekhta d'Beshallah, parashah* 2.

9. *Me'am Lo'az* to Exodus 19:22.

10. Sforno to Exodus 19:9, and *Yalkut Shimoni,* vol. 1, *remez* 276.

11. *Midrash ha-Gadol* to Exodus 19:19.

12. Morrell and Capparell, *Shackleton's Way,* p. 191.

13. See Rashi to Exodus 19:19, based on *Mekhilta d'Rabbi Ishmael, Massekhta d' Bahodesh, parashah* 4.

14. See, among many traditions, Rashi to Exodus 19:2; *Midrash Tanhuma Buber, Yitro* 9; *Pirkei d'Rabbi Eliezer,* chap. 41; *Yalkut Shimoni,* vol. 1, *remez* 273; and especially *Me'am Lo'az* to Exodus 19:2.

15. Benno Jacob's Commentary on Exodus 19:8.

16. *Mekhilta d'Rabbi Ishmael, Massekhta d'Bahodesh, parashah* 2.

17. See, for example, Amos Hacham, *Sefer Shemot,* to Exodus 19:4.

18. Woolfe, *Leadership Secrets from the Bible,* p. 90.

19. Among many parallel texts throughout the breadth of the rabbinic tradition, see *Mekhilta d'Rabbi Ishmael, Massekhta d'Bahodesh, parashah* 2; Rashi to Exodus 19:3; *Yalkut Shimoni,* vol. 1, *remez* 276; *Midrash Lekah Tov, Midrash Sekhel Tov,* and *Midrash Aggadah* to Exodus 19:3.

20. *Me'am Lo'az* to Exodus 19:3.

21. *Shemot Rabbah* 28:2 and *Tzena U'Rena* to Exodus 19:3.

22. *Midrash Lekah Tov* to Exodus 19:7 and the Ramban to 19:8.

23. *Midrash Ha-Gadol* to Exodus 19:7; Abraham Ibn Ezra to Exodus 19:3; Benno Jacob's Commentary on Exodus 19:7; and Sarna, *JPS Torah Commentary to Exodus* 19:7.

24. *Me'am Lo'az* to Exodus 19:7. Benno Jacob's Commentary on Exodus 19:7; and Visotzky, *The Road to Redemption,* p. 209.

25. Hayward, *Churchill on Leadership,* pp. 68–69.

26. *Midrash ha-Hefetz* to Exodus 19:17, and Hizkuni to 19:17.

27. Benno Jacob's Commentary to Exodus 19:17.

28. Benno Jacob, Ibid., and *Pirkei d'Rabbi Eliezer,* chap. 41.

29. *Midrash ha-Hefetz* to Exodus 19:24, and especially, Zornberg, *The Particulars of Rapture,* pp. 261–262.

30. Sforno to Exodus 19:21.

31. Among many parallel traditions, see *Yalkut Shimoni,* vol. 1, *remez* 285.

32. Rashi to Exodus 19:23; Rashbam to Exodus 19:24; and *Me'am Lo'az* to Exodus 19:24.

33. B.T. *Shabbat* 86b.

34. See, among several parallel traditions, *Yalkut Shimoni,* vol. 1, *remez* 276; *Midrash ha-Gadol* to Exodus 19:5; and *Midrash Sekhel Tov* to Exodus 19:5.

35. Benno Jacob's Commentary on Exodus 19:3.

36. *Midrash ha-Gadol* to Exodus 19:9. This midrash plays on the seemingly superfluous word *kol* used in verse 19, which some translations render as "thunder."

37. *Yalkut Shimoni,* vol. 1, *remez* 276.

38. *Me'am Lo'az* to Exodus 19:9.

39. Sforno to Exodus 19:8; Hizkuni to Exodus 19:8; and Benno Jacob's Commentary on Exodus 19:8–9.

40. Rashi to Exodus 19:9; *Midrash Sekhel Tov* to Exodus 9:9; *Midrash Aggadah* to Exodus 19:8; *Tzena U'Rena* to Exodus 19:7; *Me'am Lo'az* to Exodus 19:8; and Zornberg, *The Particulars of Rapture,* p. 259.

41. Zornberg, *The Particulars of Rapture,* p. 259.

42. Neff and Citrin, *Lessons from the Top,* p. 291.

43. See *Mekhilta d'Rabbi Ishmael, Massekhta d' Beshallah, parashah* 2; Rashi; Ramban; *Midrash Lekah Tov;* and the *Midrash ha-Gadol* to Exodus 19:14.

44. *Me'am Lo'az* to Exodus 19:14.

45. We see this clearly in *Pirkei d'Rabbi Eliezer,* chap. 41, and Sforno to Exodus 19:24.

46. *Shemot Rabbah* 28:3; *Akeidat Yitzhak,* chap. 44; and Moshe Alshich's Commentary to Exodus 19:21–24.

47. Levering and Moskowitz, *The 100 Best Companies,* p. 122.

CHAPTER 11: IN THE FACE OF CHALLENGE AND REJECTION

1. Zornberg, *The Particulars of Rapture,* pp. 400–401.

2. Rashi to Exodus 32:1.

3. Zornberg, *The Particulars of Rapture,* p. 407.

4. Ramban on Exodus 32:1.

5. *Me'am Lo'az* to Exodus 32:5–6 and Hizkuni to Exodus 32:1.

6. Yehuda ha-Levi, *Kuzari,* 1:97; and *Pirkei d'Rabbi Eliezer,* chap. 45.

7. Zornberg, *The Particulars of Rapture,* pp. 409–411.

8. *Meshech Chochmah* to Exodus 32:19 and Zornberg, *The Particulars of Rapture,* p. 403.

9. Hizkuni to Exodus 32: 4.

10. Among many parallel traditions, see *Tanhuma ha-Nidpas, Tezaveh* 11; *Bamidbar Rabbah* 15:21; and *Me'am Lo'az* to Exodus 32:1.

11. Woolfe, *Leadership Secrets from the Bible,* p. 154.

12. Meier, *Moses: The Prince, the Prophet,* p. 158.

13. Hayward, *Churchill on Leadership,* pp.445–446, 449.

14. B.T. *Sanhedrin* 7a; *Vayikra Rabbah* 10:3; and *Tanhuma ha-Nidpas, Ki Tissa* 19, among several parallel traditions.

15. *Vayikra Rabbah* 10:3; Rashi to Exodus 32:5; *Shemot Rabbah* 37:2; and *Me'am Lo'az* to Exodus 32:2–5.

16. Hizkuni to Exodus 32:5.

17. *Shemot Rabbah* 42:8.

18. For example, B.T. *Berachot* 32b; *Pirkei d'Rabbi Eliezer,* chap. 45; and Rashi to Exodus 32:7.

19. *Shemot Rabbah* 42:2.

20. *Pesikta Rabbati* 10:6.

21. Zornberg, *The Particulars of Rapture,* p. 415.

22. *Midrash Tanhuma ha-Nidpas, Beshallah* 22.

23. Cassuto, *A Commentary on the Book of Exodus* 32:8, and Nehama Leibowitz, *Studies in Shemot, Ki Tissa* 3.

24. *Yalkut Shimoni,* vol. 1, *remez* 391; *Midrash ha-Gadol* to Exodus 32:7; and *Me'am Lo'az* to Exodus 32:10.

25. Among many parallel versions, see *Devarim Rabbah* 3:15; Rashi to Exodus 32:10; Sarna, *JPS Torah Commentary to Exodus* 32:10; and Zornberg, *The Particulars of Rapture,* p. 413.

26. *Shemot Rabbah* 42:9.

27. See, for example, B.T. *Berachot* 32a; and *Yalkut Shimoni,* vol. 1, *remez* 391.

28. Cassuto, *A Commentary on the Book of Exodus* 32:12.

29. *Pirkei d'Rabbi Eliezer,* chap. 45; *Shemot Rabbah* 46:4; *Midrash Aggadah* to Exodus 32:7; and *Me'am Lo'az* to Exodus 32:7.

30. *Midrash Aggadah* to Exodus 32:11.

31. See, for example, Abravanel to Exodus 32: 11.

32. *Shemot Rabbah* 43:7.

33. *Midrash ha-Gadol* to Exodus 32:11.

34. Leibowitz, *Studies in Exodus, Ki Tissa* 2.

35. *Shemot Rabbah* 43:9; *Tzena U'Rena, Ki Tissa.*

36. *Deuteronomy Rabbah* 3:11; *Yalkut Shimoni,* vol. 1, *remez* 392; *Me'am Lo'az* to Exodus 32:19; and Leibovitz, *Studies in Exodus, Ki Tissa* 5.

37. Sforno to Exodus 32:19; and Isaac Arama, *Akeidat Yitzhak,* to Exodus 32.

38. *Shemot Rabbah* 43:6; *Bamidbar Rabbah* 2:15; and *Midrash ha-Gadol* to Exodus 32:11.

39. Zornberg, *The Particulars of Rapture,* p. 421.

40. *Shemot Rabbah* 43:3; Cassuto, *A Commentary on the Book of Exodus* 32:11; Wiesel, *Messengers of God,* p. 198; and Zornberg, *The Particulars of Rapture,* p. 417.

41. Hayward, *Churchill on Leadership,* p. 125.

42. Zornberg, *The Particulars of Rapture,* p.424.

43. *Shemot Rabbah* 43:1; and *Midrash ha-Gadol* to Exodus 32:19.

44. Sforno to Exodus 32:15; and Leibovitz, *Studies in Exodus, Ki Tissa* 5.

45. *Shemot Rabbah* 46:1.

46. Lewis, *Models and Meanings in the History of Jewish Leadership,* p. 13.

47. Woolfe, *Leadership Secrets from the Bible,* p. 116.

48. *Pesikta Rabbati* 22:4; and *Yalkut Shimoni,* vol. 1, *remez* 391.

49. Rashi to Exodus 32:32.

50. *Me'am Lo'az* to Exodus 32:32.

51. Ramban and Rashbam to Exodus 32:32.

52. See, for example, Sforno and Abravanel to Exodus 32:32; Saadia Gaon's Commentary to Job 251; and *Me'am Lo'az* to Exodus 32:33.

53. *Midrash Tanhuma ha-Nidpas, Ki Tissa* 21; Rashi to Exodus 32:7; and *Me'am Lo'az* to Exodus 32:5.

54. Cassuto, *A Commentary on the Book of Exodus* 32:30.

55. *Tzena U'Rena, Ki Tissa.*

56. Ramban to Exodus 32:18.

CHAPTER 12: HEARING CRITICISM—KNOWING HOW TO RESPOND

1. Isaac Arama, *Akeidat Yitzhak* to parashat *Beha'alotecha,* and the comments of Martin Noth, *Numbers: A Commentary* (Philadelphia: The Westminster Press, 1968), p. 93.

2. Milgrom, *JPS Torah Commentary to Numbers* 12:1 (Philadelphia: Jewish Publication Society, 1990).

3. Yehiel Tzvi Moskovitz, *Sefer Bamidbar* (Jerusalem: Mosad ha-Rav Kook, 1988), to Numbers 12:1.

4. *Sifrei Bamidbar, pisqa* 99; Rashi to Numbers 12:1; *Yalkut Shimoni,* vol. 1, *remez* 738; *Midrash Lekah Tov* to Numbers 12:1; and *Me'am Lo'az* to Numbers 12:2.

5. See, for example, *Avot de-Rabbi Natan,* A, chap. 9, and *Midrash ha-Gadol* to Numbers 12:1.

6. *Sifrei Bamidbar, pisqa* 99; Abraham Ibn Ezra to Numbers 12:1; and Leibowitz, *Studies in Bamidbar,* p. 29.

7. See, for example, Josephus, *Jewish Antiquities,* vol. 2: 243–253.

8. *Sifrei Bamidbar pisqa* 99; Rashi to Numbers 12:1; *Yalkut Shimoni,* vol. 1, *remez* 738; Noth, *Numbers: A Commentary,* p. 94; and Milgrom, *JPS Torah Commentary to Numbers* 12:1.

9. Milgrom, *JPS Torah Commentary to Numbers.*

10. Noth, *Numbers: A Commentary,* pp. 92–93.

11. *Avot d'Rabbi Natan,* A, chap. 9.

12. See Hizkuni's comment on Numbers 12:2, which alludes to Miriam's prophecy of Moses's birth, e.g., *Shemot Rabbah* 1:22.

13. See also *Devarim Rabbah* 11:10 and *Midrash Tanhuma Buber, Metzorah* 6.

14. Note, in this regard, *Sifrei Bamidbar, pisqa* 99; *Yalkut Shimoni,* vol. 1, *remez* 738; *Tzena U'Rena* to Numbers 12:1; and *Me'am Lo'az* to Numbers 12:1.

15. *Sifrei Zuta* to Numbers 12:1; *Midrash Lekah Tov* to Numbers 12:2; and *Midrash Aggadah* to Numbers 12:1.
16. *Sifrei Bamidbar, pisqa* 99; and *Yalkut Shimoni*, vol. 1, *remez* 738.
17. Milgrom, *JPS Torah Commentary to Numbers* 12:1
18. Hayward, *Churchill on Leadership*, pp. 45–51.
19. *Midrash Tanhuma ha-Nidpas, Mezorah* 2; Alshich's comments on Numbers 12:2; and Noth, *Numbers: A Commentary*, p. 94.
20. *Avot d'Rabbi Natan*, A, chap. 9; and *Tzena U'Rena* to Numbers, *Parashah Beha'alotecha*.
21. Moskovitz, *Sefer Bamidbar* to Numbers 12:3.
22. See *Me'am Lo'az* to Numbers 12:3, which spotlights the connection between *anav* and *anah*.
23. *Mekhilta d'Rabbi Ishmael, Massekhta d'Bahodesh, parashah* 9.
24. Patrick Lencioni, "The Trouble with Humility," *Leader to Leader* (Winter 1999): 44.
25. *Sifrei Bamidbar, pisqa* 100; Ramban to Numbers 12:3; *Yalkut Shimoni*, vol. 1, *remez* 738; *Midrash ha-Gadol* to Numbers 12:2; and *Midrash Aggadah* to Numbers 12:3, among many other parallels.
26. The Rabbis make a point of stressing Moses's sensitivity to Miriam (and, by extension, to Aaron), when afterwards, he prays on her behalf. See, for example, *Sifrei Bamidbar, pisqa* 105.
27. Moscovitz, *Sefer Bamidbar* to Numbers 12:6.
28. *Sifrei Bamidbar, pisqa* 103.
29. Morrell and Capparrell, *Shackleton's Way*, p. 84.
30. *Sifrei Zuta* to Numbers 12:9.
31. *Sifrei Bamidbar, pisqaot* 104–105; and *Avot d'Rabbi Natan*, A, chap. 9.
32. *Midrash Rabbenu Bahya ben Asher* to Numbers 12:1.
33. B.T. *Shabbat* 97a.
34. *Me'am Lo'az* to Numbers 12:11; Alshich's Commentary to Numbers 12:9.
35. *Avot d'Rabbi Natan*, A, chap. 9.
36. Noth, *Numbers: A Commentary*, pp. 94–95.
37. *Sifrei Zuta* to Numbers 12:13 and *Midrash ha-Gadol* to Numbers 12:13.
38. Abraham Ibn Ezra to Numbers 12;13; *Midrash Rabbenu Bachya* to Numbers 12:13; and Ginzberg, *Legends of the Jews*, vol. 3, p. 200.
39. Milgrom, *JPS Torah Commentary to Numbers* 12:13.
40. Hizkuni to Numbers 12:13.
41. Morrell and Capparrell, *Shackleton's Way*, p. 48.

42. *Sifrei Bamidbar, pisqaot* 105–106; and *Avot d'Rabbi Natan,* A, chap. 9.

43. *Sifrei Bamidbar, pisqa* 105; Rashi to Numbers 12:13; and *Yalkut Shimoni,* vol. 1, *remez* 742.

44. *Midrash Aggadah* to Numbers 12:13; Alshich's Commentary to Numbers 12:13; and Noth, *Numbers: A Commentary,* p. 97.

45. Levering and Moskowitz, *The 100 Best Companies,* p. 408.

46. *Sifrei Bamidbar, pisqa* 106; *Sifrei Zuta* to Numbers 12:15; B.T. *Sotah* 9b; and *Midrash ha-Gadol* to Numbers 12:15.

CHAPTER 13: MAKING TOUGH DECISIONS; MEETING CHALLENGES

1. Milgrom, *JPS Torah Commentary to Numbers* 16:2.

2. *Bamidbar Rabbah* 18:5 and *Me'am Lo'az* to Numbers 16:4.

3. Noth, *Numbers: A Commentary,* p. 121.

4. Nachshoni, *Studies in the Weekly Parashah, Korah.* The two motives are embraced in the commentaries of Abraham Ibn Ezra and the Ramban.

5. Plaut, *The Torah,* p. 1131.

6. Milgrom, *JPS Torah Commentary to Numbers* 16:2, who points out that Zelophedad, the Manassahite chieftain, does not join the rebellion as implied in Numbers 27:3.

7. Alshich's Commentary to Numbers 16:1.

8. Noth, *Numbers: A Commentary,* p. 124.

9. *Yalkut Shimoni,* vol. 1, *remez* 750; and *Midrash ha-Gadol* to Numbers 16:19.

10. Noel Tichy, *The Leadership Engine* (New York: Harper Business, 1977), pp. 125–126.

11. Josephus, *Jewish Antiquities* 4, 36–37; and the Ramban to Numbers 16:14.

12. Milgrom, *JPS Torah Commentary to Numbers* 16:1; Josephus, *Jewish Antiquities,* 4:19–20; *Bamidbar Rabbah* 18:2; Rashi to Numbers 16:1; and *Yalkut Shimoni,* vol. 1, *remez* 750. See the genealogical chart of the Kohat line in Exodus 6:16–22.

13. Rashi to Numbers 16:3, quoting *Tanhuma ha-Nidpas.*

14. Josephus, *Jewish Antiquities,* 4:14; B.T. *Pesachim* 119b; *Bamidbar Rabbah* 18:16; and *Midrash ha-Gadol* to Numbers 16:1.

15. *Midrash Tanhuma Buber, Korah* 12; *Bamidbar Rabbah* 18:8; and *Me'am Lo'az* to Numbers 16:8.

16. *Targum Onkolos* to Numbers 16:1; *Midrash Tanhuma Buber, Korah* 5; Rashi and Ramban to Numbers 16:1.

17. *Bamidbar Rabbah* 18:3.

18. Plaut, *The Torah, Gleanings,* p. 1134.

19. *Midrash Tanhuma Buber, Korah* 2; Rashi to Numbers 16:1; and *Bamidbar Rabbah* 18:2, among many other traditions.

20. Milgrom, *JPS Torah Commentary to Numbers* 16:1 and Hizkuni's commentary to Numbers 16:2.

21. Plaut, *The Torah,* pp. 1132–1133.

22. Rashi to Numbers 16:19 and *Me'am Lo'az* to Numbers 16:16–18.

23. *Bamidbar Rabbah* 18:10. See also Isaac Arama's commentary, *Akeidat Yitzhak* to *Parashat Korah* and *Me'am Lo'az* to Numbers 16:3.

24. Milgrom, *JPS Torah Commentary to Numbers,* 16:14; and *Me'am Lo'az* to Numbers 16:14.

25. Arama, *Akeidat Yitzhak* to *Parashat Korah.*

26. *Yalkut Shimoni,* vol. 1, *remez* 750; *Midrash Aggadah* to Numbers 16:19; and *Me'am Lo'az* to Numbers 16:1.

27. Ramban to Numbers 16:3.

28. Josephus, *Jewish Antiquities,* 4:59–60; Sforno to Numbers 16:2; and *Me'am Lo'az* to Numbers 16:20–22.

29. Josephus, *Jewish Antiquities,* 4:20–23; and *Bamidbar Rabbah* 18:4.

30. Sforno to Numbers 16:15.

31. Milgrom, *JPS Torah Commentary to Numbers* 16:8.

32. Rashi to Numbers 16:8, 12; and Ramban to Numbers 16:12; and *Midrash ha-Gadol* to Numbers 16:8.

33. Arama's *Akeidat Yitzhak* on *Parashat Korah,* and the Alshich's commentary to Numbers 16:1.

34. Josephus, *Jewish Antiquities,* 4:24–25.

35. Ramban to Numbers 16:4 and the Alshich's commentary to Numbers 16:8.

36. Rashi to Numbers 16:5; and *Bamidbar Rabbah* 18:7.

37. Ramban and *Midrash Aggadah* to Numbers 16:25.

38. Rashi and *Bamidar Rabbah,* 18:7.

39. Hayward, *Churchill on Leadership,* pp. 118–119.

40. *Midrash Tanhuma ha-Nidpas, Korah* 6; *Midrash Tanhuma Buber, Korah,* 15; and *Bamidbar Rabbah* 18:9.

41. *Yalkut Shimoni,* vol. 1, *remez* 750.

42. *Bamidbar Rabbah* 18:9; and Isaac Arama, *Akeidat Yitzhak* on *Parashat Korah.*

43. Nachshoni, *Studies in the Weekly Parashah, Korah; Yalkut Shimoni,* vol. 1, *remez* 750; and *Me'am Lo'az* to Numbers 16:11.

44. Levering and Moskowitz, *The 100 Best Companies*, p. 223.
45. Noth, *Numbers: A Commentary*, p. 127; and *Me'am Lo'az* to Numbers 16:25.
46. Alshich's Commentary to Numbers 16:25.
47. Josephus, *Jewish Antiquities*, 4:46–49.
48. Rashi to Numbers 16:15; *Yalkut Shimoni*, vol. 1, *remez* 750; and *Midrash ha-Gadol* to Numbers 16:25.
49. Noel Tichy, *The Leadership Engine*, pp. 113–114.
50. Noth, *Numbers: A Commentary*, p. 129.
51. *Bamidbar Rabbah* 18:10.
52. Arama, *Akeidat Yitzhak* on *Parashat Korah*.
53. Milgrom, *JPS Torah Commentary to Numbers* 16:6.
54. Ibid., 17:5.
55. Neff and Citrin, *Lessons from the Top*, p. 278.
56. *Me'am Lo'az* to Numbers 16, "Beur."

CHAPTER 14: BALANCING THE PERSONAL AND THE PROFESSIONAL

1. Micah 6:4.
2. B.T. *Ta'anit* 9a; *Yalkut Shimoni*, vol. 1, *remez* 763; *Midrash Aggadah* to Numbers 20:2; and *Me'am Lo'az* to Numbers 20:1.
3. B.T. *Moed Katan* 28a; Rashi to Numbers 20:1; *Yalkut Shimoni*, vol. 1, *remez* 763; and *Tzena U'Rena* to Numbers, *Parashat Hukkat*.
4. For example, Rashi to Numbers 20:1.
5. B.T. *Ta'anit* 9a and *Midrash ha-Gadol* to Numbers 20:1, to name just two of many sources.
6. Rambam and Hizkuni to Numbers 20:1; and Milgrom, *JPS Torah Commentary to Numbers* 20:1.
7. For example, Rashbam to Numbers 20:1.
8. For example, Rashi to Numbers 20:2; and *Yalkut Shimoni*, vol. 1, *remez* 763.
9. See above, chapter 5. Note also *Mekhilta d'Rabbi Ishmael, Va-Yassa, parashah* 5; and *Midrash ha-Gadol* to Numbers 21:16.
10. Abraham Ibn Ezra to Numbers 20:1.
11. *Yalkut Shimoni*, vol. 1, *remez* 763; Alshich's commentary to Numbers 20:1; and *Me'am Lo'az* to Numbers 20:1.
12. Ginzberg, *Legends of the Jews*, vol. 3, pp. 310, 317–318; and *Tzena U'Rena* to Numbers, *Parashat Hukkat*.
13. Morrell and Capparell, *Shackleton's Way*, pp. 186–87.

14. Abraham Ibn Ezra to Numbers 20:6; *Yalkut Shimoni,* vol. 1, *remez* 763; and *Midrash ha-Gadol* to Numbers 20:6.

15. Lewis, *Models and Meanings in the History of Jewish Leadership,* p. 18.

16. Hayward, *Churchill on Leadership,* pp. 148–149.

17. For example, *Yalkut Shimoni,* vol. 1, *remez* 763.

18. *Midrash ha-Gadol* to Numbers 20:7.

19. *Yalkut Shimoni,* vol. 1, *remez* 763; and *Tzena U'Rena* to *Parashat Hukkat.*

20. Neff and Citrin, *Lessons from the Top,* p. 191.

21. Rashbam to Numbers 20:12 and *Me'am Lo'az* to Numbers 20:11. Martin Noth, in his *Numbers: A Commentary,* as other modern Bible scholars, notes the parallelism with Exodus 17:17 and the striking of the rock.

22. See, for example, *Midrash Lekah Tov* to Numbers 21:11.

23. *Yalkut Shimoni,* vol. 1, *remez* 763; and Alshich's comments to Numbers 20:8.

24. *Midrash Tanhuma ha-Nidpas, Hukkat* 29; *Midrash Tanhuma Buber, Hukkat* 9; and *Yalkut Shimoni,* vol. 1, *remez* 763.

25. *Midrash ha-Gadol* to Numbers 20:10.

26. *Bamidbar Rabbah* 19:9; Rashi and *Midrash Aggadah* to Numbers 20:10.

27. Morrell and Capparell, *Shackleton's Way,* pp. 191–192.

28. For example, Sforno to Numbers 20:8 and the Alshich's commentary to Numbers 20:8.

29. *Yalkut Shimoni,* vol. 1, *remez* 763; and Hizkuni to Numbers 20:9.

30. *Midrash Tanhuma ha-Nidpas, Hukkat* 10; *Midrash Tanhuma Buber, Hukkat* 31; and *Tzena U'Rena* to *Parashat Hukkat.*

31. *Bereshit Rabbah* 99:5; Ramban to Numbers 20:10; *Yalkut Shimoni,* vol. 1, *remez* 763; and *Midrash ha-Gadol* to Numbers 20:12.

32. *Midrash Petirat Aharon.*

33. "Leading through Rough Times: An Interview with Novell's Eric Schmidt," *Harvard Business Review* (March 2001), pp. 116–123.

34. *Vayikra Rabbah* 13:1.

35. Milgrom, *JPS Torah Commentary to Numbers* 20:13.

36. *Bamidbar Rabbah* 19:13–14; Ramban to Numbers 20:13; Alshich's commentary to Numbers 20:8; and *Tzena U'Rena* to Numbers 20:13.

37. According to the Rabbis, God performs miracles for the People of Israel at the Arnon similar to those that they have experienced at the Red Sea. See, for example, *Midrash Tanhuma ha-Nidpas, Hukkat* 20; *Midrash Tanhuma Buber, Hukkat* 47; and *Yalkut Shimoni,* vol. 1, *remez* 764.

This tradition seems to anticipate the repetition of wording found in the Song at the Sea here in Numbers 21 at Be'er.

38. Rashi to Numbers 21:17.
39. *Midrash Tanhuma ha-Nidpas, Hukkat* 21; *Yalkut Shimoni,* vol. 1, *remez* 764; and Alshich's commentary to Numbers 20:8.
40. *Midrash Lekah Tov* to Numbers 21:17.
41. *Bamidbar Rabbah* 19:26.
42. Rashi and *Midrash Lekah Tov* to Numbers 21:18.
43. B.T. *Shabbat* 35a.

CHAPTER 15: LEADERS STRUGGLE WITH THEIR MORTALITY

1. Jeffrey Tigay, *JPS Torah Commentary to Deuteronomy* 3:25 (Philadelphia: Jewish Publication Society, 1996); and *Yalkut Shimoni,* vol. 1, *remez* 811.
2. Nachshoni, *Studies in the Weekly Parashah, Ve-Ethanan.*
3. *Me'am Lo'az* to Deuteronomy 3:24–25.
4. *Devarim Rabbah* 2:1,7; *Midrash Tanhuma ha-Nidpas, Ve-Ethanan* 3; *Midrash ha-Gadol* to Deuteronomy 3:24; and *Midrash Aggadah* to Deuteronomy 3:26.
5. Rashi to Deuteronomy 3:26; *Midrash Rabbenu Bahya ben Asher* to Deuteronomy 3:26; and *Me'am Lo'az* to Deuteronomy 3:26.
6. Nachshoni, *Studies in the Weekly Parashah, Ve-Ethanan.*
7. For example, *Yalkut Shimoni,* vol. 1, *remez* 816.
8. *Devarim Rabbah* 2:6, based on a play on the seeming superfluous word *leimor* in the phrase, "I pleaded with Adonai ... saying (*leimor*)" in Deuteronomy 3:23.
9. *Me'am Lo'az* to Deuteronomy 3:23.
10. Rashi and *Midrash Rabbenu Bahya* to Deuteronomy 3:23.
11. *Devarim Rabbah* 11:1 and *Midrash Petirat Moshe.*
12. *Devarim Rabbah* 2:5; *Ramban to Deuteronomy* 3:23; *Yalkut Shimoni,* vol. 1, *remez* 812; and Nachshoni, *Studies in the Weekly Parashah, Ve-Ethanan.*
13. *Devarim Rabbah* 2:4 and *Me'am Lo'az* to Deuteronomy 3:23.
14. *Midrash Tanhuma ha-Nidpas, Ve-Ethanan* 6; and *Midrash Tanhuma Buber, Ve-Ethanan* 6.
15. *Devarim Rabbah* 2:3.
16. Janet Lowe, *Jack Welch Speaks* (New York: John Wiley & Sons, 2001), p. 202.

17. Tigay, *JPS Torah Commentary to Deuteronomy* 3:23–26a.

18. *Pirkei d'Rabbi Eliezer,* chap. 45.

19. *Sifrei Bamidbar, pisqa* 135; Rashi to Deuteronomy 3:26; and *Midrash Petirat Moshe.*

20. *Midrash Aggadah* to Deuteronomy 3:26.

21. Morrell and Capparell, *Shackleton's Way,* p. 207.

22. *Yalkut Shimoni,* vol. 1, *remez* 817; Isaac Arama, *Akeidat Yitzhak, Ve-Ethanan;* and Nachshoni, *Studies in the Weekly Parashah, Ve-Ethanan.*

23. *Midrash Tanhuma ha-Nidpas, Ve-Ethanan* 6; *Midrash Tanhuma Buber, Ve-Ethanan* 6; *Yalkut Shimoni,* vol. 1, *remez* 820–821; *Midrash ha-Gadol* to Deuteronomy 3:24; and *Me'am Lo'az* to Deuteronomy 3:24.

24. *Sifrei Devarim, pisqa* 27; and *Me'am Lo'az* to Deuteronomy 3:23.

25. See, for example, *Yalkut Shimoni,* vol. 1, *remez* 820–821, among several sources.

26. *Yalkut Shimoni,* vol. 1, *remez* 817.

27. Meier, *Moses: The Prince, the Prophet,* p. 164.

28. *Yalkut Shimoni,* vol. 1, *remez* 819; and Aaron Wildavsky, *The Nursing Father: Moses as a Political Leader* (Birmingham: The University of Alabama Press, 1984), p. 166.

29. Dave Ulrich, Jack Zenger, and Norm Smallwood, *Results-Based Leadership* (Boston: Harvard Business School Press, 1999), p. 214.

30. Isaac Arama, *Akeidat Yitzhak, Ve-Ethanan;* and Wildavsky, *Nursing Father,* p. 165.

31. For example, Rashi to Deuteronomy 3:28; and Wildavsky, *The Nursing Father,* p. 143.

32. *Bamidbar Rabbah* 7:6 and *Me'am Lo'az* to Deuteronomy 3:28.

33. Hesselbein, Goldsmith, and Beckhard, eds., *The Leader of the Future* (San Francisco: Jossey-Bass, 1996), p. 258.

34. *Sifrei Bamidbar, pisqa* 135; and Nachshoni, *Studies in the Weekly Parashah, Ve-Ethanan.*

35. *Tzena U'Rena* to *Parashat Ve'Ethanan.*

36. Woolfe, *Leadership Secrets from the Bible,* p. 215.

37. This midrash is a composite based on several compilations, including *Devarim Rabbah* 11:10 and *Midrash Petirat Moshe.*

38. Elisabeth Kübler-Ross, *On Death and Dying* (New York: Touchtone Press, 1969).

39. Wildavsky, *Nursing Father,* pp. 150–151.

CHAPTER 16: RAISING UP THE NEXT GENERATION OF LEADERS

1. Lewis, *Models and Meanings in the History of Jewish Leadership,* p. 20. As early as the Israelites' battle with the Amalekites in Exodus 17, Joshua already is charged with significant responsibility.

2. Ibid., p. 22.

3. Rashi to Deuteronomy 31:2.

4. Woolfe, *Leadership Secrets from the Bible,* p. 214.

5. Tigay, *JPS Torah Commentary* to Deuteronomy 31:1–6.

6. Josephus, *Jewish Antiquities* 4:177–179; and *Me'am Lo'az* to Deuteronomy 31:1.

7. Morrell and Capparell, *Shackleton's Way,* p. 196.

8. Josephus, *Jewish Antiquities* 4:320–323.

9. For example, Ibn Ezra and *Me'am Lo'az* to Deuteronomy 31:1; and Alshich's commentary on *parashah Va-Yelech.*

10. Sforno to Deuteronomy 31:1; Ramban, *Midrash Rabbenu Bachya,* and *Me'am Lo'az* to Deuteronomy 31:2.

11. Hayward, *Churchill on Leadership,* p. 152.

12. *Yalkut Shimoni,* vol. 1, *remez* 941; *Midrash ha-Gadol* to Deuteronomy 31:8; *Midrash Lekah Tov* to Deuteronomy 31:14; and Nachshoni, *Studies in the Weekly Parashah, Va-Yelech.*

13. Dennis C. Carey and Dayton Ogden, *CEO Succession* (Oxford: Oxford University Press, 2000), p. 15.

14. The tradition indicates that Moses also gathers all the people into the *Ohel Mo'ed.* See, in this regard, *Midrash ha-Gadol* to Deuteronomy 31:7.

15. Alshich's Commentary to Deuteronomy 31:14.

16. Katharine Q. Seelye, "An Announcement Today Passes the Torch at the House of Luce," the *New York Times* (October 17, 2005), C1, 4.

17. For example, Sforno and Saadia Gaon, as well as *Midrash Lekah Tov* to Deuteronomy 31:23.

18. Tigay, *JPS Torah Commentary* to Deuteronomy 31:23.

19. *Midrash Lekah Tov* to Deuteronomy 31:23.

20. Ramban to Deuteronomy 31:19; and Nachshoni, *Studies in the Weekly Parashah, Va-Yelech.*

21. Robert Rosen, *Leading People* (New York: Viking, 1996), p. 192.

22. For example, *Midrash ha-Gadol* to Deuteronomy 31:19.

23. *Midrash Petirat Moshe.*

24. Ibid.

25. *Devarim Rabbah* 9:9.
26. *Devarim Rabbah* 9:9 and *Midrash Petirat Moshe.*
27. *Devarim Rabbah* 9:9.

CONCLUSION

1. Meier, *Moses: The Prince, the Prophet,* p. 63.
2. Lewis, *Models and Meaning in the History of Jewish Leadership,* p. 12.
3. Wildavsky, *Nursing Father,* p. 201.
4. Lewis, *Models and Meaning in the History of Jewish Leadership,* p. 10.
5. Ibid., pp. 12, 21–22.
6. Wildavsky, *Nursing Father,* p. 86.
7. Ibid., p. 123.
8. Meier, *Moses: The Prince, the Prophet,* p. 181.
9. Ari Zivitofsky, "The Leadership Qualities of Moses," *Judaism* 43, no. 3 (Summer 1992): 259–263.
10. Lewis, *Models and Meaning in the History of Jewish Leadership,* pp. 15–16.
11. Wildavsky, *Nursing Father,* p. 89.
12. *Midrash Petirat Aaron.*
13. Lewis, *Models and Meaning in the History of Jewish Leadership,* p. 22.
14. Wildavsky, *Nursing Father,* pp. 34, 39.
15. See Abraham Zaleznik, "Managers and Leaders—Are They Different?" in *On Leadership* (Boston: Harvard Business School Press, 1990), pp. 61–88.
16. Lewis, *Models and Meaning in the History of Jewish Leadership,* p. 13.
17. Meier, *Moses: The Prince, the Prophet,* p. 179.
18. Wildavsky, *Nursing Father,* p. 175.

Suggestions for Further Reading

Alter, Robert. *The Art of Biblical Narrative.* New York: Basic Books, 1981.

Bennis, Warren, and Nanus, Burt. *Leaders.* New York: Harper Business, 1997.

Cohen, Norman. *Self, Struggle and Change: Family Conflict Stories in Genesis and Their Healing Insights for Our Lives.* Woodstock, Vt.: Jewish Lights Publishing, 1996.

———. *The Way Into Torah.* Woodstock, Vt.: Jewish Lights Publishing, 2000.

Elazar, Daniel. *Authority, Power and Leadership in the Jewish Polity.* Lanham, Md.: University Press of America, 1991.

Haywood, Steven. *Churchill on Leadership.* New York: Gramercy Books, 1997.

Laufer, Nathan. *The Genesis of Leadership: What the Bible Teaches Us about Vision, Values and Leading Change.* Woodstock, Vt.: Jewish Lights Publishing, 2006.

Leibowitz, Nehama. *Studies in Shemot.* Jerusalem: WZO Dept. for Torah Education and Culture in the Diaspora, 1978.

———. *Studies in Bamidbar.* Jerusalem: WZO, 1980.

Levering, Robert, and Moskowitz, Milton. *The 100 Best Companies to Work For in America.* New York: Plume/Penguin, 1994.

Lewis, Hal. *Models and Meanings in the History of Jewish Leadership, Jewish Studies,* vol. 26. Lewiston: Edwin Mellon Press, 2004.

Meier, Levi. *Moses: The Prince, the Prophet: His Life, Legend and Message for Our Lives.* Woodstock, Vt.: Jewish Lights Publishing, 1998.

Milgrom, Jacob. *The JPS Torah Commentary to Numbers.* Philadelphia: Jewish Publication Society, 1990.

Morell, Margot, and Capparell, Stephanie. *Shackleton's Way*. London: Penguin Books, 2001.

Neff, Thomas, and Citrin, James M. *Lessons from the Top*. New York: Currency/Doubleday, 2001.

Sarna, Nahum. *The JPS Torah Commentary to Exodus*. Philadelphia: Jewish Publication Society, 1991.

Senge, Peter. *The Fifth Discipline: The Art & Practice of the Learning Organization*. New York: Currency and Doubleday, 2006.

Tigay, Jeffrey. *The JPS Torah Commentary to Deuteronomy*. Philadelphia: Jewish Publication Society, 1996.

Visotzky, Burton. *The Road to Redemption*. New York: Crown Publishers Inc., 1998.

Walzer, Michael. *Exodus and Revolution*. New York: Basic Books, 1986.

Wiesel, Elie. *Messengers of God: Biblical Portraits and Legends*. New York: Random House, 1976.

Wildavsky, Aaron. *The Nursing Father: Moses as a Political Leader*. Birmingham: The University of Alabama Press, 1984.

Woolfe, Lorin. *Leadership Secrets from the Bible*. New York: MJF Books, 2002.

Zornberg, Aviva. *The Particulars of Rapture: Reflections on Exodus*. New York: Doubleday, 2000.

Notes

Notes

Bar/Bat Mitzvah

The JGirl's Guide: The Young Jewish Woman's Handbook for Coming of Age
By Penina Adelman, Ali Feldman, and Shulamit Reinharz
An inspirational, interactive guidebook designed to help pre-teen Jewish girls
address the spiritual, educational, and psychological issues surrounding coming of
age in today's society.   6 x 9, 240 pp, Quality PB, 978-1-58023-215-9 **$14.99**
  Also Available: **The JGirl's Teacher's and Parent's Guide**
  8½ x 11, 56 pp, PB, 978-1-58023-225-8 **$8.99**

Bar/Bat Mitzvah Basics: A Practical Family Guide to Coming of Age Together
  Edited by Cantor Helen Leneman 6 x 9, 240 pp, Quality PB, 978-1-58023-151-0 **$18.95**

The Bar/Bat Mitzvah Memory Book, 2nd Edition: An Album for Treasuring the
Spiritual Celebration *By Rabbi Jeffrey K. Salkin and Nina Salkin*
8 x 10, 48 pp, Deluxe HC, 2-color text, ribbon marker, 978-1-58023-263-0 **$19.99**

For Kids—Putting God on Your Guest List: How to Claim the Spiritual Meaning
of Your Bar or Bat Mitzvah *By Rabbi Jeffrey K. Salkin*
6 x 9, 144 pp, Quality PB, 978-1-58023-015-5 **$14.99** *For ages 11–13*

Putting God on the Guest List, 3rd Edition: How to Reclaim the Spiritual
Meaning of Your Child's Bar or Bat Mitzvah *By Rabbi Jeffrey K. Salkin*
6 x 9, 224 pp, Quality PB, 978-1-58023-222-7 **$16.99**; HC, 978-1-58023-260-9 **$24.99**
  Also Available: **Putting God on the Guest List Teacher's Guide**
  8½ x 11, 48 pp, PB, 978-1-58023-226-5 **$8.99**

Tough Questions Jews Ask: A Young Adult's Guide to Building a Jewish Life
By Rabbi Edward Feinstein 6 x 9, 160 pp, Quality PB, 978-1-58023-139-8 **$14.99** *For ages 12 & up*
  Also Available: **Tough Questions Jews Ask Teacher's Guide**
  8½ x 11, 72 pp, PB, 978-1-58023-187-9 **$8.95**

Bible Study/Midrash

**Abraham's Bind & Other Bible Tales of Trickery, Folly, Mercy
and Love** *By Michael J. Caduto*
Re-imagines many biblical characters, retelling their stories and highlighting their
foibles and strengths, their struggles and joys. Readers will learn that God has a
way of working for them and through them, even today.
6 x 9, 224 pp, HC, 978-1-59473-186-0 **$19.99** *(A SkyLight Paths book)*

Ancient Secrets: Using the Stories of the Bible to Improve Our Everyday Lives
  By Rabbi Levi Meier, PhD 5½ x 8½, 288 pp, Quality PB, 978-1-58023-064-3 **$16.95**

The Genesis of Leadership: What the Bible Teaches Us about Vision,
Values and Leading Change *By Rabbi Nathan Laufer; Foreword by Senator Joseph I. Lieberman*
Unlike other books on leadership, this one is rooted in the stories of the Bible, and
teaches the values that the Bible believes are prerequisites for true leadership.
6 x 9, 288 pp, HC, 978-1-58023-241-8 **$24.99**

Hineini in Our Lives: Learning How to Respond to Others through 14 Biblical Texts and
  Personal Stories *By Norman J. Cohen* 6 x 9, 240 pp, Quality PB, 978-1-58023-274-6 **$16.99**

Moses and the Journey to Leadership: Timeless Lessons of Effective Management from
  the Bible and Today's Leaders *By Dr. Norman J. Cohen* 6 x 9, 250 pp, HC, 978-1-58023-227-2 **$21.99**

Self, Struggle & Change: Family Conflict Stories in Genesis and Their Healing Insights for
  Our Lives *By Norman J. Cohen* 6 x 9, 224 pp, Quality PB, 978-1-879045-66-8 **$18.99**

The Triumph of Eve & Other Subversive Bible Tales *By Matt Biers-Ariel*
5½ x 8½, 192 pp, HC, 978-1-59473-040-5 **$19.99** *(A SkyLight Paths book)*

Voices from Genesis: Guiding Us through the Stages of Life *By Norman J. Cohen*
6 x 9, 192 pp, Quality PB, 978-1-58023-118-3 **$16.95**

Or phone, fax, mail or e-mail to: **JEWISH LIGHTS Publishing**
Sunset Farm Offices, Route 4 • P.O. Box 237 • Woodstock, Vermont 05091
Tel: (802) 457-4000 • Fax: (802) 457-4004 • www.jewishlights.com
Credit card orders: (800) 962-4544 (8:30AM–5:30PM ET Monday–Friday)
Generous discounts on quantity orders. SATISFACTION GUARANTEED. Prices subject to change.

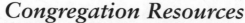

Congregation Resources

The Art of Public Prayer, 2nd Edition: Not for Clergy Only *By Lawrence A. Hoffman*
6 x 9, 272 pp, Quality PB, 978-1-893361-06-5 **$19.99** *(A SkyLight Paths book)*

Becoming a Congregation of Learners: Learning as a Key to Revitalizing
Congregational Life *By Isa Aron, PhD; Foreword by Rabbi Lawrence A. Hoffman*
6 x 9, 304 pp, Quality PB, 978-1-58023-089-6 **$19.95**

Finding a Spiritual Home: How a New Generation of Jews Can Transform the
American Synagogue *By Rabbi Sidney Schwarz*
6 x 9, 352 pp, Quality PB, 978-1-58023-185-5 **$19.95**

Jewish Pastoral Care, 2nd Edition: A Practical Handbook from Traditional &
Contemporary Sources *Edited by Rabbi Dayle A. Friedman*
6 x 9, 528 pp, HC, 978-1-58023-221-0 **$40.00**

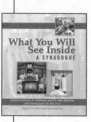

Jewish Spiritual Direction: An Innovative Guide from Traditional and Contemporary
Sources *Edited by Rabbi Howard A. Addison and Barbara Eve Breitman*
6 x 9, 368 pp, HC, 978-1-58023-230-2 **$30.00**

The Self-Renewing Congregation: Organizational Strategies for Revitalizing
Congregational Life *By Isa Aron, PhD; Foreword by Dr. Ron Wolfson*
6 x 9, 304 pp, Quality PB, 978-1-58023-166-4 **$19.95**

Spiritual Community: The Power to Restore Hope, Commitment and Joy
By Rabbi David A. Teutsch, PhD 5½ x 8½, 144 pp, HC, 978-1-58023-270-8 **$19.99**

The Spirituality of Welcoming: How to Transform Your Congregation into a
Sacred Community *By Dr. Ron Wolfson* 6 x 9, 224 pp, Quality PB, 978-1-58023-244-9 **$19.99**

Rethinking Synagogues: A New Vocabulary for Congregational Life
By Rabbi Lawrence A. Hoffman 6 x 9, 240 pp, Quality PB, 978-1-58023-248-7 **$19.99**

Children's Books

What You Will See Inside a Synagogue
By Rabbi Lawrence A. Hoffman and Dr. Ron Wolfson; Full-color photos by Bill Aron
A colorful, fun-to-read introduction that explains the ways and whys of Jewish
worship and religious life.
8½ x 10¼, 32 pp, Full-color photos, HC, 978-1-59473-012-2 **$17.99** *For ages 6 & up* *(A SkyLight Paths book)*

The Kids' Fun Book of Jewish Time
By Emily Sper 9 x 7½, 24 pp, Full-color illus., HC, 978-1-58023-311-8 **$16.99**

In God's Hands
By Lawrence Kushner and Gary Schmidt 9 x 12, 32 pp, HC, 978-1-58023-224-1 **$16.99**

Because Nothing Looks Like God
By Lawrence and Karen Kushner
Introduces children to the possibilities of spiritual life.
11 x 8½, 32 pp, Full-color illus., HC, 978-1-58023-092-6 **$16.95** *For ages 4 & up*

Also Available: **Because Nothing Looks Like God Teacher's Guide**
8½ x 11, 22 pp, PB, 978-1-58023-140-4 **$6.95** *For ages 5–8*

Board Book Companions to *Because Nothing Looks Like God*
5 x 5, 24 pp, Full-color illus., SkyLight Paths Board Books *For ages 0–4*

What Does God Look Like? 978-1-893361-23-2 **$7.99**

How Does God Make Things Happen? 978-1-893361-24-9 **$7.95**

Where Is God? 978-1-893361-17-1 **$7.99**

The Book of Miracles: A Young Person's Guide to Jewish Spiritual Awareness
By Lawrence Kushner. All-new illustrations by the author
6 x 9, 96 pp, 2-color illus., HC, 978-1-879045-78-1 **$16.95** *For ages 9 and up*

In Our Image: God's First Creatures
By Nancy Sohn Swartz 9 x 12, 32 pp, Full-color illus., HC, 978-1-879045-99-6 **$16.95** *For ages 4 & up*

Also Available as a Board Book: **How Did the Animals Help God?**
5 x 5, 24 pp, Board, Full-color illus., 978-1-59473-044-3 **$7.99** *For ages 0–4* *(A SkyLight Paths book)*

Children's Books
by Sandy Eisenberg Sasso

Adam & Eve's First Sunset: God's New Day
Engaging new story explores fear and hope, faith and gratitude in ways that will
delight kids and adults—inspiring us to bless each of God's days and nights.
9 x 12, 32 pp, Full-color illus., HC, 978-1-58023-177-0 **$17.95** *For ages 4 & up*

Also Available as a Board Book: **Adam and Eve's New Day**
5 x 5, 24 pp, Full-color illus., Board, 978-1-59473-205-8 **$7.99** *For ages 0–4 (A SkyLight Paths book)*

But God Remembered
Stories of Women from Creation to the Promised Land
Four different stories of women—Lillith, Serach, Bityah, and the Daughters of
Z—teach us important values through their faith and actions.
9 x 12, 32 pp, Full-color illus., HC, 978-1-879045-43-9 **$16.95** *For ages 8 & up*

Cain & Abel: Finding the Fruits of Peace
Shows children that we have the power to deal with anger in positive ways.
Provides questions for kids and adults to explore together.
9 x 12, 32 pp, Full-color illus., HC, 978-1-58023-123-7 **$16.95** *For ages 5 & up*

God in Between
If you wanted to find God, where would you look? This magical, mythical tale
teaches that God can be found where we are: within all of us and the relationships
between us.
9 x 12, 32 pp, Full-color illus., HC, 978-1-879045-86-6 **$16.95** *For ages 4 & up*

God's Paintbrush: Special 10th Anniversary Edition
Wonderfully interactive, invites children of all faiths and backgrounds to
encounter God through moments in their own lives. Provides questions adult and
child can explore together.
11 x 8½, 32 pp, Full-color illus., HC, 978-1-58023-195-4 **$17.95** *For ages 4 & up*

Also Available: **God's Paintbrush Teacher's Guide**
8½ x 11, 32 pp, PB, 978-1-879045-57-6 **$8.95**

God's Paintbrush Celebration Kit
A Spiritual Activity Kit for Teachers and Students of All Faiths, All Backgrounds
Additional activity sheets available:
8-Student Activity Sheet Pack (40 sheets/5 sessions), 978-1-58023-058-2 **$19.95**
Single-Student Activity Sheet Pack (5 sessions), 978-1-58023-059-9 **$3.95**

In God's Name
Like an ancient myth in its poetic text and vibrant illustrations, this
award-winning modern fable about the search for God's name celebrates
the diversity and, at the same time, the unity of all people.
9 x 12, 32 pp, Full-color illus., HC, 978-1-879045-26-2 **$16.99** *For ages 4 & up*

Also Available as a Board Book: **What Is God's Name?**
5 x 5, 24 pp, Board, Full-color illus., 978-1-893361-10-2 **$7.99** *For ages 0–4 (A SkyLight Paths book)*

Also Available: **In God's Name video and study guide**
Computer animation, original music, and children's voices. 18 min. **$29.99**

Also Available in Spanish: **El nombre de Dios**
9 x 12, 32 pp, Full-color illus., HC, 978-1-893361-63-8 **$16.95** *(A SkyLight Paths book)*

Noah's Wife: The Story of Naamah
When God tells Noah to bring the animals of the world onto the ark, God also calls
on Naamah, Noah's wife, to save each plant on Earth. Based on an ancient text.
9 x 12, 32 pp, Full-color illus., HC, 978-1-58023-134-3 **$16.95** *For ages 4 & up*

Also Available as a Board Book: **Naamah, Noah's Wife**
5 x 5, 24 pp, Full-color illus., Board, 978-1-893361-56-0 **$7.95** *For ages 0–4 (A SkyLight Paths book)*

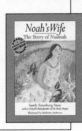

For Heaven's Sake: Finding God in Unexpected Places
9 x 12, 32 pp, Full-color illus., HC, 978-1-58023-054-4 **$16.95** *For ages 4 & up*

God Said Amen: Finding the Answers to Our Prayers
9 x 12, 32 pp, Full-color illus., HC, 978-1-58023-080-3 **$16.95** *For ages 4 & up*

Current Events/History

The Story of the Jews: A 4,000-Year Adventure—A Graphic History Book
Written & illustrated by Stan Mack
Witty, illustrated narrative of all the major happenings from biblical times to the twenty-first century. 6 x 9, 288 pp, illus., Quality PB, 978-1-58023-155-8 **$16.95**

Hannah Senesh: Her Life and Diary, the First Complete Edition
By Hannah Senesh; Foreword by Marge Piercy; Preface by Eitan Senesh
6 x 9, 352 pp, HC, 978-1-58023-212-8 **$24.99**

The Jewish Prophet: Visionary Words from Moses and Miriam to Henrietta Szold and A. J. Heschel *By Rabbi Dr. Michael J. Shire*
6½ x 8½, 128 pp, 123 full-color illus., HC, 978-1-58023-168-8
Special gift price $14.95

Foundations of Sephardic Spirituality: The Inner Life of Jews of the Ottoman Empire
By Rabbi Marc D. Angel, PhD 6 x 9, 224 pp, HC, 978-1-58023-243-2 **$24.99**

Judaism and Justice: The Jewish Passion to Repair the World
By Rabbi Sidney Schwarz
6 x 9, 250 pp, HC, 978-1-58023-312-5 **$24.99**

Ecology

Ecology & the Jewish Spirit: Where Nature & the Sacred Meet
Edited by Ellen Bernstein 6 x 9, 288 pp, Quality PB, 978-1-58023-082-7 **$16.95**

Torah of the Earth: Exploring 4,000 Years of Ecology in Jewish Thought
Vol. 1: Biblical Israel: One Land, One People; Rabbinic Judaism: One People, Many Lands
Vol. 2: Zionism: One Land, Two Peoples; Eco-Judaism: One Earth, Many Peoples
Edited by Arthur Waskow
Vol. 1: 6 x 9, 272 pp, Quality PB, 978-1-58023-086-5 **$19.95**
Vol. 2: 6 x 9, 336 pp, Quality PB, 978-1-58023-087-2 **$19.95**

The Way Into Judaism and the Environment
By Jeremy Benstein 6 x 9, 224 pp, HC, 978-1-58023-268-5 **$24.99**

Grief/Healing

Against the Dying of the Light: A Parent's Story of Love, Loss and Hope
By Leonard Fein
5½ x 8½, 176 pp, Quality PB, 978-1-58023-197-8 **$15.99**

Grief in Our Seasons: A Mourner's Kaddish Companion *By Rabbi Kerry M. Olitzky*
4½ x 6½, 448 pp, Quality PB, 978-1-879045-55-2 **$15.95**

Healing of Soul, Healing of Body: Spiritual Leaders Unfold the Strength & Solace in Psalms *Edited by Rabbi Simkha Y. Weintraub, CSW*
6 x 9, 128 pp, 2-color illus. text, Quality PB, 978-1-879045-31-6 **$14.99**

Jewish Paths toward Healing and Wholeness: A Personal Guide to Dealing with Suffering *By Rabbi Kerry M. Olitzky; Foreword by Debbie Friedman.*
6 x 9, 192 pp, Quality PB, 978-1-58023-068-1 **$15.95**

Mourning & Mitzvah, 2nd Edition: A Guided Journal for Walking the Mourner's Path through Grief to Healing *By Anne Brener, LCSW*
7½ x 9, 304 pp, Quality PB, 978-1-58023-113-8 **$19.99**

The Perfect Stranger's Guide to Funerals and Grieving Practices
A Guide to Etiquette in Other People's Religious Ceremonies *Edited by Stuart M. Matlins*
6 x 9, 240 pp, Quality PB, 978-1-893361-20-1 **$16.95** *(A SkyLight Paths book)*

Tears of Sorrow, Seeds of Hope: A Jewish Spiritual Companion for Infertility and Pregnancy Loss *By Rabbi Nina Beth Cardin*
6 x 9, 192 pp, HC, 978-1-58023-017-9 **$19.95**

A Time to Mourn, A Time to Comfort, 2nd Edition: A Guide to Jewish Bereavement *By Dr. Ron Wolfson*
7 x 9, 384 pp, Quality PB, 978-1-58023-253-1 **$19.99**

When a Grandparent Dies: A Kid's Own Remembering Workbook for Dealing with Shiva and the Year Beyond *By Nechama Liss-Levinson, PhD*
8 x 10, 48 pp, 2-color text, HC, 978-1-879045-44-6 **$15.95** *For ages 7–13*

Holidays/Holy Days

Rosh Hashanah Readings: Inspiration, Information and Contemplation
Yom Kippur Readings: Inspiration, Information and Contemplation
Edited by Rabbi Dov Peretz Elkins with Section Introductions from Arthur Green's These Are the Words
An extraordinary collection of readings, prayers and insights that enable the modern worshiper to enter into the spirit of the High Holy Days in a personal and powerful way, permitting the meaning of the Jewish New Year to enter the heart.
RHR: 6 x 9, 400 pp, HC, 978-1-58023-239-5 **$24.99**
YKR: 6 x 9, 368 pp, HC, 978-1-58023-271-5 **$24.99**

Jewish Holidays: A Brief Introduction for Christians
By Rabbi Kerry M. Olitzky and Rabbi Daniel Judson
5½ x 8½, 144 pp, Quality PB, 978-1-58023-302-6 **$16.99**

Leading the Passover Journey: The Seder's Meaning Revealed, the Haggadah's Story Retold By Rabbi Nathan Laufer
Uncovers the hidden meaning of the Seder's rituals and customs.
6 x 9, 224 pp, HC, 978-1-58023-211-1 **$24.99**

Reclaiming Judaism as a Spiritual Practice: Holy Days and Shabbat
By Rabbi Goldie Milgram
7 x 9, 272 pp, Quality PB, 978-1-58023-205-0 **$19.99**

7th Heaven: Celebrating Shabbat with Rebbe Nachman of Breslov
By Moshe Mykoff with the Breslov Research Institute
5⅛ x 8¼, 224 pp, Deluxe PB w/flaps, 978-1-58023-175-6 **$18.95**

The Women's Passover Companion: Women's Reflections on the Festival of Freedom Edited by Rabbi Sharon Cohen Anisfeld, Tara Mohr, and Catherine Spector
Groundbreaking. A provocative conversation about women's relationships to Passover as well as the roots and meanings of women's seders.
6 x 9, 352 pp, Quality PB, 978-1-58023-231-9 **$19.99**

The Women's Seder Sourcebook: Rituals & Readings for Use at the Passover Seder Edited by Rabbi Sharon Cohen Anisfeld, Tara Mohr, and Catherine Spector
Gathers the voices of more than one hundred women in readings, personal and creative reflections, commentaries, blessings, and ritual suggestions that can be incorporated into your Passover celebration.
6 x 9, 384 pp, Quality PB, 978-1-58023-232-6 **$19.99**

Creating Lively Passover Seders: A Sourcebook of Engaging Tales, Texts & Activities
By David Arnow, PhD 7 x 9, 416 pp, Quality PB, 978-1-58023-184-8 **$24.99**

Hanukkah, 2nd Edition: The Family Guide to Spiritual Celebration
By Dr. Ron Wolfson. Edited by Joel Lurie Grishaver.
7 x 9, 240 pp, illus., Quality PB, 978-1-58023-122-0 **$18.95**

The Jewish Family Fun Book: Holiday Projects, Everyday Activities, and Travel Ideas with Jewish Themes By Danielle Dardashti and Roni Sarig. Illus. by Avi Katz.
6 x 9, 288 pp, 70+ b/w illus. & diagrams, Quality PB, 978-1-58023-171-8 **$18.95**

The Jewish Gardening Cookbook: Growing Plants & Cooking for Holidays
& Festivals By Michael Brown 6 x 9, 224 pp, 30+ b/w illus., Quality PB, 978-1-58023-116-9 **$16.95**

The Jewish Lights Book of Fun Classroom Activities: Simple and Seasonal
Projects for Teachers and Students By Danielle Dardashti and Roni Sarig
6 x 9, 240 pp, Quality PB, 978-1-58023-206-7 **$19.99**

Passover, 2nd Edition: The Family Guide to Spiritual Celebration
By Dr. Ron Wolfson with Joel Lurie Grishaver 7 x 9, 352 pp, Quality PB, 978-1-58023-174-9 **$19.95**

Shabbat, 2nd Edition: The Family Guide to Preparing for and Celebrating the Sabbath
By Dr. Ron Wolfson 7 x 9, 320 pp, illus., Quality PB, 978-1-58023-164-0 **$19.99**

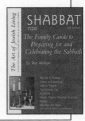

Sharing Blessings: Children's Stories for Exploring the Spirit of the Jewish Holidays
By Rahel Musleah and Rabbi Michael Klayman
8½ x 11, 64 pp, Full-color illus., HC, 978-1-879045-71-2 **$18.95** *For ages 6 & up*

Inspiration

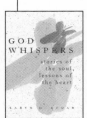

God's To-Do List: 103 Ways to Be an Angel and Do God's Work on Earth
By Dr. Ron Wolfson 6 x 9, 150 pp, Quality PB, 978-1-58023-301-9 **$15.99**

God in All Moments: Mystical & Practical Spiritual Wisdom from Hasidic Masters
Edited and translated by Or N. Rose with Ebn D. Leader
5½ x 8½, 192 pp, Quality PB, 978-1-58023-186-2 **$16.95**

Our Dance with God: Finding Prayer, Perspective and Meaning in the Stories of Our
Lives By Karyn D. Kedar 6 x 9, 176 pp, Quality PB, 978-1-58023-202-9 **$16.99**

Also Available: **The Dance of the Dolphin** (HC edition of *Our Dance with God*)
6 x 9, 176 pp, HC, 978-1-58023-154-1 **$19.95**

The Empty Chair: Finding Hope and Joy—Timeless Wisdom from a Hasidic Master,
Rebbe Nachman of Breslov *Adapted by Moshe Mykoff and the Breslov Research Institute*
4 x 6, 128 pp, 2-color text, Deluxe PB w/flaps, 978-1-879045-67-5 **$9.95**

The Gentle Weapon: Prayers for Everyday and Not-So-Everyday Moments—
Timeless Wisdom from the Teachings of the Hasidic Master, Rebbe Nachman of Breslov
Adapted by Moshe Mykoff and S. C. Mizrahi, together with the Breslov Research Institute
4 x 6, 144 pp, 2-color text, Deluxe PB w/flaps, 978-1-58023-022-3 **$9.99**

God Whispers: Stories of the Soul, Lessons of the Heart By Karyn D. Kedar
6 x 9, 176 pp, Quality PB, 978-1-58023-088-9 **$15.95**

An Orphan in History: One Man's Triumphant Search for His Jewish Roots
By Paul Cowan; Afterword by Rachel Cowan. 6 x 9, 288 pp, Quality PB, 978-1-58023-135-0 **$16.95**

Restful Reflections: Nighttime Inspiration to Calm the Soul, Based on Jewish Wisdom
By Rabbi Kerry M. Olitzky & Rabbi Lori Forman 4½ x 6½, 448 pp, Quality PB, 978-1-58023-091-9 **$15.95**

Sacred Intentions: Daily Inspiration to Strengthen the Spirit, Based on Jewish Wisdom
By Rabbi Kerry M. Olitzky and Rabbi Lori Forman 4½ x 6½, 448 pp, Quality PB, 978-1-58023-061-2 **$15.95**

Kabbalah/Mysticism/Enneagram

Awakening to Kabbalah: The Guiding Light of Spiritual Fulfillment
By Rav Michael Laitman, PhD 6 x 9, 192 pp, HC, 978-1-58023-264-7 **$21.99**

Seek My Face: A Jewish Mystical Theology By Arthur Green
6 x 9, 304 pp, Quality PB, 978-1-58023-130-5 **$19.95**

Zohar: Annotated & Explained
Translation and annotation by Daniel C. Matt; Foreword by Andrew Harvey
5½ x 8½, 176 pp, Quality PB, 978-1-893361-51-5 **$15.99** (A SkyLight Paths book)

Cast in God's Image: Discover Your Personality Type Using the Enneagram and Kabbalah
By Rabbi Howard A. Addison
7 x 9, 176 pp, Quality PB, Layflat binding, 20+ journaling exercises, 978-1-58023-124-4 **$16.95**

Ehyeh: A Kabbalah for Tomorrow
By Arthur Green 6 x 9, 224 pp, Quality PB, 978-1-58023-213-5 **$16.99**

The Enneagram and Kabbalah, 2nd Edition: Reading Your Soul
By Rabbi Howard A. Addison 6 x 9, 192 pp, Quality PB, 978-1-58023-229-6 **$16.99**

Finding Joy: A Practical Spiritual Guide to Happiness By Dannel I. Schwartz with Mark Hass
6 x 9, 192 pp, Quality PB, 978-1-58023-009-4 **$14.95**

The Flame of the Heart: Prayers of a Chasidic Mystic By Reb Noson of Breslov. Translated by
David Sears with the Breslov Research Institute 5 x 7¼, 160 pp, Quality PB, 978-1-58023-246-3 **$15.99**

The Gift of Kabbalah: Discovering the Secrets of Heaven, Renewing Your Life on Earth
By Tamar Frankiel, PhD 6 x 9, 256 pp, Quality PB, 978-1-58023-141-1 **$16.95;**
HC, 978-1-58023-108-4 **$21.95**

Kabbalah: A Brief Introduction for Christians
By Tamar Frankiel, PhD 5½ x 8½, 208 pp, Quality PB, 978-1-58023-303-3 **$16.99**

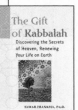

The Lost Princess and Other Kabbalistic Tales of Rebbe Nachman of Breslov
The Seven Beggars and Other Kabbalistic Tales of Rebbe Nachman of Breslov
Translated by Rabbi Aryeh Kaplan; Preface by Rabbi Chaim Kramer
Lost Princess: 6 x 9, 400 pp, Quality PB, 978-1-58023-217-3 **$18.99**
Seven Beggars: 6 x 9, 192 pp, Quality PB, 978-1-58023-250-0 **$16.99**

See also *The Way Into Jewish Mystical Tradition* in Spirituality / The Way Into… Series

Life Cycle
Marriage / Parenting / Family / Aging

Jewish Fathers: A Legacy of Love
Photographs by Lloyd Wolf. Essays by Paula Wolfson. Foreword by Rabbi Harold Kushner.
Honors the role of contemporary Jewish fathers in America. Each father tells in his own words what it means to be a parent and Jewish, and what he learned from his own father. Insightful photos.
10¾ x 9⅞, 144 pp with 100+ duotone photos, HC, 978-1-58023-204-3 **$30.00**

The New Jewish Baby Album: Creating and Celebrating the Beginning of a Spiritual Life—A Jewish Lights Companion
By the Editors at Jewish Lights. Foreword by Anita Diamant. Preface by Rabbi Sandy Eisenberg Sasso.
A spiritual keepsake that will be treasured for generations. More than just a memory book, *shows you how—and why it's important*—to create a Jewish home and a Jewish life. 8 x 10, 64 pp, Deluxe Padded HC, Full-color illus., 978-1-58023-138-1 **$19.95**

The Jewish Pregnancy Book: A Resource for the Soul, Body & Mind during Pregnancy, Birth & the First Three Months
By Sandy Falk, MD, and Rabbi Daniel Judson, with Steven A. Rapp
Includes medical information, prayers and rituals for each stage of pregnancy, from a liberal Jewish perspective. 7 x 10, 208 pp, Quality PB, b/w photos, 978-1-58023-178-7 **$16.95**

Celebrating Your New Jewish Daughter: Creating Jewish Ways to Welcome Baby Girls into the Covenant—New and Traditional Ceremonies *By Debra Nussbaum Cohen; Foreword by Rabbi Sandy Eisenberg Sasso* 6 x 9, 272 pp, Quality PB, 978-1-58023-090-2 **$18.95**

The New Jewish Baby Book, 2nd Edition: Names, Ceremonies & Customs—A Guide for Today's Families *By Anita Diamant* 6 x 9, 336 pp, Quality PB, 978-1-58023-251-7 **$19.99**

Parenting As a Spiritual Journey: Deepening Ordinary and Extraordinary Events into Sacred Occasions *By Rabbi Nancy Fuchs-Kreimer*
6 x 9, 224 pp, Quality PB, 978-1-58023-016-2 **$16.95**

Parenting Jewish Teens: A Guide for the Perplexed
By Joanne Doades 6 x 9, 200 pp, Quality PB, 978-1-58023-305-7 **$16.99**

Judaism for Two: A Spiritual Guide for Strengthening and Celebrating Your Loving Relationship *By Rabbi Nancy Fuchs-Kreimer and Rabbi Nancy H. Wiener; Foreword by Rabbi Elliot N. Dorff* Addresses the ways Jewish teachings can enhance and strengthen committed relationships. 6 x 9, 224 pp, Quality PB, 978-1-58023-254-8 **$16.99**

Embracing the Covenant: Converts to Judaism Talk About Why & How
By Rabbi Allan Berkowitz and Patti Moskovitz 6 x 9, 192 pp, Quality PB, 978-1-879045-50-7 **$16.95**

The Guide to Jewish Interfaith Family Life: An InterfaithFamily.com Handbook
Edited by Ronnie Friedland and Edmund Case 6 x 9, 384 pp, Quality PB, 978-1-58023-153-4 **$18.95**

Introducing My Faith and My Community
The Jewish Outreach Institute Guide for the Christian in a Jewish Interfaith Relationship
By Rabbi Kerry M. Olitzky 6 x 9, 176 pp, Quality PB, 978-1-58023-192-3 **$16.99**

Making a Successful Jewish Interfaith Marriage: The Jewish Outreach Institute Guide to Opportunities, Challenges and Resources *By Rabbi Kerry M. Olitzky with Joan Peterson Littman*
6 x 9, 176 pp, Quality PB, 978-1-58023-170-1 **$16.95**

The Creative Jewish Wedding Book: A Hands-On Guide to New & Old Traditions, Ceremonies & Celebrations *By Gabrielle Kaplan-Mayer*
9 x 9, 288 pp, b/w photos, Quality PB, 978-1-58023-194-7 **$19.99**

Divorce Is a Mitzvah: A Practical Guide to Finding Wholeness and Holiness When Your Marriage Dies *By Rabbi Perry Netter; Afterword by Rabbi Laura Geller.*
6 x 9, 224 pp, Quality PB, 978-1-58023-172-5 **$16.95**

A Heart of Wisdom: Making the Jewish Journey from Midlife through the Elder Years
Edited by Susan Berrin; Foreword by Harold Kushner
6 x 9, 384 pp, Quality PB, 978-1-58023-051-3 **$18.95**

So That Your Values Live On: Ethical Wills and How to Prepare Them
Edited by Jack Riemer and Nathaniel Stampfer
6 x 9, 272 pp, Quality PB, 978-1-879045-34-7 **$18.99**

Meditation

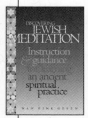

The Handbook of Jewish Meditation Practices
A Guide for Enriching the Sabbath and Other Days of Your Life
By Rabbi David A. Cooper Easy-to-learn meditation techniques.
6 x 9, 208 pp, Quality PB, 978-1-58023-102-2 **$16.95**

Discovering Jewish Meditation: Instruction & Guidance for Learning an Ancient Spiritual Practice By Nan Fink Gefen
6 x 9, 208 pp, Quality PB, 978-1-58023-067-4 **$16.95**

A Heart of Stillness: A Complete Guide to Learning the Art of Meditation
By David A. Cooper 5½ x 8½, 272 pp, Quality PB, 978-1-893361-03-4 **$16.95** (A SkyLight Paths book)

Meditation from the Heart of Judaism: Today's Teachers Share Their Practices, Techniques, and Faith Edited by Avram Davis
6 x 9, 256 pp, Quality PB, 978-1-58023-049-0 **$16.95**

Silence, Simplicity & Solitude: A Complete Guide to Spiritual Retreat at Home
By David A. Cooper 5½ x 8½, 336 pp, Quality PB, 978-1-893361-04-1 **$16.95**
(A SkyLight Paths book)

The Way of Flame: A Guide to the Forgotten Mystical Tradition of Jewish
Meditation By Avram Davis 4½ x 8, 176 pp, Quality PB, 978-1-58023-060-5 **$15.95**

Ritual/Sacred Practice/Journaling

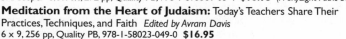

The Jewish Dream Book: The Key to Opening the Inner Meaning of
Your Dreams By Vanessa L. Ochs with Elizabeth Ochs; Full-color illus. by Kristina Swarner
Instructions for how modern people can perform ancient Jewish dream practices
and dream interpretations drawn from the Jewish wisdom tradition.
8 x 8, 128 pp, Full-color illus., Deluxe PB w/flaps, 978-1-58023-132-9 **$16.95**

The Jewish Journaling Book: How to Use Jewish Tradition to Write
Your Life & Explore Your Soul By Janet Ruth Falon
Details the history of Jewish journaling throughout biblical and modern times, and
teaches specific journaling techniques to help you create and maintain a vital journal,
from a Jewish perspective. 8 x 8, 304 pp, Deluxe PB w/flaps, 978-1-58023-203-6 **$18.99**

The Book of Jewish Sacred Practices: CLAL's Guide to Everyday & Holiday
Rituals & Blessings Edited by Rabbi Irwin Kula and Vanessa L. Ochs, PhD
6 x 9, 368 pp, Quality PB, 978-1-58023-152-7 **$18.95**

Jewish Ritual: A Brief Introduction for Christians
By Rabbi Kerry M. Olitzky and Rabbi Daniel Judson
5½ x 8½, 144 pp, Quality PB, 978-1-58023-210-4 **$14.99**

The Rituals & Practices of a Jewish Life: A Handbook for Personal Spiritual
Renewal Edited by Rabbi Kerry M. Olitzky and Rabbi Daniel Judson
6 x 9, 272 pp, illus., Quality PB, 978-1-58023-169-5 **$18.95**

The Sacred Art of Lovingkindness: Preparing to Practice
By Rabbi Rami Shapiro 5½ x 8½, 176 pp, Quality PB, 978-1-59473-151-8 **$16.99**
(A SkyLight Paths book)

Science Fiction/Mystery & Detective Fiction

Mystery Midrash: An Anthology of Jewish Mystery & Detective Fiction
Edited by Lawrence W. Raphael; Preface by Joel Siegel
6 x 9, 304 pp, Quality PB, 978-1-58023-055-1 **$16.95**

Criminal Kabbalah: An Intriguing Anthology of Jewish Mystery & Detective Fiction
Edited by Lawrence W. Raphael; Foreword by Laurie R. King
6 x 9, 256 pp, Quality PB, 978-1-58023-109-1 **$16.95**

Wandering Stars: An Anthology of Jewish Fantasy & Science Fiction
Edited by Jack Dann; Introduction by Isaac Asimov
6 x 9, 272 pp, Quality PB, 978-1-58023-005-6 **$16.95**

More Wandering Stars: An Anthology of Outstanding Stories of Jewish Fantasy and
Science Fiction Edited by Jack Dann; Introduction by Isaac Asimov
6 x 9, 192 pp, Quality PB, 978-1-58023-063-6 **$16.95**

Spirituality

The Adventures of Rabbi Harvey: A Graphic Novel of Jewish Wisdom and Wit in the Wild West *By Steve Sheinkin*
Jewish and American folktales combine in this witty and original graphic novel collection. Creatively retold and set on the western frontier of the 1870s.
6 x 9, 144 pp, Full-color illus., Quality PB, 978-1-58023-310-1 **$16.99**
Also Available: **The Adventures of Rabbi Harvey Teacher's Guide**
8½ x 11, 32 pp, PB, 978-1-58023-326-2 **$8.99**

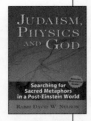

Ethics of the Sages: *Pirke Avot*—Annotated & Explained
Translation and Annotation by Rabbi Rami Shapiro
5½ x 8½, 192 pp, Quality PB, 978-1-59473-207-2 **$16.99** *(A SkyLight Paths book)*

A Book of Life: Embracing Judaism as a Spiritual Practice
By Michael Strassfeld 6 x 9, 528 pp, Quality PB, 978-1-58023-247-0 **$19.99**

Meaning and Mitzvah: Daily Practices for Reclaiming Judaism through Prayer, God, Torah, Hebrew, Mitzvot and Peoplehood *By Rabbi Goldie Milgram*
7 x 9, 336 pp, Quality PB, 978-1-58023-256-2 **$19.99**

The Soul of the Story: Meetings with Remarkable People
By Rabbi David Zeller 6 x 9, 288 pp, HC, 978-1-58023-272-2 **$21.99**

Aleph-Bet Yoga: Embodying the Hebrew Letters for Physical and Spiritual Well-Being
By Steven A. Rapp. Foreword by Tamar Frankiel, PhD and Judy Greenfeld. Preface by Hart Lazer.
7 x 10, 128 pp, b/w photos, Quality PB, Layflat binding, 978-1-58023-162-6 **$16.95**

Entering the Temple of Dreams: Jewish Prayers, Movements, and Meditations for the End of the Day *By Tamar Frankiel, PhD, and Judy Greenfeld*
7 x 10, 192 pp, illus., Quality PB, 978-1-58023-079-7 **$16.95**

Does the Soul Survive? A Jewish Journey to Belief in Afterlife, Past Lives & Living with Purpose *By Rabbi Elie Kaplan Spitz; Foreword by Brian L. Weiss, MD*
6 x 9, 288 pp, Quality PB, 978-1-58023-165-7 **$16.99**

First Steps to a New Jewish Spirit: Reb Zalman's Guide to Recapturing the Intimacy & Ecstasy in Your Relationship with God *By Rabbi Zalman M. Schachter-Shalomi with Donald Gropman* 6 x 9, 144 pp, Quality PB, 978-1-58023-182-4 **$16.95**

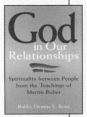

God in Our Relationships: Spirituality between People from the Teachings of Martin Buber *By Rabbi Dennis S. Ross* 5½ x 8½, 160 pp, Quality PB, 978-1-58023-147-3 **$16.95**

Judaism, Physics and God: Searching for Sacred Metaphors in a Post-Einstein World
By Rabbi David W. Nelson 6 x 9, 368 pp, Quality PB, inc. reader's discussion guide, 978-1-58023-306-4 **$18.99**;
HC, 352 pp, 978-1-58023-252-4 **$24.99**

The Jewish Lights Spirituality Handbook: A Guide to Understanding, Exploring & Living a Spiritual Life *Edited by Stuart M. Matlins*
What exactly is "Jewish" about spirituality? How do I make it a part of my life? Fifty of today's foremost spiritual leaders share their ideas and experience with us.
6 x 9, 456 pp, Quality PB, 978-1-58023-093-3 **$19.99**

Bringing the Psalms to Life: How to Understand and Use the Book of Psalms
By Daniel F. Polish 6 x 9, 208 pp, Quality PB, 978-1-58023-157-2 **$16.95**;
HC, 978-1-58023-077-3 **$21.95**

God & the Big Bang: Discovering Harmony between Science & Spirituality
By Daniel C. Matt 6 x 9, 216 pp, Quality PB, 978-1-879045-89-7 **$16.99**

Minding the Temple of the Soul: Balancing Body, Mind, and Spirit through Traditional Jewish Prayer, Movement, and Meditation *By Tamar Frankiel, PhD, and Judy Greenfeld*
7 x 10, 184 pp, illus., Quality PB, 978-1-879045-64-4 **$16.95**
Audiotape of the Blessings and Meditations: 60 min. **$9.95**
Videotape of the Movements and Meditations: 46 min. **$20.00**

One God Clapping: The Spiritual Path of a Zen Rabbi *By Alan Lew with Sherril Jaffe*
5½ x 8½, 336 pp, Quality PB, 978-1-58023-115-2 **$16.95**

There Is No Messiah ... and You're It: The Stunning Transformation of Judaism's Most Provocative Idea *By Rabbi Robert N. Levine, DD*
6 x 9, 192 pp, Quality PB, 978-1-58023-255-5 **$16.99**

These Are the Words: A Vocabulary of Jewish Spiritual Life
By Arthur Green 6 x 9, 304 pp, Quality PB, 978-1-58023-107-7 **$18.95**

Spirituality/Lawrence Kushner

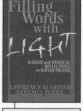

Filling Words with Light: Hasidic and Mystical Reflections on Jewish Prayer
By Lawrence Kushner and Nehemia Polen
5½ x 8½, 176 pp, HC, 978-1-58023-216-6 **$21.99**

The Book of Letters: A Mystical Hebrew Alphabet
Popular HC Edition, 6 x 9, 80 pp, 2-color text, 978-1-879045-00-2 **$24.95**
Collector's Limited Edition, 9 x 12, 80 pp, gold foil embossed pages, w/limited edition silkscreened
print, 978-1-879045-04-0 **$349.00**

The Book of Miracles: A Young Person's Guide to Jewish Spiritual Awareness
6 x 9, 96 pp, 2-color illus., HC, 978-1-879045-78-1 **$16.95** *For ages 9 and up*

The Book of Words: Talking Spiritual Life, Living Spiritual Talk
6 x 9, 160 pp, Quality PB, 978-1-58023-020-9 **$16.95**

Eyes Remade for Wonder: A Lawrence Kushner Reader *Introduction by Thomas Moore*
6 x 9, 240 pp, Quality PB, 978-1-58023-042-1 **$18.95**

God Was in This Place & I, i Did Not Know: Finding Self, Spirituality and Ultimate
Meaning 6 x 9, 192 pp, Quality PB, 978-1-879045-33-0 **$16.95**

Honey from the Rock: An Introduction to Jewish Mysticism
6 x 9, 176 pp, Quality PB, 978-1-58023-073-5 **$16.95**

Invisible Lines of Connection: Sacred Stories of the Ordinary
5½ x 8½, 160 pp, Quality PB, 978-1-879045-98-9 **$15.95**

Jewish Spirituality—A Brief Introduction for Christians
5½ x 8½, 112 pp, Quality PB, 978-1-58023-150-3 **$12.95**

The River of Light: Jewish Mystical Awareness
6 x 9, 192 pp, Quality PB, 978-1-58023-096-4 **$16.95**

The Way Into Jewish Mystical Tradition
6 x 9, 224 pp, Quality PB, 978-1-58023-200-5 **$18.99**; HC, 978-1-58023-029-2 **$21.95**

Spirituality/Prayer

Pray Tell: A Hadassah Guide to Jewish Prayer
By Rabbi Jules Harlow, with contributions from many others
8½ x 11, 400 pp, Quality PB, 978-1-58023-163-3 **$29.95**

Witnesses to the One: The Spiritual History of the *Sh'ma* *By Rabbi Joseph B. Meszler;
Foreword by Rabbi Elyse Goldstein* 6 x 9, 176 pp, HC, 978-1-58023-309-5 **$19.99**

My People's Prayer Book Series

Traditional Prayers, Modern Commentaries *Edited by Rabbi Lawrence A. Hoffman*
Provides diverse and exciting commentary to the traditional liturgy, helping modern
men and women find new wisdom in Jewish prayer, and bring liturgy into their lives.
Each book includes Hebrew text, modern translation, and commentaries from all
perspectives of the Jewish world.

Vol. 1—The *Sh'ma* and Its Blessings
7 x 10, 168 pp, HC, 978-1-879045-79-8 **$24.99**
Vol. 2—The *Amidah*
7 x 10, 240 pp, HC, 978-1-879045-80-4 **$24.95**
Vol. 3—*P'sukei D'zimrah* (Morning Psalms)
7 x 10, 240 pp, HC, 978-1-879045-81-1 **$24.95**
Vol. 4—*Seder K'riat Hatorah* (The Torah Service)
7 x 10, 264 pp, HC, 978-1-879045-82-8 **$23.95**
Vol. 5—*Birkhot Hashachar* (Morning Blessings)
7 x 10, 240 pp, HC, 978-1-879045-83-5 **$24.95**
Vol. 6—*Tachanun* and Concluding Prayers
7 x 10, 240 pp, HC, 978-1-879045-84-2 **$24.95**
Vol. 7—Shabbat at Home
7 x 10, 240 pp, HC, 978-1-879045-85-9 **$24.95**
Vol. 8—*Kabbalat Shabbat* (Welcoming Shabbat in the Synagogue)
7 x 10, 240 pp, HC, 978-1-58023-121-3 **$24.99**
Vol. 9—Welcoming the Night: *Minchah* and *Ma'ariv* (Afternoon and
Evening Prayer) 7 x 10, 272 pp, HC, 978-1-58023-262-3 **$24.99**
Vol. 10—Shabbat Morning: *Shacharit* and *Musaf* (Morning and
Additional Services) 7 x 10, 240 pp, HC, 978-1-58023-240-1 **$24.99**

Spirituality/Women's Interest

The Quotable Jewish Woman: Wisdom, Inspiration & Humor from the Mind & Heart
Edited and compiled by Elaine Bernstein Partnow
6 x 9, 496 pp, HC, 978-1-58023-193-0 **$29.99**

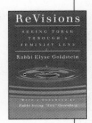

The Knitting Way: A Guide to Spiritual Self-Discovery *By Linda Skolnick and Janice MacDaniels* 7 x 9, 240 pp, Quality PB, 978-1-59473-079-5 **$16.99** *(A SkyLight Paths book)*

The Quilting Path: A Guide to Spiritual Self-Discovery through Fabric, Thread and Kabbalah
By Louise Silk 7 x 9, 192 pp, Quality PB, 978-1-59473-206-5 **$16.99** *(A SkyLight Paths book)*

The Divine Feminine in Biblical Wisdom Literature: Selections Annotated &
Explained *Translated and Annotated by Rabbi Rami Shapiro*
5½ x 8½, 240 pp, Quality PB, 978-1-59473-109-9 **$16.99** *(A SkyLight Paths book)*

Lifecycles, Vol. 1: Jewish Women on Life Passages & Personal Milestones
Edited and with Introductions by Rabbi Debra Orenstein
6 x 9, 480 pp, Quality PB, 978-1-58023-018-6 **$19.95**

Lifecycles, Vol. 2: Jewish Women on Biblical Themes in Contemporary Life
Edited and with Introductions by Rabbi Debra Orenstein and Rabbi Jane Rachel Litman
6 x 9, 464 pp, Quality PB, 978-1-58023-019-3 **$19.95**

Moonbeams: A Hadassah Rosh Hodesh Guide *Edited by Carol Diament, PhD*
8½ x 11, 240 pp, Quality PB, 978-1-58023-099-5 **$20.00**

ReVisions: Seeing Torah through a Feminist Lens *By Rabbi Elyse Goldstein*
5½ x 8½, 224 pp, Quality PB, 978-1-58023-117-6 **$16.95**

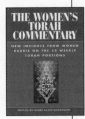

The Women's Haftarah Commentary: New Insights from Women Rabbis on the
54 Weekly Haftarah Portions, the 5 Megillot & Special Shabbatot
Edited by Rabbi Elyse Goldstein 6 x 9, 560 pp, HC, 978-1-58023-133-6 **$39.99**

The Women's Torah Commentary: New Insights from Women Rabbis on the 54
Weekly Torah Portions *Edited by Rabbi Elyse Goldstein*
6 x 9, 496 pp, HC, 978-1-58023-076-6 **$34.95**

The Year Mom Got Religion: One Woman's Midlife Journey into Judaism
By Lee Meyerhoff Hendler 6 x 9, 208 pp, Quality PB, 978-1-58023-070-4 **$15.95**

See Holidays for *The Women's Passover Companion: Women's Reflections on
the Festival of Freedom* and *The Women's Seder Sourcebook: Rituals &
Readings for Use at the Passover Seder.* Also see Bar/Bat Mitzvah for *The JGirl's
Guide: The Young Jewish Woman's Handbook for Coming of Age.*

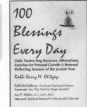

Travel

Israel—A Spiritual Travel Guide, 2nd Edition
A Companion for the Modern Jewish Pilgrim
By Rabbi Lawrence A. Hoffman 4¾ x 10, 256 pp, Quality PB, illus., 978-1-58023-261-6 **$18.99**

Also Available: **The Israel Mission Leader's Guide** 978-1-58023-085-8 **$4.95**

12-Step

100 Blessings Every Day: Daily Twelve Step Recovery Affirmations, Exercises for
Personal Growth & Renewal Reflecting Seasons of the Jewish Year
By Rabbi Kerry M. Olitzky; Foreword by Rabbi Neil Gillman
4½ x 6½, 432 pp, Quality PB, 978-1-879045-30-9 **$15.99**

Recovery from Codependence: A Jewish Twelve Steps Guide to Healing Your Soul
By Rabbi Kerry M. Olitzky 6 x 9, 160 pp, Quality PB, 978-1-879045-32-3 **$13.95**

Renewed Each Day: Daily Twelve Step Recovery Meditations Based on the Bible
By Rabbi Kerry M. Olitzky and Aaron Z.
Vol. 1—Genesis & Exodus: 6 x 9, 224 pp, Quality PB, 978-1-879045-12-5 **$14.95**
Vol. 2—Leviticus, Numbers & Deuteronomy: 6 x 9, 280 pp, Quality PB, 978-1-879045-13-2 **$18.99**

Twelve Jewish Steps to Recovery: A Personal Guide to Turning from Alcoholism &
Other Addictions—Drugs, Food, Gambling, Sex...
By Rabbi Kerry M. Olitzky and Stuart A. Copans, MD; Preface by Abraham J. Twerski, MD
6 x 9, 144 pp, Quality PB, 978-1-879045-09-5 **$14.95**

Theology/Philosophy/The Way Into... Series

The Way Into... series offers an accessible and highly usable "guided tour" of the Jewish faith, people, history and beliefs—in total, an introduction to Judaism that will enable you to understand and interact with the sacred texts of the Jewish tradition. Each volume is written by a leading contemporary scholar and teacher, and explores one key aspect of Judaism. The Way Into... series enables all readers to achieve a real sense of Jewish cultural literacy through guided study.

The Way Into Encountering God in Judaism
By Neil Gillman
For everyone who wants to understand how Jews have encountered God throughout history and today.
6 x 9, 240 pp, Quality PB, 978-1-58023-199-2 **$18.99**; HC, 978-1-58023-025-4 **$21.95**
Also Available: **The Jewish Approach to God:** A Brief Introduction for Christians
By Neil Gillman
5½ x 8¼, 192 pp, Quality PB, 978-1-58023-190-9 **$16.95**

The Way Into Jewish Mystical Tradition
By Lawrence Kushner
Allows readers to interact directly with the sacred mystical text of the Jewish tradition. An accessible introduction to the concepts of Jewish mysticism, their religious and spiritual significance and how they relate to life today.
6 x 9, 224 pp, Quality PB, 978-1-58023-200-5 **$18.99**; HC, 978-1-58023-029-2 **$21.95**

The Way Into Jewish Prayer
By Lawrence A. Hoffman
Opens the door to 3,000 years of Jewish prayer, making available all anyone needs to feel at home in the Jewish way of communicating with God.
6 x 9, 224 pp, Quality PB, 978-1-58023-201-2 **$18.99**

The Way Into Judaism and the Environment
By Jeremy Benstein
Explores the ways in which Judaism contributes to contemporary social-environmental issues, the extent to which Judaism is part of the problem and how it can be part of the solution.
6 x 9, 288 pp, HC, 978-1-58023-268-5 **$24.99**

The Way Into Tikkun Olam (Repairing the World)
By Elliot N. Dorff
An accessible introduction to the Jewish concept of the individual's responsibility to care for others and repair the world.
6 x 9, 320 pp, HC, 978-1-58023-269-2 **$24.99**

The Way Into Torah
By Norman J. Cohen
Helps guide in the exploration of the origins and development of Torah, explains why it should be studied and how to do it.
6 x 9, 176 pp, Quality PB, 978-1-58023-198-5 **$16.99**; HC, 978-1-58023-028-5 **$21.95**

The Way Into the Varieties of Jewishness
By Sylvia Barack Fishman
Explores the religious and historical understanding of what it has meant to be Jewish from ancient times to the present controversy over "Who is a Jew?"
6 x 9, 250 pp, HC, 978-1-58023-030-8 **$24.99**

Theology/Philosophy

Christians and Jews in Dialogue: Learning in the Presence of the Other
By Mary C. Boys and Sara S. Lee; Foreword by Dr. Dorothy Bass
6 x 9, 240 pp, HC, 978-1-59473-144-0 **$21.99** *(A SkyLight Paths book)*

The Death of Death: Resurrection and Immortality in Jewish Thought
By Neil Gillman 6 x 9, 336 pp, Quality PB, 978-1-58023-081-0 **$18.95**

Ethics of the Sages: Pirke Avot—Annotated & Explained
Translation & Annotation by Rabbi Rami Shapiro
5½ x 8½, 208 pp, Quality PB, 978-1-59473-207-2 **$16.99** *(A SkyLight Paths book)*

Evolving Halakhah: A Progressive Approach to Traditional Jewish Law
By Rabbi Dr. Moshe Zemer 6 x 9, 480 pp, Quality PB, 978-1-58023-127-5 **$29.95**;
HC, 978-1-58023-002-5 **$40.00**

Hasidic Tales: Annotated & Explained
By Rabbi Rami Shapiro; Foreword by Andrew Harvey
5½ x 8½, 240 pp, Quality PB, 978-1-893361-86-7 **$16.95** *(A SkyLight Paths Book)*

Healing the Jewish-Christian Rift: Growing Beyond our Wounded History
By Ron Miller and Laura Bernstein; Foreword by Dr. Beatrice Bruteau
6 x 9, 288 pp, Quality PB, 978-1-59473-139-6 **$18.99** *(A SkyLight Paths book)*

A Heart of Many Rooms: Celebrating the Many Voices within Judaism
By David Hartman 6 x 9, 352 pp, Quality PB, 978-1-58023-156-5 **$19.95**

The Hebrew Prophets: Selections Annotated & Explained
Translation & Annotation by Rabbi Rami Shapiro; Foreword by Zalman M. Schachter-Shalomi
5½ x 8½, 224 pp, Quality PB, 978-1-59473-037-5 **$16.99** *(A SkyLight Paths book)*

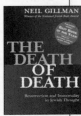

A Jewish Understanding of the New Testament
By Rabbi Samuel Sandmel; Preface by Rabbi David Sandmel
5½ x 8½, 368 pp, Quality PB, 978-1-59473-048-1 **$19.99** *(A SkyLight Paths book)*

Keeping Faith with the Psalms: Deepen Your Relationship with God Using the Book
of Psalms *By Daniel F. Polish* 6 x 9, 320 pp, Quality PB, 978-1-58023-300-2 **$18.99**;
HC, 978-1-58023-179-4 **$24.95**

A Living Covenant: The Innovative Spirit in Traditional Judaism
By David Hartman 6 x 9, 368 pp, Quality PB, 978-1-58023-011-7 **$20.00**

Love and Terror in the God Encounter
The Theological Legacy of Rabbi Joseph B. Soloveitchik
By David Hartman 6 x 9, 240 pp, Quality PB, 978-1-58023-176-3 **$19.95**;
HC, 978-1-58023-112-1 **$25.00**

The Personhood of God: Biblical Theology, Human Faith and the Divine Image
By Dr. Yochanan Muffs; Foreword by Dr. David Hartman
6 x 9, 240 pp, HC, 978-1-58023-265-4 **$24.99**

Tormented Master: *The Life and Spiritual Quest of Rabbi Nahman of Bratslav*
By Arthur Green 6 x 9, 416 pp, Quality PB, 978-1-879045-11-8 **$19.99**

Traces of God: Seeing God in Torah, History and Everyday Life
By Neil Gillman 6 x 9, 240 pp, HC, 978-1-58023-249-4 **$21.99**

We Jews and Jesus: Exploring Theological Differences for Mutual Understanding
By Rabbi Samuel Sandmel; Preface by Rabbi David Sandmel
6 x 9, 176 pp, Quality PB, 978-1-59473-208-9 **$16.99** *(A SkyLight Paths book)*

Your Word Is Fire: The Hasidic Masters on Contemplative Prayer
Edited and translated by Arthur Green and Barry W. Holtz
6 x 9, 160 pp, Quality PB, 978-1-879045-25-5 **$15.95**

I Am Jewish
Personal Reflections Inspired by the Last Words of Daniel Pearl
Almost 150 Jews—both famous and not—from all walks of life, from all around
the world, write about Identity, Heritage, Covenant / Chosenness and Faith,
Humanity and Ethnicity, and *Tikkun Olam* and Justice.
Edited by Judea and Ruth Pearl
6 x 9, 304 pp, Deluxe PB w/flaps, 978-1-58023-259-3 **$18.99**; HC, 978-1-58023-183-1 **$24.99**
**Download a free copy of the *I Am Jewish Teacher's Guide* at our website:
www.jewishlights.com**

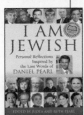

About Jewish Lights

People of all faiths and backgrounds yearn for books that attract, engage, educate, and spiritually inspire.

Our principal goal is to stimulate thought and help all people learn about who the Jewish People are, where they come from, and what the future can be made to hold. While people of our diverse Jewish heritage are the primary audience, our books speak to people in the Christian world as well and will broaden their understanding of Judaism and the roots of their own faith.

We bring to you authors who are at the forefront of spiritual thought and experience. While each has something different to say, they all say it in a voice that you can hear.

Our books are designed to welcome you and then to engage, stimulate, and inspire. We judge our success not only by whether or not our books are beautiful and commercially successful, but by whether or not they make a difference in your life.

For your information and convenience, at the back of this book we have provided a list of other Jewish Lights books you might find interesting and useful. They cover all the categories of your life:

Bar/Bat Mitzvah
Bible Study / Midrash
Children's Books
Congregation Resources
Current Events / History
Ecology
Fiction: Mystery, Science Fiction
Grief / Healing
Holidays / Holy Days
Inspiration
Kabbalah / Mysticism / Enneagram

Life Cycle
Meditation
Parenting
Prayer
Ritual / Sacred Practice
Spirituality
Theology / Philosophy
Travel
12-Step
Women's Interest

Stuart M. Matlins

Stuart M. Matlins, Publisher

Or phone, fax, mail or e-mail to: **JEWISH LIGHTS Publishing**
Sunset Farm Offices, Route 4 • P.O. Box 237 • Woodstock, Vermont 05091
Tel: (802) 457-4000 • Fax: (802) 457-4004 • www.jewishlights.com
Credit card orders: (800) 962-4544 (8:30AM–5:30PM ET Monday–Friday)
Generous discounts on quantity orders. SATISFACTION GUARANTEED. Prices subject to change.